AFTERMATH:FRANCE 1945-54
NEW IMAGES OF MAN

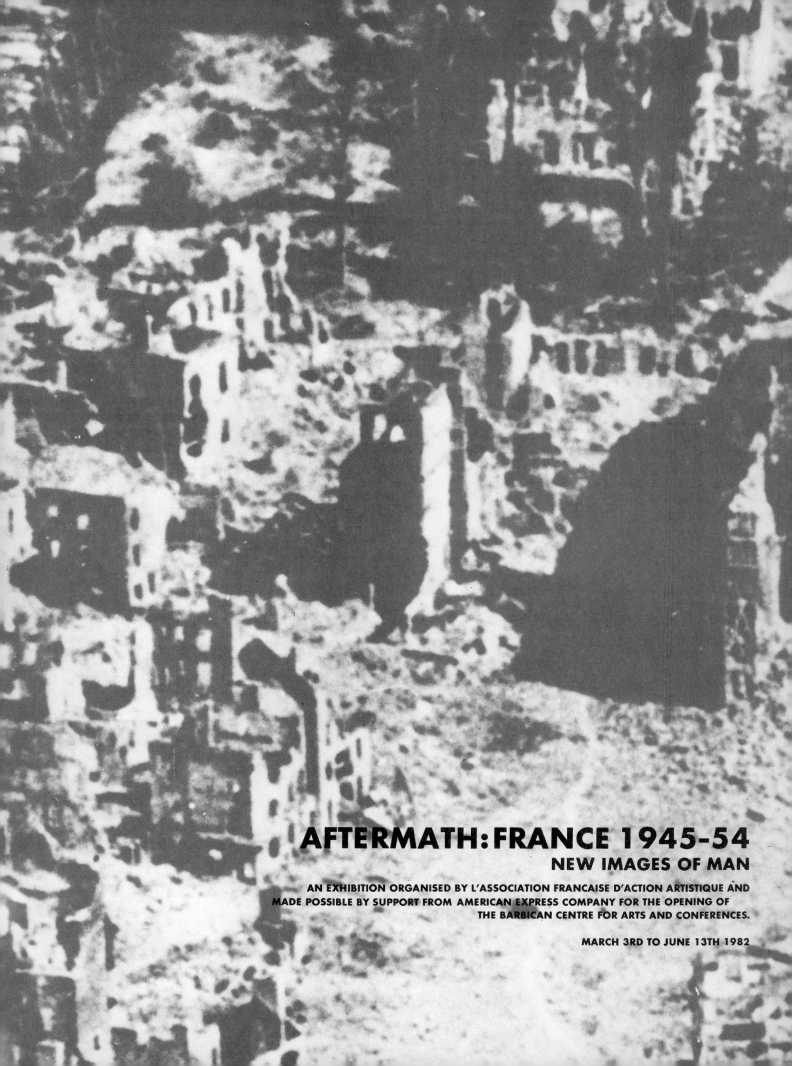

AFTERMATH: FRANCE 1945-54
NEW IMAGES OF MAN

AN EXHIBITION ORGANISED BY L'ASSOCIATION FRANCAISE D'ACTION ARTISTIQUE AND
MADE POSSIBLE BY SUPPORT FROM AMERICAN EXPRESS COMPANY FOR THE OPENING OF
THE BARBICAN CENTRE FOR ARTS AND CONFERENCES.

MARCH 3RD TO JUNE 13TH 1982

Foreword

As plans for the Barbican Centre materialised, it became evident to all those involved in the arts world-wide that the Centre would inevitably and rightly play as important a role as any other major arts complex in the Western world. In the mid-1970s, the cultural attaché at the French Embassy, Yves Mabin, proposed that a major exhibition from Paris should open the new Barbican Art Gallery. The result of this far-sighted proposal is this exhibition: *Aftermath France 1945 – 1954 New Images of Man*. The exhibition has become an important factor in Franco-British artistic co-operation, and I would like to express my gratitude to L'Association Française d'Action Artistique for their help and organisation and the Arts Council of Great Britain for their encouragement.

The origin of this exhibition is the very successful *Paris-Paris* exhibition at the Centre Pompidou in the spring of 1981. The organiser of that exhibition was Germain Viatte, and happily he accepted the appointment of director for the *Aftermath* exhibition at the Barbican. I am very grateful to him and to Sarah Wilson of the Barbican Centre staff for their initiative and imagination.

Aftermath provides a unique appraisal of post-war paintings and sculpture. Never before has such a collection of French art from this period been seen in this country. The post-war theme of the exhibition is particularly relevant to the Barbican, which itself rose like a phoenix from the ashes of World War II.

I would also like to express my deep appreciation to the American Express Company, without whose generosity this magnificent exhibition would not have been possible.

Henry Wrong
General Administrator, Barbican Centre
March 1982

Patrons

The Right Honourable The Lord Carrington KCMG MC
Minister for Foreign and Commonwealth Affairs

The Right Honourable Paul Channon
Minister for the Arts

The Right Honourable the Lord Mayor Sir Christopher Leaver
Lord Mayor of London

The Right Honourable Kenneth Robinson
Chairman of the Arts Council of Great Britain

Joanna Drew
Director of Art – Arts Council of Great Britain

Godfrey Thompson
*City Librarian and Director of Art Gallery
– Corporation of London*

Henry Wrong
General Administrator – Barbican Centre

This exhibition has been organised for the opening of the Barbican Art Gallery in the Barbican Centre for Arts and Conferences, as part of the programme of cultural exchanges organised between France and the United Kingdom, under the auspices of the Minister for External Affairs and of the Minister of Culture of the French Republic, for the Association Francaise d'Action Artistique with the support of the Musée National d'Art Moderne, Centre National d'Art et de Culture Georges Pompidou, Paris.

The exhibition will also be shown at the Louisiana Museum, Humlebaek, Denmark.

Committee of honour

M. Claude Cheysson
Ministre des relations extérieures

M. Jack Lang
Ministre de la Culture

S. Exc. M. Emmanuel Jacquin de Margerie
Ambassadeur de France en Grande-Bretagne

Coordinating Committee

M. Louis Joxe
*Ambassadeur de France – Président de l'Association
Française d'Action Artistique*

M. Jacques Thibau
*Directeur Général des Relations Culturelles,
Scientifiques et Techniques au Ministère
des relations extérieures*

M. Jacques Sallois
Directeur du Cabinet du Ministre de la Culture

M. Hubert Landais
Directeur des Musées de France

M. Jean-Claude Groshens
*Président du Centre National d'Art et
du Culture Georges Pompidou*

M. Dominique Bozo
*Directeur du Musée National d'Art Moderne,
Centre d'Art et de Culture Georges Pompidou*

M. André Gadaud
*Sous-Directeur des Echanges Artistiques au Ministère
des relations extérieures – Directeur de l'Association
Française d'Action Artistique*

M. Michel Huriet
*Conseiller Culturel près l'Ambassade de France
en Grande-Bretagne*

M. Yves Mabin
*Chef du Bureau des Arts Plastiques à la Sous-Direction
des Echanges Artistiques du Ministère des
relations extérieures*

Director of Exhibition

M. Germain Viatte

Organisation

M. Germain Viatte
*Conservateur du Musée National d'Art Moderne –
Centre Georges Pompidou*

Mlle Sarah Wilson
Visual Arts Consultant Barbican Centre

Administrator

M. Max Moulin
*Bureau des Arts Plastiques, Association Française
d'Action Artistique*

CONTENTS

Acknowledgements

This exhibition would not have been possible without the valuable assistance of the Musée National d'Art Moderne, Centre d'Art et de National Culture Georges Pompidou, and without the generous agreement and support of the following museums, galleries and individuals:

Musée de l'Abbaye Sainte Croix, les Sables d'Olonne

Musée d'Art Moderne de la Ville de Paris

Centre d'étude de l'expression, Hôpital Sainte Anne Paris

East Ham Library, London

Fonds National d'art contemporain, Paris

Fondation Maeght, St Paul de Vence

Haags Gemeente Museum, The Hague

Hirshhorn Museum, Washington

Musée de l'Ile de France, Sceaux

Kunsthaus, Zurich

Kunstmuseum, Bern

Musée National Fernand Léger, Biot

Leverhulme Foundation

Menil Foundation, Houston, Texas

Museum of Modern Art, New York

Musée Picasso, Paris

Tate Gallery, London

Robert and Lisa Sainsbury Collection, University of East Anglia

Galerie Claude Bernard, Paris

Galerie Bonnier, Geneva

Galerie Jeanne Bucher, Paris

Galerie Jean Fournier, Paris

Galerie Krugier, Geneva

Galerie Louise Leiris, Paris

Galerie Albert Loeb, Paris

Galerie Maeght, Paris

Galerie Adrien Maeght, Paris

Galerie Pierre Matisse, New York

Galerie de Messine, Paris

Galerie Nova Spectra, The Hague

Galerie André François Petit, Paris

Monsieur le Prefet des Hauts de Seine

Monsieur le Maire de Paris

Monsieur le Maire des Sables-d'Olonne

Bernard Anthonioz

Monique Barbier

Félix Baumann

Georges Bauquier

Michel Boutinard Rouelle

Alan Bowness

Dominique Bozo

Pierre Brache

Brassaï

Elisa Breton

Dominique Cheniveuse

Bernard Colin

Bernardette Contensou

Henry-Claude Cousseau

Jacques Donnars

Jean Dypreau

Etienne-Martin

Docteur R. Ferdière

André Fougeron

Françoise Fritschy

Stephen Gilbert

Henri Goetz

Henriette Gomes

Thomas Le Guillou

Jean-François Jaeger

Edouard Jaguer

Sylvain Lecombre

Nadia Leger

Daniel Lelong

Michel Lequesne

Madame Jean Leymarie

Albert Loeb

Florence Loeb

Madeleine Malraux

Florence Malraux-Resnais

Alexander Margulies

Alain Massiaux

Georges Mathieu

Sebastian Matta

Edward May

Dominique de Menil

Jean Yves Mock

Bernard Noel

Richard Oldenbuy

Yves Orecchioni

Olga Picabia

Georges Poisson

Annie Raison

Michèle Richet

Henny Riemens

William Rubin

Bruno de Saint Victor

J.W.N. Segaar

L. Sossountzou Serpan

Boris Taslitzky

Samy Tarica

Jean-Christophe de Tavel

Théodore van Velzen

Aline Vidal

together with those lenders who prefer to remain anonymous.

The catalogue notices have been compiled by Germain Viatte (G.V.) and Sarah Wilson (S.W.) and all translations are by Sarah Wilson. All dimensions are in centimetres, height preceding width. Unless otherwise specified, all places of birth and death are in France.

Barbican Art Gallery Curator: Roger Took

Exhibition consultants: Carlton Cleeve Ltd.

This catalogue was produced for the Barbican Centre for Arts and Conferences by Trefoil Books Ltd 15 St Johns Hill London SW11

ISBN 0 86294 006 0

Designed by Roger Davies
Set in Zapf and Futura by TNR Productions
Printed and bound by Lund Humphries

Pablo Picasso
Le Charnier (The Charnel House), 1948. *Oil on canvas.*
Museum of Modern Art, New York (not in exhibition)

AFTERMATH
A NEW GENERATION
Germain Viatte

[1] Charles de Gaulle: *Memoirs de Guerre*, Volume 3, *Le Salut* (1944-1946), Blon, Paris, 1959, p.1.

[2] *Westkunst, Zeitgenossische Kunst seit 1939*, May 30 – August 16, 1981, Messehallé, Cologne. Director: Laszlo Glozer. Catalogue of 524 pages by Laszlo Glozer Du Mont Buchverlag Cologne, 1981.

[3] *Paris-Paris, Creations en France, 1937-1957*, Centre Georges Pompidou, Paris, May 26 – November 2, 1981. Director: Germain Viatte. Catalogue of 528 pages including much hitherto unpublished material, and extensive reproduction of contemporary texts and documents. German edition reviewed and corrected published by Prestel-Verlag, Munich, 1981.

[4] Peter Selz: *New Images of Man*, Museum of Modern Art, New York, 1959.

'The withdrawing tide revealed all at once, from end to end of the country, the ravaged body of France.'[1] Following the Allied landings of June 6th 1944, and the Liberation of Paris in August, the waiting, the sense of failure, and the fighting of the Occupation gave way to a long period of uncertainty. The victory celebrations were soon forgotten as the population faced the problems of reconstruction and economic crisis. The capitulation of the Germans on May 8th 1945, meant the opening up of the concentration camps, while Hiroshima, in all its horror, finally put an end to the World War the following August.

From the autumn of 1944 onwards, the arts in Paris started to flourish once more. In October, Picasso was seen as the symbol of Resistance when a retrospective exhibition was held in his honour at the Salon de la Libération. Among the many exhibitions that heralded the rebirth of modern art in all its forms, the Galerie René Drouin's showings of Dubuffet, Fautrier and Wols marked a definitive break with the past. The violent and provocative nature of these works challenged and reflected the fears and anxieties of contemporary society. A new generation had appeared.

Aftermath: France 1945-1954, New Images of Man, attempts to resituate this art, by taking a longer look at certain areas of painting and sculpture which were recently included in two major international exhibitions: *Westkunst* in Cologne,[2] and *Paris-Paris* at the Centre Georges Pompidou.[3] These were very different in their emphases, and *Aftermath* has chosen to develop specific aspects of *Paris-Paris*, restricting itself to the first decade in France after the war. It does not aim to define movements, to look for influences, or to present a complete panorama of art in Paris at the time. Instead it hopes to discover the thoughts, the feelings, the questions that redefined man and his relationship to a universe irrevocably changed by World War II. The moral dilemmas of the Occupation, the clandestine violence and the sense of suppression it engendered are equally essential to the understanding of the climate of Paris in 1945.

Aftermath has been divided into four sections, which echo and contrast with each other. The first, entitled 'Masters of the Older Generation' recalls the presence of the 'Founding fathers' of modern art, a symbol of continuity in postwar Paris. Their work at this time was remarkably innovative, but this could have a very inhibiting effect on younger artists. Picasso, for example, a twentieth-century Proteus, found solutions to most contemporary plastic problems in his own work. The second section, 'Aspects of Realism' contrasts the contemporary notions of realism in all their contradictions. Dramatic illustrations of the period vie with images of militant political engagement and attempts to portray man's inner, existential being. The third section, 'Primitivism and Art Brut' demonstrates how instinctive, non-cultural values inspired many of the most significant contemporary artists, while the fourth section, 'Frontiers of Identity' is linked to the idea of 'transgression'. It tries to show how, by surpassing certain limits fixed by society or the individual, a deeper understanding of human identity might be achieved. The artist, and through his work Man himself, is perceived as a phenomenological being, while the painting becomes a new womb-like space, visceral, organic, a network of emotions, at once 'being and nothingness', an empty and infinite pictorial plane.

'New Images of Man', our subtitle, was used as early as 1959 by Peter Selz to describe the work of certain major figures of postwar European art, many of whom appear in this exhibition.[4] Now, however, more than three decades after the 1940s, we can see this period in all its complexity as one of the first expressions of the crisis of 'post-modernism'. The phenomenon was nothing new of course: in the same way the First World War had given rise to twin reactions, the 'anti-Art' of the Dadaists and simultaneously the 'Retour à l'ordre' which advocated a new realism and restraint. Now the same questions were repeated, the same answers too at times, but the problem of styles became more urgent, and was intimately related to the movement of ideas. In the 'réfus global' of this period, many ideas originally put forward by the Surrealists were now given new currency, thanks to the philosophical systems that sprang up around existentialism. These ideas influenced the work of certain artists usually considered quite remote from such preoccupations. It is surprising to find the work of Bissière, Lapicque, de Staël, or Vieira da Silva in *Aftermath*, but it suggests at once an underlying unity within the rich variety of the contemporary scene in Paris.

The break with the immediate past was such that the very precepts of modernism were questioned, when the old 'Querelle du Réalisme' started up again.[5] This dispute, which began in the late 1930s as a movement for politically engaged, realist art, accessible to the working classes, assumed new dimensions the following decade, when the French Communist Party decided to advocate a hard-line socialist realism, as proposed by Zhdanov, Stalin's cultural mouthpiece. In addition, a bitter, more general debate raged in Paris throughout the period, between the figurative painters and the advocates of abstraction.

Aftermath has therefore chosen a particular emphasis, and has deliberately ignored certain movements which made the art scene so very complicated, whatever their importance. Geometric abstract art underwent a considerable development for example, while the new 'Ecole de Paris' painters were greeted enthusiastically throughout Europe. Many artists in this last category felt it was necessary to reestablish links with the firm traditions of modern art. Once more, reason should be associated with artistic sensibility. The innate and transcendental qualities of 'le peintre français' should be rediscovered, new systems should be constructed on the sure foundations of Fauvism, Cubism and abstraction. Both in his public lectures from 1946-1948, and in his role as teacher at his painting academy, André Lhôte advocated a conciliatory form of modernism, capable of soothing contemporary neuroses. His position was equally that of the officials and self-appointed spokesmen associated with modern French art.[6]

But to André Lhôte's declaration 'Blasphemy isn't French', the writer Jean Paulhan replied 'Why not? If I were a painter, that's what would immediately make me want to blaspheme'.[7] For many artists and intellectuals life could never be the same again. These were the people who were subjected to Antonin Artaud's terrible invective at the Théâtre du Vieux Colombier on January 13th, 1947. 'Reason beat a retreat . . . Artaud forced us into his tragic game of revolt against all that we accepted, which for him, in his purity was unacceptable: . . . "We are not yet in the world . . . things have not yet been created, the raison d'être has not yet been found." '[8] Pierre Loeb, who presented Artaud's drawings in his gallery, declared later in a conference at the Sorbonne: 'I'm waiting for an art that's ungrateful, ugly, crude, as painful as giving birth, because it's a question of birth, not of games any longer, here as elsewhere.'[9] One of the most enthusiastic disciples of this art that broke with the past, Michel Tapié, who managed the Foyer de l'Art Brut at the Galerie René Drouin, later

[5] See Louis Aragon: *Pour un Réalisme Socialiste*, Editions Denoel & Steele, Paris, 1935, and ed. *La Querelle du Réalisme*, Editions Sociales et Internationales, Paris, 1936.

[6] Bernard Dorival, Pierre Francastel and René Huyghe for example.

[7] Jean Paulhan: letter to André Lhôte, in *Jean Paulhan à travers ses peintres*, Grand Palais, Paris, 1974, p.55.

[8] *84*, no. 5-6, p.151, quoted by André Berne Joffroy: 'Quand les Belles-Lettres touchent aux Beaux-Arts.' in *Paris-Paris*, op cit, p.37.

[9] Pierre Loeb: *Regards sur la peinture*, lecture given December 13 1949, published by the Librarie-Galerie La Hune, Paris, 1950.

recalled what seemed to him to unify the protagonists of this 'other art' he had called 'un art autre': 'One needed temperaments ready to break up everything, whose works were disturbing, stupefying, full of magic and violence to reroute the public. To reroute into a real future that mass of a so-called advanced public, hardened like a sclerosis around a cubism finished long ago, (but much prolonged), a misplaced geometric abstraction, and a limited puritanism which above anything else blocks the way to any possible, authentically fertile future.'[10] Finally Jean Dubuffet, reacting to Jean Paulhan's *La Lettre sur la Paix* published in 1949, wrote to him saying: 'To Paracelsus' regime for living (quotidie defecare, hebdomare coire, mensue ebriare, anne peregrinare) one should add pillage, kill, and set things on fire once every ten years, and find yourself in extreme danger.'[11] And indeed, Dubuffet was tirelessly provocative, abandoning the world of art for that of literature, creating quite a cruel, but very amusing portrait gallery of the best-known writers of the time. The relationship between art and literature had never been so intense, and it is doubtless one of the most significant features of the period. Although in the case of Louis Aragon this was rather disturbing – the ex-Surrealist writer became the prestigious mouthpiece of the Communist-inspired socialist realism movement – it was generally crucial for the new generation, who were discovered and brought to the public's attention thanks to certain writers: Jean Paulhan, André Malraux, Jean-Paul Sartre and André Breton are the most notable examples. The double role of artist and writer was played not only by Antonin Artaud and Henri Michaux, but by Dubuffet himself, Gaston Chaissac, and in a slightly different capacity by the Surrealist painter André Masson. Finally, there were those very deep sympathies which were equally important: between Michel Leiris or Jean Genêt and Giacometti, between the writer Georges Bataille and Hans Bellmer, between Samuel Beckett and Bram Van Velde.[12]

If the immediate postwar period in Paris now seems far away in terms of its political and philosophical preoccupations, it is astonishingly near when the violence of its desire to break with the past is considered. There was a need for direct and brutal communication – obscene if necessary – to supplant dead forms of language, a need to explore the force and the potential of the human body, to question the predetermined, and an exasperation with the materials and forms associated with all artistic traditions, including modernism. It was a 'monstrous art', as Severo Sardung has called today's creations.[13] Parallel to the purely visual, 'retinal' traditions of French painting, and often in violent opposition with them, this refusal developed: with its celebration of crude, ephemeral materials, of frenetic gestuality, of the forbidden. A 'behavioural' art, one might almost say. These outrageous provocations were reflected simultaneously in the influential work of Isidore Isou, and his 'lettriste' friends.[14]

This art excluded no one. In 1945, and for a few more years, Paris was the only major capital cosmopolitan and receptive enough to become the focus and the promoter of new ideas. From the beginning of the 1950s, this exclusivity was challenged. A second pole of attraction, New York was finally established, and progressively other cities asserted their national identity in the field of the arts. In 1953, Robert Lebel, in a moment of exceptional foresight, was able to predict the situation that is familiar today: 'This unknown factor is starting to appear before us with the presence of the American continent in the territory of artistic creation. This is an event whose probable consequences cannot be overestimated. The

[10] Michel Tapié: 'Espaces et Expressions', in *Premier bilan de l'art actuel*, Le Soleil Noir, Positions, nos 3 and 4, 1953, p. 102.

[11] Jean Dubuffet, Letter to Jean Paulhan, quoted in *Jean Paulhan à travers ses peintres*, op cit, p.104.

[12] See André Berne Joffroy: 'Quand les Belles Lettres touchent les Beaux-Arts,' in *Paris-Paris*, op cit. pp.34-40.

[13] Severo Sardung: 'Un art monstre', preface to the catalogue of the exhibition: 'Baroques 81, les débordements d'une avant-garde internationale', ARC, Musée d'Art Moderne de la Ville de Paris, Oct 1 – Nov 15, 1981.

[14] The review *La Dictature Lettriste* appeared in 1946. In 1952, *L'Internationale Lettriste* came to share the position taken by Jorn in the *Cobra* review and then those of the *Bauhaus Imaginiste*. This led to the creation of the *Internationale Situationniste* review in 1957.

fascination which Europe has always had for distant civilisations which has been manifested in the last fifty years by a particularly thorough exploration of primitive and native art could turn into a living reality at any moment. If indeed, the so-called Ecole de Paris is still dominant, a Mexican imprint is already obvious in much figurative work in Europe, and the oriental calligraphy and lay-out which stamps the work of Mark Tobey and the Pacific School is noticeable in works of the Parisian avant-garde. And it would be unwise, to say the least, to treat socialist realism as a non-event. Thanks to this spectacular enlargement of our frontiers and our perspectives, we are doubtless heading for an even more profound upheaval in what has been for so long the ritual of art in a sovereign continent.'[15]

Man was no longer the question: at last the war seemed almost forgotten.

GERMAIN VIATTE

[15] Robert Lebel: 'Confrontations' in *Premier bilan de l'Art actuel*, op cit, p.16.

Poster for the first exhibition of works by the insane.

THE SEARCH FOR NEW ORIGINS

Henry-Claude Cousseau

Culture Versus History

In an era so deeply marked by the passionate opposition between figurative and abstract art, it is not surprising that the traditional and indeed the 'professional' values of art itself came under fire – even from those who supposedly represented them. The profound transformations that took place in the immediate aftermath of World War II in France clearly had their source in the climate of guilt and anxiety resulting from that conflict. The postwar period witnessed a return to the values of the past, just as had been the case at the beginning of the century (and for identical reasons) but this time the reaction was more violent and finally more decisive. It happened on a scale which placed the very origins of culture under scrutiny, which questioned all its lessons and put them to the test.

As André Breton himself declared,[1] this comprehensive re-evaluation could be interpreted as a break with the Graeco-Roman tradition of European culture, a break which led to a celebration of primitive art in general, above all art of national origin: in the case of France prehistoric, Celtic and early Medieval art in particular. But this purely archaeological phenomenon could also be seen as a systematic and fundamental process of questioning, which in every case took on the guise of a manifesto. This art, which had at the beginning of the century been merely an aesthetic revelation, became a mirror for the postwar generation. It responded to their angst and, against a background of general bankruptcy, became a means of testing the truth of inherited values and of discovering their essential meaning. The process did not simply question the origin of forms and techniques of painting, but what had hitherto constituted its basis, namely that state of consciousness and freedom in which a work is created. If, in consequence, the postwar return to the sources of primitive art has rightly been seen as nostalgia for an idealised past, as a kind of confirmation of a primeval 'French tradition', complementary aspects of the phenomenon must not be overlooked. The idea of the *primitive*, which crops up so often in the writings of Breton, Jean Dubuffet, and contemporary art critics, as well as in that of psychiatrists and ethnologists, appeared as a logical consequence of this historical reassessment. So did the growing interest in popular art.[2] It was this same idea of a previous state of existence, this fascination with man's primal origins, his 'ante-cultural' stage, which accounted for the concurrent renaissance in psychology and psychiatry. The study of mental illness was to become the central forum for contemporary anxieties. Madness could, of course, be interpreted as a primitive, elementary condition of man, as the scientific establishment agreed at the time.[3] So, by logical extension, could childhood. The psychiatrists and psychologists, as much as the artists, were hoping to find in the drawings of children and mental patients – who were seemingly untouched by history – the secret of human expression and its formulations.

All this seemed to call for a type of creation not so much nostalgically orientated towards the past as capable of proving its authenticity via its purity, its spontaneity, its virginity. This is above all the key to Jean Dubuffet's involvement with Art Brut, and to Gaston Chaissac's work. Dubuffet was seeking an illusory stage of creation in its 'primal state', Chaissac a creation totally at one with his powers of intuition – attitudes which in both cases excluded neither violence nor subversion. Subversion is in fact the ultimate message of Art Brut. It is equally the central motivation of Antonin Artaud, whose drawings express the transgression of his own 'madness', and of Henri Michaux, whose works similarly violate the conventions of language. The timing was propitious. Just at the moment when the historical process was at its lowest ebb, the purity of art in its primitive version came into its own. It was as though the aftermath of World War II demanded that any idea of continuity or of starting again could only be conceived and justified in confrontation with man's origins, and could only be developed if it pursued the one morally acceptable course – the break which could become a new point of departure.

Psychotic Art and Art Brut

The questioning of art as such was underlined by the emergence of Art Brut and 'art psychopathologique' – psychotic art. These two notions were at once completely different and complementary, widely separated in context, yet sometimes strangely akin. The fascination with graphic expression after the war, with the work of children and the mentally ill in particular, must also be seen independently of any developments in psychology. It was a reaction in favour of precisely those elements specific to art that the Nazis had classed as degenerate. Their defeat naturally encouraged the re-emergence of the works they had rejected. But even more to the point, these works not only rendered obsolete the distinction between normal and degenerate, but also drew attention towards pathological elements of expression.

It was quite typical, in this postwar atmosphere then, that in 1946 the St Anne psychiatric hospital in Paris should have held a large exhibition of works by the mentally ill, an exhibition which revealed for the first time to a very large public a whole body of work hitherto ignored. The exhibition, which lasted from February 16 to 28, opened with a lecture given by Dr Gaston Ferdière, and its catalogue was prefaced by Professor Henri Mondor and the art critic Waldemar George. Four years later, in 1950, Paris was chosen as the venue for the first World Congress of Psychiatry. On this occasion 2000 items from collections in seventeen countries were brought together for the first ever international exhibition of works by the mentally ill. The exhibition was an enormous success and achieved considerable press coverage. It can most certainly be considered as an authentic revelation.[4] This show formed the basis of the research which led Dr Robert Volmat to formulate his view of what he called 'art psychopathologique' – psychotic art.[5]

By this time, it must be noted, the art of the mentally ill possessed a long, well-documented history reaching back to the end of the nineteenth century.[6] Formerly one had spoken of the art of the insane (l'art des fous), or the art of the mentally ill, but by keeping strictly to the term 'psychopathologique' Volmat took the work out of a sociological context, by adopting a more abstract theoretical attitude. He managed to structure and define what had until then been merely a number of loose observations concerning a particular body of work. The basis of medical investigations into the art of the mentally ill was generally orientated towards classification, comparing the structure of the work with the symptoms of the patient. However, what concerns us here are the questions posed by the notion of psychotic art in the fields of both art and psychiatry, together with the purely aesthetic implications of the problem. Jean Dubuffet, for example, energetically questioned its premises when he denied that creatures with a common destiny could produce works with classifiably different characteristics. He refused to accept a distinction between the normal and the abnormal.[7] In fact, he regarded the work of art as something created in conceptual isolation, while for the medical establishment, on the contrary, it existed purely as a sociological document. For Dubuffet psychotic art seemed far richer than it might at first appear, because he was above all concerned with the aesthetic aspect of the works.

For all the impeccable scientific methods of Volmat's research, his book poses fundamental questions, as his predecessors' work had done, as to the very notion of art. Besides, the aim of the World Congress of 1950, as Volmat himself declared, was to 'assemble significant works of scientific interest . . . and to enable a wider public to perceive the aesthetic and thus the human value of the works of the mentally ill'.[8] It was indeed this quality which had attracted the attention of various doctors at the end of the nineteenth century, and was the reason why collections of 'l'art des fous' had originally been formed.[9] But now the notion of psychotic art not only took those with genuine artistic talent into consideration (this has been estimated as twenty per cent of the total), but in its concern to distinguish the 'artistic' from the 'pathological' or psychotic element, it gave to these artists a means of social communication, thus acknowledging their existence as individuals.[10] The fascination exerted by psychotic art on the public at the time must also be seen as an instance of the age-old dialogue between genius and madness: the similarity between the artist's creative trance and that of the madman has always formed the crux of the debate. Hence, psychotic art in the postwar period took on the aspect of a strange mirror in which contemporary art searched for its own image.

Initially, certain critics exploited the formal parallels between the works of mental patients and those of professional artists in order to prove the decadence of the latter. Such was the case with Waldemar George, who went so far as to speak of 'an eclipse of the Western world'.[11] It is significant, however, that among those who best understood or tolerated the avant-garde were precisely those doctors who had long since been examining the artistic productions of mental patients, with their violent, and far from traditional approach. They saw contemporary art almost as a result, if not a confirmation, of their research.[12] The reciprocity was bizarre: contemporary art found its most daring practices justified, and was incited to go even further. The relationship between the art of the mentally ill and 'the art of savages' – despite the pejorative tone of Waldemar George's preface to the St Anne exhibition catalogue – was precisely that link between psychotic art and that of primitive tribes, which the doctors had noted and which André Breton would comment on a little later. If madness could be seen as an original phase of mankind, psychotic art became increasingly necessary, if not indispensable, to its interpretation, through its affirmation of the primitive, which contemporary art was also reflecting.[13]

It was exactly at this moment, around 1945, that Jean Dubuffet began researching what he was later to call Art Brut:[14] a term which may be seen solely to apply to the collection he started at the time, and which is housed today at the Château de Beaulieu in Lausanne. Although psychotic art was based on certain social and cultural criteria that were precise and relatively limited, Art Brut on the contrary tended to exalt an ideal of creation untainted by any social concessions or by forms of expression recognised as psychotic, surrealist or naive, indeed by anything that was part and parcel of culture as Dubuffet saw it.

L'ART BRUT PRÉFÉRÉ AUX ARTS CULTURELS

Catalogue cover for the Art Brut exhibition, 1949.

It seems that Dubuffet began to be interested in works by people on the fringes of society in 1923, when he was doing his military service. At that time he happened to discover the work of a medium.[15] It was not until the end of the war, however, that intending to write a book about such works he made a trip to Switzerland; important collections of works by the mentally ill having already been constituted in Swiss psychiatric hospitals. When, in November 1947, the Foyer de l'Art Brut opened in the basement of the Galerie René Drouin in Paris, it was Dubuffet's collection and documents, amassed since 1945, which were shown to the public. Exhibitions of the works of Crépin, Aloïse, Juva, Salinguardes and Hernandez were also held at the time.[16] In June 1948, an association called the Compagnie de l'Art Brut was created to manage the Foyer de l'Art Brut, which was then transferred to the pavilion at the back of the garden belonging to Editions Gallimard, at 17 rue de l'Université, premises of the *Nouvelle Revue Française*. The inaugural exhibition showed works by Wölfli, Aloïse and Gironella.[17] Dubuffet wrote the first *Notice sur la Compagnie de l'Art Brut*,[18] in which he specified the aims of the association: 'To seek out the artistic productions of humble people which have a special quality of personal creation, spontaneity, and liberty with regard to convention and received ideas. To draw the public's attention towards this sort of work, to create a taste for it and encourage it to flourish.' The founder members were Jean Dubuffet, André Breton, Jean Paulhan, Charles Ratton, Henri-Pierre Roché and Michel Tapié.

In October and November 1949, the important exhibition L'Art Brut préféré aux arts culturels' took place in the Galerie Drouin. It included more than 200 works by 63 artists. This was in a way the official consecration of Art Brut, and Dubuffet's preface to the catalogue assumed the proportions of a manifesto.[19] The association held regular sessions up until September 1951, when Dubuffet, maintaining that certain problems were disrupting the smooth running of the Compagnie de l'Art Brut, demanded its dissolution and the authority to reconstitute it on an alternative basis. André Breton protested vigorously against this plan, and – making his differences of opinion quite clear – submitted his resignation. By October 8 of that year the Compagnie had been dissolved and its collections transported to the United States, where Alfonso Ossorio gave them shelter in the New York apartment he had previously offered the association. There they rested until 1962, when they returned to Paris.

It is obvious that Jean Dubuffet based his research on the collections of psychiatric hospitals from the very outset, and that the diversity and complexity of investigations of a strictly medical nature always held his attention, as the 'Appel aux médecins psychiatres' in the *Notice* of 1948 demonstrates.[20] However, from an early date Dubuffet was careful to remove any traces of his identification with this area, as indeed he proceded to do with Surrealist and naive art. He was sensitive to any reductive notions which might limit the ambitious concept he was elaborating, and he was in any case broadening his investigations to include the work of mediums and isolated individuals on the fringe of society. As he justly remarked, a really creative talent is as rare to find in 'insane' persons as in those considered normal. He pointed to the arbitrary nature of the distinction between insanity and normality and went so far as to say: 'There's no more an art of the insane than there's an art of dyspeptics or of people with sore knees',[21] thus totally refuting the existence of psychotic art. The validity of Dubuffet's attitude will not be discussed here,

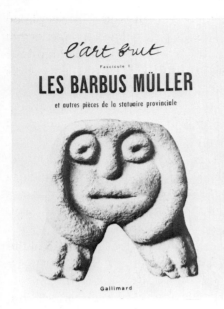

Cover of the first issue of Art Brut, 1947.

Back cover of the first issue of Art Brut.

but let it be remarked that the forcefulness and the coherence of his opinions were most influential in the context of the times.

By enlarging the notion of creation to include works that had hitherto been considered strictly marginal and outside culture, and by enriching it to include the drawings of mediums and clairvoyants, Dubuffet was working towards an idealistic vindication of absolute art.[22] Art Brut as a general concept leads one directly into a realm of nostalgia where the act of creation is envisaged in all its innate violence, stripped bare of everything that travesties its principles, that makes it artificial, a cultural parade. It is obvious that here one is encountering, on a utopian level, parallel to Dubuffet's own research as a creative artist, an ultimate form of the quest for origins: the fantasy of 'individual creation without precedent'.[24]

Marginality as a Source of Creation: Artaud, Michaux, Chaissac

If psychotic art and Art Brut resort to notions that are essentially sociological on the one hand, and purely subjective on the other, it is certain that some isolated or deliberately solitary individuals find a means of expression through their own social and cultural independence. In particular, through painting and writing, activities which may often be inseparable, they arrive at a statement of their community of origin. Here, the cases of Antonin Artaud, Henri Michaux and Gaston Chaissac are of particular interest.

Drawing as an activity for Artaud was essentially linked with his period of hospitalisation at the psychiatric clinic at Rodez, from 1943 onwards. He had in fact done some drawings before, the theatrical decors of 1924 for example, but he did not regard these as at all important. It is interesting to note that his drawings appeared at the very moment he started to write again in 1945,[25] firstly in the margins of his exercise books, then as points and geometrical figures spread out over the whole page. Artaud continued to draw symbolic and obsessive forms, intimately connected with his work as a writer up until his death in 1948. Besides this type of drawing, there were a number of others, relating to his experiences with the Tarahumas tribe in 1936, which used the same syntax, but were very much larger in format, and heightened with colour. At the same period, around 1945, he drew a self portrait, the first of the feverish series of portraits which he undertook on his return to Paris in 1946. He described his obsession with the human face in the catalogue to the exhibition at the Galerie Pierre in July 1947, where he showed portraits of all his friends.

Artaud's last drawings are of totemic figures, bizarrely crowded together, dead or alive, and dominated by his own face. If their violent technique, an expression of his personal life, especially the ravages of consumption, very definitely evokes the Art Brut aesthetic of Jean Dubuffet, it is obvious that Artaud's personality excludes his drawings from this category. Yet Artaud took up drawing on doctors' orders, submitting his works for their diagnosis, and hence their therapeutic origin would rather indicate a form of psychotic art. Above all, however, having 'definitively broken with art, style or talent'[26] the drawings appeared as a desperate attempt to achieve an elementary, total language, with which to 'manifest sorts of latent, linear truths which are equally valuable as words or written phrases, as graphic expression and features of perspective'.[26]

The work of Henri Michaux, another explorer of imaginary realms, shows again the inseparable relationship between painting and writing. A discourse evolves, which modifies both modes and finally transcends them. His use of automatic, spontaneous, experimental techniques, his nonchalant attitude towards academic practice and his imperious need to listen to the 'space within', separates Henri Michaux irrevocably from the caste of the 'professionals'. His work as a whole tends to reach back to the original source of his utterances. Between 1946 and 1950, with his 'frottages' and watercolours of a powerfully mediumistic character, where faces and bodies unceasingly emerge from the shadows, he constituted an imaginary language, primordial, expressive, the consequence of the first 'alphabets' he created. Thus, when Michaux exhibited for the first time at the Galerie René Drouin in 1948, his drawings appeared the equal of his literary works. For many they evoked an 'archaic emotion', the 'original encounter'.[27] Michaux continued in this vein from 1950-1956 in Indian ink paintings and gouaches achieved through movement, as a long poem of 1951 explains. The poem announced the gouaches which were to follow, where 'throngs' and 'melées' multiplied silhouettes suggestive of prehistoric painting. A magic fusion was established between the world of signs and that of the body. This was the moment when drugs influenced Michaux's work, in the mescaline drawings of 1954. Here he approaches a level of pure experience, as did Antonin Artaud, in the rituals of a communion with total knowledge.

The case of Gaston Chaissac, another painter and writer is an important one. He was encouraged to draw by Otto Freundlich in Paris around 1937, and thanks to his remarkable talent he came in 1942 to the notice of Robert Delaunay, the circle attached to the *Nouvelle Revue Française*, and Jean Dubuffet. He entered into a long correspondence with them, and in 1951, a series of his letters and poems, *Hippobosque au bocage*, was edited by Jean Dubuffet and published by Gallimard. He received no other significant recognition before 1961. Yet Chaissac was to spend all his life as a recluse in the rural setting of the Vendée, where he suffered intensely from a sense of isolation – though this was his raison d'être as a creator – and in addition he became the butt of local wits. His work is resolutely directed towards the aesthetic of 'bricolage', the imaginative use of odds and ends. Nothing could sum it up better than his own expression: 'modern rustic painting'. Original, provocative, violently expressive, sentimental, Chaissac's work has a sort of everyday urgency about it. It unfolds as a series of metamorphoses, sometimes tragic, sometimes comic, tender, ingenious, and with a total indifference to professional formulae. With its sense of humour, its enjoyment of the found object, his work demonstrates an uncommon intelligence and self-assurance. Because of his poverty, but also as a matter of choice, Chaissac's materials are almost always humble, and often the fruit of the most haphazard discoveries. His graphic expression, a mixture of drawing and writing, with its digressive, associative quality very often makes use of automatism and chance, in an improvised, unpremeditated manner. The expressively awkward, clumsy style, whether deliberate or spontaneous – like that of Paul Klee, whose work he knew – helped give his drawings the allure of graffiti, 'scribbles', as he said himself. They are related to drawings made by children, which he often took as a point of departure for his own work. His chromatic systems are closely related to these structures, but with a variety, and wide range of media and techniques, that make Chaissac, without a doubt, one of the most gifted colourists of the period. His work as a whole has a proliferating, organic character. Chance and the ephemeral come together in an ideal

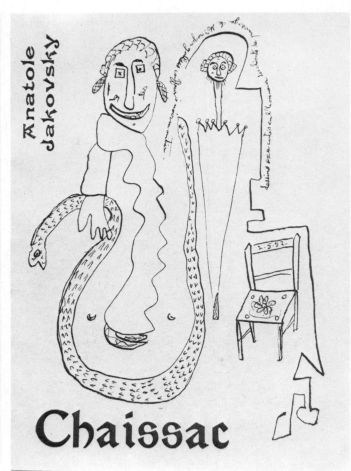

Cover for the catalogue of Chaissac's exhibition at the Galerie l'Arc en Ciel, 1947.

Cover of Jakovsky's *Chaissac – l'homme orchestre*, published 1952.

fusion of the artist with his environment and with nature, the nature which he so often used as a metaphor. From the first drawings of 1937-1938, their forms separated by black contours and ornamented with scale motifs inspired by prehistoric paintings and objects, to the abstract period of the 1960s, his work pursues a logic whose syntax is based on small, well-defined areas, and whose themes constantly revert to the human face and body. The inclusion of writing in his drawings which was an original compromise between figuration and abstraction around 1950, and the collages and assemblages which appeared so prolifically at that moment, make Chaissac one of the most significant artists of his time. He was not indifferent to his contemporaries, notably Picasso, but he was always most directly inspired by traditional craft techniques, and concerned above all with communication and reaching a popular audience. His work at once prefigured and contained in itself all the explosive force of the Cobra group. In this postwar period, it was a perfect example of creative resourcefulness.

The 'Professional' Reaction

It is equally important that contemporary movements themselves had been influenced by the return to primitive sources. The significance of the publication in 1942 of *Les Arts primitifs français* by Leon Gischia and Lucien Mazenod, and its influence on the coloration and technique of contemporary work has recently been noted.[28] Estève, Bazaine, Bissière, Lapicque, Manessier, Beaudin, Matisse, Dubuffet and many other artists were well aware of the monumental power and the expressive and decorative potential of the frescoes and illuminated manuscripts of the Romanesque period. The avant-garde painting of the 'French tradition' on occasion took much of its inspiration from history: it created a nostalgia for an idealised, vanished world where the medieval painter enjoyed a social status in the community corresponding with his role as the mediator of spiritual truth. This sentiment encouraged many artists, Dubuffet, Léger and Chaissac included, to believe in the reality of popular painting. At the same time, and in consequence perhaps, the contemporary taste for craft works, the use of found objects, rubbish, odds and ends left lying around, was to influence a certain number of works by Picasso and Miro during the period: towards 1950, 'assemblages' made from various odd objects and bits of rubbish could no longer be interpreted as mere survivors of Surrealism.

Bissière, for example, who created 'assemblages' and 'tapestries' of stray pieces of cloth during the war, could be seen to wage a sort of 'offensive' of materials, which one finds at the same moment in Victor Brauner, and this was evidently one of Dubuffet's activating principles too. With other artists, Fautrier for example, the promotion of matter for its own sake could become an autonomous principle. It is interesting to note that this need to break with the traditional painting of the immediate past through the glorification of pure matter or gesture alone, was succinctly expressed by Michel Tapié, when, in 1951, he gave his book on the first generation of 'informel' painters the title 'Un art Autre'.

It was André Breton, however, returning to Paris in 1946, who formulated and defined the tendencies which had hitherto been simply phenomena to be observed in the work of certain painters. Through his direct involvement with them and through his writings, he was eventually able to pinpoint the logic of events and the various forces at work, allowing them a scope that corresponded to the emphatic position of Dubuffet. Before the war, with *Le Surréalisme et la Peinture* (1928), and *Genèse et perspective artistique du Surréalisme* (1941) Breton had already elaborated the notions of primitivism and automatism, and in *Autodidactes dits Naïfs* (1942) he proclaimed 'the vital necessity of a myth to oppose that of Odin and a few others . . . in view of today's conflicts'. This article, in which Breton gives first place to the Douanier Rousseau, is central to the reinterpretation of the mythical sources of art, which was to breathe new life into Surrealism, finally leading via automatism into gestural and 'informel' painting. At the time, Breton cultivated marginal artists with enthusiasm: he wrote about naive painters such as Hyppolite (1947), Demonchy (1949), Vivancos (1950), Crépin (1954), and most important of all, in 1948 he wrote *'L'Art des fous, la Clé des Champs'*. Here he makes a totally convincing comparison between the mentally ill and the art of primitive peoples: 'This absolute liberty confers a grandeur upon the art of the mentally sick which we can only rediscover with any certitude among primitive tribes.' In 1954 and 1955, with *Triomphe de l'Art Gaulois* and *Présent des Gaules*, Breton drew the parallel between contemporary artistic development and the Romanesque style, concluding in each case that there had been a break with the classical, Graeco-Roman world. Extending the concept of primitivism in this way, Breton not only defined the origins of the new painting in terms of a precise territory but he helped to establish that apparently contradictory movements did spring from the same source. Thus he explained and even gave new impetus to contemporary painting. Previously, enlarging the

[1] André Breton: 'Présent des Gaules' in *Le Surréalisme et la Peinture*, Gallimard, Paris, 1965, p.333.

[2] See Henry-Claude Cousseau, 'L'origine et l'écart: d'un art l'autre' in *Paris-Paris, créations en France, 1937-1957*, Centre Georges Pompidou, Paris, May 28 to November 2, 1981, pp.158-174.

[3] The relationship between contemporary psychiatric and anthropological research is most carefully explained in Robert Volmat: *L'Art Psychopathologique*, Paris, 1956, in the chapter entitled 'Les arts et la pensée archaïque', p.196. See also Michel Foucault: *Histoire de la folie a l'âge classique*, Paris, 1972, p.538.

[4] See articles by René Bessière and Jean Bouret in *Arts*, September 22, 1950, Waldemar George in *Le Peintre*, October 25, 1950 and Julien Alvard in *Art d'aujourd'hui*, November 1950.

[5] Robert Volmat's doctoral thesis, *L'Art Psychopathologique*, was published in 1956.

[6] See Françoise Will-Levaillant: 'L'analyse des dessins d'aliénés et de mediums en France avant le surréalisme', in *Revue de l'Art* no 50, C.N.R.S., Paris, 1980, pp.24-39.

[7] In his preface to the catalogue *L'Art Brut préferé aux arts culturels*, Galerie René Drouin, Paris, 1949. See also 'Honneur aux valeurs sauvages' and 'Place à l'incivisme', in Jean Dubuffet: *Prospectus et tous écrits suivants*, Volume 1, Gallimard, Paris 1967, pp.198-202, 205-214 and 452-457.

[8] Quoted in Marie-France Bochot: *Expression plastique, méthode d'investigation et méthode thérapeutique*, Doctoral thesis in medicine, Paris, 1975, p.19 ff.

[9] Especially the collections of Auguste Marie (1856-1934), and Charles Ladame (1871-1949). See also Marcel Réja: *L'art chez les fous, le dessin, la prose, la poésie*, Paris, 1907.

[10] See Werner Spies: 'L'Art Brut avant 1967', in *Revue de l'Art*, no 1-2, C.N.R.S., Paris, 1968, pp.123-6, and Claude Wiart: 'Expression picturale des malades mentaux' in the *Petit Larousse de la Peinture*, Volume 2, Paris, 1979, pp.418-422.

[11] In the preface to the catalogue 'Exposition des oeuvres exécutées par des malades mentaux', Centre Psychiatrique Saint Anne, Paris, February 1946.

[12] See in Robert Volmat's doctoral thesis, *L'Art Psychopathologique*, op cit., p.215, the chapter called 'Positions de l'art moderne' for an excellent synthesis.

[13] Werner Spies: 'L'Art Brut avant 1967', op. cit., note 10. It must be noted that for Hans Prinzhorn, who wrote *Bildnerei der Geisteskranken* (Berlin, 1922), it was on the contrary the study of art which afforded the most valuable lessons for psychiatry.

[14] For Art Brut in general, see the very full documentation and the collected articles in Jean Dubuffet: *Prospectus et tous écrits suivants*, Volume 1, part 3, Gallimard, Paris 1967. See also Michel Thévoz, *L'Art Brut*, Geneva, 1975.

[15] The story is related in Georges Limbour: *Tableau bon levain à vous de cuir la pâte, l'art brut de Jean Dubuffet*, Paris, 1953, p.56. See also François Gagnon, 'Coupures de presse' in *Dubuffet*, L'Herne, Paris, 1975, p.121.

[16] For these artists, see the *Fascicules de l'Art Brut*, published from 1964 onwards.

[17] Idem.

[18] Jean Dubuffet: *Prospectus* op. cit., p.489. Dubuffet was to write a second 'Notice' in January 1963, when the Compagnie de l'Art Brut was reconstituted at the Rue de Sevres, Paris (*Prospectus* op. cit., p.167).

[19] *Prospectus* op. cit., p.198.

[20] See note 18.

[21] See note 19.

** On this subject, see Dubuffet, 'Place à l'incivisme', op. cit. note 7.

[23] In 'Place à l'incivisme' idem.

[24] Quoted in Gaetan Picon: *Le travail de Jean Dubuffet*, Geneva, 1973, p.188.

[25] As Paule Thévenin explains in *Antonin Artaud*, Cahiers de l'Abbaye Sainte-Croix, no 37, Les Sables d'Olonne, 1980, but it seems that Artaud had tried his hand at this type of drawing as early as 1944, if we believe his letters to Dr. Ferdière in *Antonin Artaud*, La Tour de Feu, no 136, December 1977, p.16.

[26] Quoted in *Paris-Paris*, op. cit., p.157.

[27] Jean Starobinski: 'Le monde physionomique' in the catalogue *Henri Michaux*, Centre Georges Pompidou, Paris, 1968, p.65.

[28] Sarah Wilson: 'Les jeunes peintres de tradition française', in the catalogue *Paris-Paris*, op. cit., p.106.

[29] It was at the Galerie René Drouin, in the same year, 1945, that Fautrier's 'Otages' and Dubuffet's 'Hautes pâtes' were exhibited.

[30] Gaetan Picon, op. cit., p.208.

area of his research, he had investigated the medium-inspired automatism of Crépin and Lesage, and magic art with Hyppolite, in order to broaden his interpretation of creative phenomena and widen its frontiers. It was in fact because he refused to limit Art Brut to a definition closely associated with the art of the mentally ill that he resigned from the 'Compagnie de l'Art Brut'.

The second offensive against culture was the result of a movement which was born to oppose the conventions of Parisian taste. This movement stemmed curiously enough from foreign artists, who came originally from Copenhagen, Brussels and Amsterdam, and who, taking the initials of these towns, called themselves 'Cobra'. While Breton and the Surrealist movement had adopted a largely historical, highly intellectual viewpoint, Cobra was to adopt a more immediate – and effective – attitude, instantly appropriating popular art, childrens' drawings, graffiti and raw and waste materials for their repertory of motifs and techniques. The group had a review called *Cobra* which ran for eight issues between 1948 and 1951. With its deliberate iconoclasm, its desire to disrupt both figurative and abstract conventions, to enlarge the official frontiers of art, in particular when they insisted on writing as a form of autonomous artistic expression, the Cobra movement assumed a scope which ultimately embraced many French avant-garde artists, from Dubuffet to Atlan, from Etienne-Martin to Wols and Mathieu, inasmuch as their own work was based on the same sources. Thus Cobra precipitated a movement which had initially been stimulated by the elementary principles of Surrealism. In its attempts at synthesis, extremely influential at the time, where popular, craft values took their place alongside traditional and psychotic art, Cobra was to impose an aesthetic of intuition, inspiration, spontaneity and violence which could be seen as the opposite, 'cultural' version of Dubuffet's attempts at subversion with Art Brut.

If the Surrealist effort to return to primitive sources was, with a few exceptions narrowly iconographical, Cobra broadened the whole enterprise, with an immediacy capable of abolishing the traditional techniques of painting. Hence the group's interest in the work of Jean Dubuffet, and their plan to make him the subject of the eighth number of their review. But Dubuffet's research was already taking him well ahead, and the interdependence he established between matter and the graphic element in his work made him, no less than Fautrier, a prophet of the most significant contemporary developments.[29] In confrontation with Surrealism, Dubuffet with his subversive and uncompromising approach linked the magic of the image not so much to its own power of reference, but to its mysterious apparition within matter itself. With his desire to 'take things up again from their point of departure', to be at the source of 'what has not yet begun',[30] Dubuffet saw his own work confirmed, as he himself had vindicated Art Brut: it was 'an individual creation without precedent'.[24]

**The ceremony
for which all ceremonies
exist: the ceremony of the
physical union between man and the world.**

(AIMÉ CESAIRE)

MASTERS OF THE OLDER GENERATION

BONNARD
BRAQUE
CHAGALL
LAURENS
LÉGER
MATISSE
PICASSO
ROUAULT
VILLON

In November 1945, the cinema newsreel 'Actualités Françaises' produced a film called 'L'Art retrouvé', which showed museum masterpieces on display once more after years of storage, the renewal of artistic activity in Montmartre and Montparnasse, and the return of the 'Masters': Braque, Matisse, Picasso, Rouault and Laurens. Utrillo was preferred to Dufy, and Bonnard was forgotten: he was living almost as a recluse at Le Cannet, where he died in 1947.

Just before the war, the Expostion Internationale of 1937 had impressively demonstrated that the State and municipal authorities of the Ville de Paris at last recognised the existence of modern art. Thanks to their new cultural policy, an important number of works were commissioned, and the Palais des Beaux Arts was built to house the future national and municipal museums of modern art. This policy however, sanctioned a long-lasting split between the French tradition inherited from the generation of the Fauves and Cubists, and the 'foreign' characteristics of the Surrealist and Abstract schools. The first tendency was officially on show at the huge exhibition 'Maitres de l'art independant' at the Petit Palais, while the 'foreign school' held a markedly more comprehensive exhibition 'Origines et développement de l'art international indépendant' at the Jeu de Paume. Ten years later, in 1947, this division was still in evidence; the situation was repeated when the collection of the new Musée Nationale d'Art Moderne in Paris was challenged by the exhibition of 'Peintures et Sculptures Contemporaines' organised by Christian Zervos at the Palais des Papes in Avignon.

During the war however, and despite certain unfortunate compromises that the erstwhile Fauves, Derain, Vlaminck, Othon Friesz and Dunoyer de Segonzac saw fit to make with the Occupant, it had been the first tendency, rooted in Cubism and Fauvism, which asserted the continuity of the French tradition, with its creative fusion of emotion and reason. It was under this aegis that 'Vingt jeunes peintres de tradition française', twenty young and not so young painters, held an exhibition with highly Resistant overtones in May 1941, at the Galerie Braun. After the war they developed what became known as 'paysagisme abstrait' (abstract landscape painting), which maintained an essentially cubist grid structure and a taste for brilliant colour. This became characteristic of the so-called 'Nouvelle Ecole de Paris', represented by such painters as Maurice Esteve, Jean Bazaine, Alfred Manessier, and Jean Le Moal. The official critics of the time who unanimously praised the moral integrity of 'La Peinture' embodied by this French Tradition continued to reject the 'intellectualism' of the great abstract Dada and Surrealist artists. Thus they repeated the pronouncements made during the Occupation when the 'Maîtres' were promoted as living witnesses of the permanence of the French tradition. In 1943, for example, Gaston Diehl's *Les Peintres d'Aujourd'hui* had perfectly summed up this shared desire to achieve 'Absolute Harmony' (Braque), 'the grandeur and sacred nature of every living thing' (Matisse), 'the lofty dignity of he who turns towards the invisible world in horror of this mechanical, over-wise, utilitarian age' (Rouault). The once disturbing figure of Picasso had joined their ranks quite naturally as 'the classic of this half-century' the master of 'plastic truths'. But though Picasso's genius was uncontested, as early as 1946, the academicism of the Picassoids was being mooted: Rene Guilly, in 'Picasso . . . et les Picassoides' (*Juin* no 19, June 1946), denounces Paris's 'odious exclusion' of Tanguy, de Chirico, Max Ernst and Masson, who were apparently considered not sufficiently 'plastic'. This enlightened point of view was at odds with the official patronage of the humanist tradition, impregnated with the material and spiritual values of French culture, and patronised moreover, in official circles. Inevitably a reaction and counterpart was found in the developments by experimental, politically active or marginal artists, who sought to create new forms corresponding to the climate of postwar Paris.

Undeniably, however, the ranks of these artists were swelled at this time because of the presence of the 'Maîtres', the masters of the older generation. Paris became once more the mecca for artists from all over the world. They arrived to discover the heritage of modern art miraculously alive . . . Thanks to the provisions of the G.I. bill for example, over one hundred American artists were able to enrol for twice-weekly sessions in the studio of Fernand Leger, who at sixty-six was still the vigorous prophet of modernism. He exhibited at the Galerie Carré from 1948 to 1953.

The oldest of the masters, Pierre Bonnard, diverging almost imperceptibly from his classic post-impressionist period, achieved in his final years a vertiginous brilliance of design and colour, where the object, glowing and yet disintegrated, reflected at once the anxieties of an era and his individual doubts and sufferings.

Georges Braque was another of the older painters whose work entered a particularly strong period in the later 1940s. The Galerie Maeght mounted almost annual exhibitions of Braque in 1947, 1948, 1950 and 1952.

During the war, Marc Chagall had been the symbol of the French creative genius in New York. He sent his salutations to Paris for the Salon de la

Libération of 1944 and on his return to the capital in 1947, the Musée National d'Art Moderne held a retrospective in his honour, having accepted a donation of some of Chagall's finest pictures.

Raoul Dufy perfected his fluid technique, surpassing mere decoration, finally reaching a degree of graphic freedom in which all becomes sign. Raoul Dufy and Jacques Villon exhibited regularly after the war at the Galerie Louis Carré in both Paris and New York. Established figures of the modern movement, their sensitive interpretations of reality evoked a bucolic world of charm and happiness. Among the sculptors, Henri Laurens rather than the lone figure of Brancusi, embodied in his work both classical plentitude and a certain audacity in his more conceptual pieces. His failure to win the Grand Prix at the Venice Biennale of 1950 aroused the sympathy of Matisse and the public support of many of his friends. The following year, both Laurens and Jacques Villon achieved the summits of official recognition with retrospectives at the Musée National d'Art Moderne. The 'Hommage a Rouault' organised by the Centre Catholique des Intellectuels at the Palais de Chaillot celebrated Rouault's eightieth birthday in 1951, and heralded retrospectives in Brussels, Amsterdam and the Musée National d'Art Moderne, Paris, the following year.

Rouault, with this untiring enthusiasm and yet uneasy temperament, continued to paint violent, almost abstract works which he refused to consider 'finished', and which he did his utmost to shield from speculation: on November 5 1948 he burnt 315 canvases after court proceedings concerning the late Ambrose Vollard.

Matisse continued to explore his sensual, delicate, enchanting universe, where pictorial metaphor united with a powerful, dynamic sense of ornament, a freedom of design repeated to the point of automatism, and the most daring juxtapositions of brilliant colour. The technique of paper cut-outs, 'drawings with scissors', on matt gouach surfaces, which he invented in 1937 for a cover of the magazine *Verve* disrupted the normal limitations of space, enabling him to find a paradoxical depth in his super-positionings of flat, coloured planes. Here he went completely beyond the represented object, achieving the ultimate in purely visual effects. Matisse's work from 1947-8 was shown in 1954 at the Musée National d'Art Moderne. But it was to be the elegant Maison de la Pensée Française, run by the French Communist Party which rendered a constant and semi-official homage to Picasso, (exhibitions in 1948, 1950 and 1953), Léger (1951 and 1954), and Matisse (1950). It was thanks to these artists in effect, that France maintained her supremacy at the Venice Biennale, with exhibitions of Braque in 1948, Matisse in 1950 and Dufy in 1952.

Picasso and Matisse, who had been first honoured by their fellow-artists with retrospectives at the Salons d'Automne of 1944 and 1945 respectively, were regularly welcomed at the new Salon de Mai where they showed their latest creations; Picasso's work during the occupation was shown at the Galerie Louis Carré in 1945 and 1946. From 1945 onwards, Picasso was hedonistically proclaiming the 'joie de vivre' of the Mediterranean – a joy shared at the time with his young companion Françoise Gilot and his two children Paloma and Claude. He became interested in sculpture again, and embarked upon a vast series of ceramic works which entailed a return to certain rigorously abstract principles he had first explored in the 1930s. The 'Joie de Vivre' and the 'Seated Figure' sculptures of 1947, both at the Musée Picasso, Antibes, illustrate these two tendencies. The Antibes ("Antipolis") period of 1945-8 was shown in 1948 at the Galerie Louise Leiris.

Slightly later, a new wilfully brutal attitude to design, colour and the application of paint, led to the creation of extremely expressionistic works, whose repercussions can be seen to mark the painters of today.

Rather than resting mere tutelary spirits of modernism, the masters of the previous generation were revealing astonishing powers of invention when confronted with the aesthetic problems of the period. Their deepest interrogations, their most daring and individual solutions, were often misunderstood at the time, and only perceived in their full importance in the 1960s and 1970s, in movements as diverse as Pop art, 'Support-Surface', and more recently in Pattern painting.

GERMAIN VIATTE

V Pierre Bonnard
L'atelier aux mimosas (The Studio with mimosas), 1939-46. *Oil on canvas, 127 x 127*
Musée National d'Art Moderne, Centre Georges Pompidou

PIERRE BONNARD

b 1867, Fontenay aux Roses,
d 1947, Le Cannet

As early as 1886 at the Académie Julian, Bonnard met Paul Serusier, Maurice Denis, Gabriel Ibel and Paul Ranson, and at the Ecole des Beaux Arts the following year he was friendly with Edouard Vuillard and Xavier Roussel. He became one of the most brilliant members of the group known as the Nabis, an ironic title, meaning 'prophets'. The group were interested in the work of Gaugin, the Japanese print, scenes from everyday life, and in particular, the poster – Bonnard's 'France Champagne' (1888) for example. From now on, Bonnard's paintings and lithographs depicted street life in all its familiar and unexpected aspects, and the world of childhood, with great sophistication and charm. His superb illustrations for Verlaine's *Parallèlement* (1900), and for Longus' *Daphnis et Chloe* (1902), published by Ambroise Vollard, showed a full-bodied, sensual use of colour which marked a change in his painting. From his Nabi period, Bonnard retained the decentralised compositions and foreshortenings based on the lessons of contemporary photography, while his magnificent colour had its source in impressionism.

While Bonnard was always in touch with the latest developments in modern painting, light and colour were always paramount for him as an artist. In 1909, he was enchanted by the light of the South of France at St Tropez, and from then onwards he returned there every year. For the rest of his life he explored tone, light and colour on a large or small scale. He worked with complete independence, keeping at first to the framework of his composition, but later letting his colour glow with a luminosity that transcended the subject, and became an almost vertiginous visual experience for the spectator. From 1906, he held regular exhibitions at the Galerie Bernheim Jeune in Paris, and achieved considerable recognition. While he was always shy and secluded, a painter of private dreams and emotions who spent the crucial years 1939-1945 in isolation at Le Cannet, he was nonetheless acclaimed during the war by the 'Jeunes peintres de Tradition française' such as Jean Bazaine, who saw his work as an example: 'a total conception of space-colour which leads painting along its most authentic path.'. His graphic work was shown in December 1944 at the Galerie Pierre Béres, and in June 1946, a retrospective exhibition was held at the Galerie Bernheim Jeune. G.V.

'I believe that the success of every painter's life depends on his pursuit of the simple figure which is infinitely variable according to individual temperaments. In the work of Matisse, who is preoccupied with the purity of his means, the simple, forceful expression of reality, the object is stripped away until, little by little, it becomes a sign or an ideogram. But Bonnard remains enamoured of the world of the flesh, aware of the material being and surface of each thing. Light, which in Matisse's painting creates a lucid and transparent universe, cannot become in Bonnard's work abstract or detached from a sensual perception of reality. It remains embodied, while the matter in the painting takes on density: light supports and animates it. The simple figure coming to terms with abstraction means for Bonnard the intimate union of light with heavy and absorbent matter. Year by year we have seen his faces become less individual yet more intense, his large scale compositions of leaves, countryside and clouds become increasingly pure areas of vibrating, balanced and intense colour and form, in which sunlight, sky and landscape are woven together into one.

Jean Bazaine, 'Bonnard et la Realité', in *Formes et couleurs*, no. 2, 1944.

GEORGES BRAQUE

b 1882, Argenteuil sur Seine, d 1963 Paris

Braque's father moved to Le Havre in 1890, and set up a paint business where the young Braque served as an apprentice, while at the same time he studied at Le Havre's Ecole des Beaux Arts. He went to Paris in 1900, where he continued his professional training, visited the museums and met Marie Laurencin and Francis Picabia at the Académie Humbert. He was impressed by the works of Raoul Dufy and Othon Friesz – both old friends from Le Havre – when they exhibited at the Salon d'Automne in the room devoted to the artists who were christened the 'fauves' or wild beasts. Braque himself then painted in the Fauvist style, before his crucial meeting with Picasso in 1907, when he saw the 'Demoiselles d'Avignon', the key work in Picasso's transition to Cubism. Braque's friendship with Picasso and the impact of the Cézanne retrospectives at the Salon d'Automne of 1907 and at the Galerie Bernheim Jeune, marked a complete change in his work, which was exhibited in 1908 by Daniel Kahnweiler, with a catalogue prefaced by the poet Guillaume Apollinaire. Maintaining all the while a very intimate, complementary relationship with Picasso, Braque explored the realms of analytical and synthetic cubism at Estaque (1908-1910), La Roche Guyon (1909), Ceret (1911-1913) and

Sorgues (1912-1914). It was a revolution in terms of pictorial space: the conceptual and tactile aspects of reality were dynamically represented in two dimensions. In September 1912, Braque invented the papier collé, the paper collage which introduced fragments of reality onto the surface of the art object. It was the beginning of an increasingly adventurous, methodical exploration of the artist's world of forms, which culminated before the war in the series 'Intérieurs', like 'le Duo', 1937, and the large 'Natures Mortes', of 1938, which were magnificently echoed in the 'Billiards' of 1944. The harsh material and domestic realities of the Occupation were later immortalized by Braque in the series of nine 'Ateliers', painted from 1949-1956. 'L'Art et le vie ne font qu'un' he said, and on the fluid paint surfaces spaces and objects appear, inextricably harmonised and animated, it seems, by the flight of a great bird which was to become a dominant symbol for Braque. After his first one-man-show at the Galerie Maeght in 1947, he exhibited at the Venice Biennale of 1948 where he won first prize for his painting. From 1956 onwards, his work began to emphasise the material quality of paint as autonomous matter, a development which paralleled the experiments of the younger generation.   G.V.

With no established precedents, and no direct descendants, Braque creates an impression at every moment of a man who gives precise instructions and who guarantees the authentic. His easel holds a world that is strangely full and autonomous to the point where each colour loses its traditional role. Green no longer suggests landscape, nor red violence nor violet ambiguity. Other critics have discussed in depth his use of sketches, his passion for artistic problems, the feminine and tender element in his work and yet its thick, rebellious paint quality: he has been called the master of visual relationships. I gladly call him the master of invisible relationships ... I would not willingly decide whether Braque is the artist endowed with the most variety and widest repertoire of our times. But if the great painter is the one who gives the most accurate and stimulating idea of painting, then with no hesitation I take Braque as my master, the 'patron'.

Jean Paulhan, *Braque le patron*, Gallimard, 1952.

I Georges Braque
La Nuit (Night), 1951-2. *Oil on canvas, 162 x 73*
Galerie Maeght, Paris

MARC CHAGALL

b 1887, Vitebsk; Russia

Throughout his life, Chagall's work has been deeply involved with the mystical, poetic universe of his childhood, spent in Vitebsk in a modest and very religious Jewish family. This small town on the river's bank, with its turrets and wooden houses, its vagabonds and violin players, its processions of life and death, its symbolic animals, were all part of the vivid world that Chagall loved. He discovered primitive sign painting, and began his formal training there in 1906 at Jehuda Penn's school of painting. He went to St Petersburg in 1907, becoming a pupil at the Imperial School for the Encouragement of the Arts; then in 1908 he went to the Zvanseva School, where Leon Bakst, the designer for the Russian Ballet, introduced him to modern art. In 1910, he arrived in Paris, and lived in the artists' community at La Ruche, where Blaise Cendrars and Max Jacob the poets, and the painters Léger, Modigliani and Roger de la Fresnaye became his friends. His fantastic memories of Vitebsk now became transposed into a universe of dreams, strengthened by the use of cubist form and orphic colour. In 1911, Chagall exhibited 'Moi et le village' in the Cubist room of the Salon des Indépendants. Apollinaire used the terms 'surnaturalisme' and then 'réalisme' for the first time with reference to Chagall's work, and introduced the artist to Herwarth Walden who gave him an exhibition at the Der Sturm gallery in Berlin. Taken by surprise when the Revolution broke out in Moscow, Chagall exhibited forty-five works at the 'Knave of Diamonds' salon in 1916, and in 1918, his name was put forward by Lounatcharsky as Commissioner for the Fine Arts for the Government of Vitebsk. There he founded a Fine Arts Academy and invited Lissitzky, Pougny and Malevitch to be teachers. In fact they soon supplanted him. In 1919 and 1920 Chagall created costumes and scenery for the New State Theatre of Jewish Art in Moscow.

Returning to France in 1923, he prepared illustrations for several luxury editions at the suggestion of Ambroise Vollard: *Les fables de la Fontaine*, 1925-1926, and Gogol's *Les âmes mortes*, 1927, which were later published by Tériade, and a series of gouaches based

1 Marc Chagall
L'Ame de la Ville (Soul of the Town), 1945. *Oil on canvas, 106 x 82*
Musée National d'Art Moderne, Centre Georges Pompidou. Gift of the artist

on the theme of the circus. In 1931 he visited Palestine as background and inspiration to his set of Bible illustrations. Yet as early as 1933, Goebbels had ordered his work to burnt at Mannheim, and the joy and tranquility of the 1930s soon gave way to an atmosphere of anti-semitism, the persecution of the Jews and the horrors of the Second World War. Chagall started to produce dramatic and visionary works; the theme of the 'Crucifixion', often side by side with the 'Chute de l'Ange' became the symbol of war and of the sufferings of his people. Chagall fled to the United States in 1941, and in October 1944 from New York he sent a message to the Salon d'Automne, called that year the Salon de la Libération: 'I bow before your universal battle, your battle against the enemy of Art and Life. With Paris free, and Art in France reborn, the world will free itself once and for all from its diabolical enemies who wished to destroy not only the body but the soul. The soul . . . without which there is neither life nor artistic creation.' Chagall returned to Paris in 1947, and the first exhibition to be held at the new Musée National d'Art Moderne was a retrospective in his honour.   G.V.

'Man is searching for something new: he must perpetually rediscover the authenticity of his own language. A language like that of primitive peoples, men who opened their mouths for the first time to speak their one, unique truth.

A painting for me is a surface covered with representations of things (objects, animals, human forms) in a certain order, in which logic and illustration have no importance whatever. A mysterious fourth or fifth dimension exists perhaps – perhaps not simply visual – which gives birth intuitively to a balance of artistic and psychic contrasts, striking the eye of the spectator with new unaccustomed concepts. In fact, what gives an object colour is neither what is called 'real colour', nor 'conventional colour'.

In the same way, depth does not seem from the supposed laws of perspective. It is life, likewise, which creates the contrasts without which art would be unimaginable and incomplete.'

Marc Chagall in the exhibition catalogue *Marc Chagall*, Musée des Arts Décoratifs, Paris, 1959.

HENRI LAURENS

b 1885, Paris, d 1954, Paris

Laurens served as an apprentice to an ornamental sculptor learning the direct carving method in stone. After his initial academic traning, he was attracted by the work of Rodin for a period. The most important influence on him, however, was that of Braque, whom he met in 1911. Laurens' first Cubist works, figures done in polychrome wood and plaster, date from 1915. He proceeded to make more subtle and complicated constructions in various materials, and from 1916 onwards, created several paper collages. Thanks to a meeting with Picasso, Laurens held an exhibition in 1916 at Leonce Rosenberg's Galerie L'Effort Moderne. Working very often in terracotta with an emphasis on bas reliefs, Laurens continued in the cubist style until the mid 1930s when his sculptures became rounder, evoking mythical figures, curvaceous bathers and mermaids, in a play of volumes and hollows. He received several commis-sions for the Exposition Internationale of 1937: one of his most notable works was a suspended monumental structure in wood, cardboard and metal, for Le Corbusier's Pavillon des Temps Nouveaux. 1937 was also the year that Laurens' major works, 'Amphion' and 'La Musicienne' were created. They preceded the more solemn sculptures of the war years, 'L'Adieu', 'La Nuit', and the joyful and dynamic work of the postwar period: 'Le Matin', 'L'Aurore' and 'L'Automne'. Laurens also illustrated two luxury editions: Theocritus' *Les Idylles* in 1945 for Verve, and Lucian's *Loukos ou L'Ane* in 1946 for Tériade. He was considered the greatest living French sculptor of the period, and in 1951 the Musée National d'Art Moderne organised a retrospective exhibition in his honour.   G.V.

'A work of art must shed its own light and not borrow it. This light is the expression of the human quality of the artist. It is a beautiful language which measures a man, which illuminates a work, and which Henri Laurens possesses to the full. His art was for all people, but so much has been done that it has become distant from them all, for everything is a question of education. (Art, historically speaking, has never been accepted by the masses except when it has been imposed on them, and what authority do they have today to guide them?.) If it is esoteric, it is so to the same extent that Olympus, Tavan, or the Portail Royal are for us. If there is a divorce between art and man, man alone, not the creator is responsible for it.

A work of art must shed its own light. What desolation, these times, in which living beauty shines, equal and eternal, in harmony with our pulses which are quicker, our days which are fewer in a sacred solitude, while a few steps away men blind to her tear themselves to pieces and die in obscurity.

Louis Gabriel Clayeux: *Le monde français*, II no. 5, February 1946, p. 312.

'Laurens' sculpture is for me, more than anything else, a veritable projection of himself into space, a bit like a shadow with three dimensions. His way of breathing, touching, feeling, thinking even, becomes an object, becomes sculpture. This sculpture is complex, it is real as a glass (I would like to say "or as a root", I'm less sure of that although certain aspects are nearer to a root than to glass); at the same time it recalls a human figure reinvented, it is above all the "double", of what makes Laurens one with himself through time, but in addition, each one of his sculptures is the crystallisation of a particular moment of this time.

Alberto Giacometti: *Labyrinthe* no. 4, Geneva, 1945.

'Look at Laurens' work: the soul or what passes for it, dilates, swells, expands, you open your eyes to endless distances, you look into boundless space, you'd think you were facing the sea. It's a poem, which like all true poems, has neither a beginning nor an end. Like any living thing, it's the networks of moving forms you see, which do not simply partake of the nature of man, but go beyond him and are life itself, organic life, enriched with vital lyricism. And above all, yes, above all, Laurens' work is a living force which is mute. What serenity and power! Infinity lies somewhere in this tragic stillness, this troubling quietude which surrounds his work like an atmosphere, haloes it with the super-human majesty of silence, not a religious silence, but a silence pure as pure water, which would be broken if one sensed some conversation starting up, if all of a sudden the sculptor could be seen creating his sculpture. For realism, however, you choose to dress it up with other names, is never anything more than naturalism looking for excuses. And it must be said incidentally, that if art were as easy as the advocates of realism would have it, if it were only a question of feeling

I Georges Braque
La Nuit (Night), 1951-2. *Oil on canvas,*
162 x 73
Galerie Maeght, Paris

2 Henri Laurens
L'automne (Autumn), 1948. *Bronze, 80 x 170*
Musée National d'Art Moderne, Centre Georges Pompidou

3 Henri Laurens
L'adieu (The Farewell), 1941. *Bronze,*
73 x 85 x 69
Musée National d'Art Moderne, Centre Georges Pompidou

reality in touch with our senses, our conscience, our sensibility, if it were simply necessary to communicate with reality by direct contact, we would have no need for artists. With Laurens there's a state of perpetual and primitive wonder at the physical forces of life.'

Maurice Raynal: 'Henri Laurens', *Le Point* Lanzac par Souillac, July 1946.

FERNAND LÉGER

b 1881, Argentan, d 1955, Gif sur Yvette

Léger came from a solid agricultural background in Normandy. In 1897 he was apprenticed to an architect in Caen and worked with an architect in Paris before entering the Ecole des Arts Décoratifs in 1903. The Cézanne retrospective at the Salon d'Automne of 1907 was crucial: 'It took me three years to get rid of Cézanne's influence . . . its grip was so strong, that to get out of it I had to go as far as abstraction'. At this period he associated with all the avant-garde painters who lived with him in the artistic community of La Ruche – Archipenko, Laurens, Lipchitz, Delaunay, Chagall and Soutine. In 1910 Leger started the series 'Toits' and 'Fumées'painted from his window, and with Delaunay, Gleizes, Metzinger, Kupka, Picabia and others he participated in the Section d'Or Salons.

His experience in the trenches in 1914 was his first contact with both the reality of war, and 'all the french people'. At the same time he was inspired by 'the breech of a 75 rifle open in full sunlight'. Léger henceforth celebrated the beauty of the machine: the dynamic technology of industrial civilisation. Man was reduced to a mere robot in his paintings. Yet after 1920 the human figure reasserted itself. In 1924, the year of his film *Le Ballet mécanique*, and his abstract painting 'Eléments mécanique', he produced 'La Lecture' for example, with its two very recognisable figures, books, and a bunch of flowers. It was the year he founded his first studio, the Académie Moderne with Ozenfant and Marie Laurençin in the rue Notre Dame des Champs. After 1933 it reopened until the outbreak of war, and it was during the 1930s that Roland Brice, later Léger's ceramicist, and Nicolas de Staël came to work in the studio, mixing with the Renault factory workers who received special evening courses. Léger's first

mural paintings had been done in 1925 for Le Corbusier's 'Pavillon de L'Esprit Nouveau' at the Exposition des Arts Décoratifs, and increasingly, the concept of mural painting became linked with his idea of the democratisation of art. He participated in the famous 'Querelle du Réalisme' of 1936, countering Louis Aragon's inclinations towards 'Socialist Realism' with his 'new realism' of the industrial object. 'Le Transport des Forces', Léger's mural for the Palais de la Découverte at the Exposition Internationale of 1937, depicts a factory, steamy clouds, a waterfall (painted in by Asger Jorn), and a rainbow — a blithely optimistic view of industrial conditions at a time of increasing unemployment. In 1945, Léger joined the French Communist party, sending a telegram to Paris from the USA where he spent the war years. America was a socialist dream 'it's big, high, wide and limitless . . . hundreds of tongues and people are gathered here to live'; he was inspired by the lights and advertising in Broadway and the idea of 'obsolescence'. His paintings became curiously weightless as in the 'Plongeurs' series, and his 'Saltimbanques'. On his return to Paris he developed these epic figure compositions with proletarian heroes – workers, picnickers, men on bicycles. There is an obvious reference here to David, painter of the French Revolution, whose huge bi-centenary exhibition was

held at the Orangeries in 1948. Léger's 'Hommage à Louis David – Les Loisirs' corresponded to contemporary 'Davidian' paintings by social realists, but was resolutely distanced from their vindictive political content and sombre style. The 'Constructeurs' of 1950, which was exhibited at De Marx à Staline in May 1953 and the third Salon des Peintres témoins de leur Temps, April 1954, optimistically looks towards the future. Above all, the 'Hommage à Maiakowski' poet of the Russian Revolution, with its drawings of hands which 'resemble their tools', which have 'worked a lot, carried, demolished, rebuilt', is a painting of solidarity, far transcending the particular violence of the cold-war arena of the 1950s. Léger's studio re-opened in 1946, even before his return from the USA, moving from Montrouge, an industrial suburb, to Montmartre in 1947. The following year the American G.I. Bills provided grants for ex-servicemen to study in Paris, and the studio became inundated with serious — and not so serious — students, including Sam Francis, Greenberg and Guido Haas. A certain number, however, went to Zadkine's studio – Kenneth Noland, Olitski, Al Held and Stankiewicz for example, a main attraction being that Zadkine spoke English. In the Macarthy period there were certain very strong objections among the G.I. students to Léger's Communism, especially in view of the hospitality he

IV Fernand Léger

Les loisirs – Hommage à Louis David (Leisure – Homage to Louis David), 1948.
Oil on canvas, 154 x 185 Musée National d'Art Moderne, Centre Georges Pompidou

left
4 Henri Laurens
Le matin (Morning), 1944. *Bronze, 118 x 80*
Musée National d'Art Moderne, Centre Georges Pompidou.
Gift of the artist, 1966

had received in the USA. However, his 'realism of conception' was far from any representational norm, and Léger remained a prophet of modernism for the generation of the 1950s.   s.w.

Léger's advice to his pupils:

'You've come to work here of your own free will. Don't be afraid of being under my influence, for a time at least. We've all been through it. Nothing falls from heaven, and you aren't born a genius. Personally, I was under the influence of Cézanne. Then, one day I said to him: "Zut! That's enough". It's up to you to do the same and say "Zut! to Léger", and take from your time in my studio all that you think's useful for the development of your own personality.'

In 1951 this is how he saw the future of painting:

'An abstract art which must adapt itself to the wall.

'A monumental art, ready for walls.

'The easel painting pursues its course.

'The reappearance of figures, of human bodies, of eyes and legs which organise themselves into real or social subjects.

'The return to collective creations.

'These are the ways which at the moment must lead to modern paintings.'

Georges Bauquier in 'L'Atelier Léger', *F. Léger*, Musée des Arts Decoratifs, Paris, 1956

HENRI MATISSE

b 1869, Le Cateau-Cambresis, d 1954, Nice

In 1882 Matisse gave up his studies in law, and went to Ecole des Beaux Arts where he became a pupil in Gustave Moreau's studio. Here he met certain painters like André Derain who later formed the group known as the Fauves.

The brilliant light of Corsica that he first saw in 1898, and his study of the writings of the divisionist painter Paul Signac the following year, meant that he became increasingly aware of the role of light and colour in his work. From 1904 onwards, Matisse's art focussed exclusively on the emotional potential of colour and the vital rhythms of the arabesque. At the Salon d'Automne of 1905 he appeared as the leader of the new Fauve painters. He visited Algeria in 1906, and was one of the first painters to become interested in African art. His masterly assurance and the audacity of his new style attracted the attention of artists like Hans Purrmann and the collectors Choukine and Morosov, Leo and Gertrude Stein, thanks to whom his reputation spread to Germany, Russia and the United States. Matisse held his first exhibitions in 1908 in New York, Moscow and Berlin, and in 1913, his 'Nu Bleu' created a scandal at the New York Armory Show.

His passion for light and pure colour, inspired anew by trips to Spain and Morocco in 1911, 1912 and 1913 made him the painter of a golden age. His work continued to celebrate peace, harmony and the world of the senses throughout his life. As early as 1916, and then every year from 1922 onwards, Matisse spent several months in Nice and on the Côte d'Azur. Here, after the forceful and productive work of the period 1908 to 1919, his art became more tranquil. His paintings attempted to describe the soft and tender light of the Riviera in all its sensuous beauty. He took up sculpture again at this time, and went to Tahiti in 1930. Both were experiences which led him to a simpler, more constructed style in his two-dimensional work. This is demonstrated in 'La Danse', the decorative mural commissioned in 1930 by Alfred Barnes for his foundation at Merion near Philadelphia. Matisse also illustrated some of the most beautiful luxury editions of the twentieth century, Mallarmé's *Poésies* (1932) and Ronsard's

Florilèges des Amours (1948) both published by Skira, Montherlant's *Pasiphae* (1942) published by Fabiani and Marianna Alcaforado's *Lettres Portugaises* (1946) and Charles d'Orleans' *Poèmes* (1950) published by Tériade. A new Matisse appeared in these years, a symbol of miraculous renewal and hope for postwar France. Besides the superb drawings, with their principle of themes and variations, the papiers découpés, cut-outs in paper painted with brilliantly coloured gouaches, epitomised this new and youthful era. He had invented the technique in 1937 for a cover of the magazine *Verve* and then used it for the costumes of the ballet *Rouge et noir*. He followed this with the magnificent papiers découpés in *Jazz* published in 1947, and a number of large-scale compositions of exceptional daring which he continued to create up until his death. Recent paintings, the 'Interieurs' series, the illustrated books,

II Henri Matisse
Grand interieur rouge (Large Red Interior), 1948. *Oil on canvas, 146 x 97*
Musée National d'Art Moderne, Centre Georges Pompidou

right
5 Henri Matisse
Interieur jaune et bleu (Yellow & Blue Interior), 1946. *Oil on canvas, 116 x 81*
Musée National d'Art Moderne, Centre Georges Pompidou

his larger drawings in paint and the first gouache cut-outs were exhibited in Paris in 1949 at the Musée National d'Art Moderne. In 1950, Louis Aragon, author of *Matisse en France* (1944), presented works relating to the projects for the decoration of a chapel in Vence at the Maison de la Pensée Française. This chapel, where the papier découpé technique was transferred to stained glass with great success, was conceived in its entirety by Matisse. The chapel was consecrated in 1951, three years before his death.   G.V.

'Giving, with no thought of giving: art surpasses love; it consumes itself in exchange for nothing, like the sun burning away, and we recall the words of the official at the crematorium in the Czech concentration camp: 'I declare that I have burnt the poet Robert Desnos'. The artist burns, made of the same matter as other men. His spectrum analysis would be the same as theirs. All these faces bear witness to distant flames; thanks to Matisse, we know that an Empire exists, fruit carved in stone. An art of autumn, and the end of autumn; just before the iron grip of winter.

Jacques Kober: *Matisse 1946*, Pierre à feu, Les memoirs profonds, Maeght, Paris 1947, pp. 86 and 88.

'Matisse, who has not ceased to develop with power and mastery, is today the creator of such beautiful, magnificent works that one feels moved to see in him the figure of the Painter incarnate. He is that very singular individual who sees the world like any one of us, but who through operations and calculations that belong to his province can draw surprising images from this vision (. . .) He is the Painter, then, because it seems that all the special and particular talents which make a painter, are united in his being, all of them, perfectly balanced, each one at its highest pitch of excellence and efficiency. He is the figure of the Painter because of all the figures which could be suggested to represent him fully, the one he offers is the most happy and harmonious.

Jean Cassou: Preface to the exhibition. *Henri Matisse, oeuvres recentes*, Musée National d'Art Moderne, Paris 1949.

PABLO PICASSO

b 1881, Malaga, Spain, d 1973, Mougins

Picasso has undoubtedly been responsible for the most significant transformations and developments in the art of this century. His influence extends from the period of fin-de-siècle symbolism up to 1900, to the 'new spirit in painting' of the 1980s. Every element of visual language, every possible technique has been explored, as Picasso reflects on the artist's relationships with reality and with the art of the past and the present. Intensely autobiographical, his work is also a mirror of his times.

The influence of Cézanne and primitive art, and the experiments with volume that marked the first, 'analytic' Cubist period, were followed by Picasso's attempt at a 'synthetic' interpretation of the real. With the 'Guitare' of 1912 he became a pioneer of twentieth-century constructive sculpture. His collages and 'papiers collés' introduced everyday objects into his work, an idea that was rapidly imitated. Picasso's use of raw materials and waste products persisted throughout his career, notably in the 'assemblages' of 1926 onwards.

The horror of the Spanish Civil War moved Picasso to create 'Songe et Mensonge de Franco' and 'Guernica', expressions of deep political engagement. During the Occupation his presence in Paris was an important symbol for other artists. At this time he created such tragic and powerful images as the bronze skull, 'Le Crâne', 1943, the 'Homme à l'Agneau' 1944, and the 'Charnier' of 1945, which expressed in a heap of distorted and mangled bodies all the atrocities of the concentration camps.

But Picasso was still a bitterly controversial figure, above all when he continued to play Surrealist games with discarded objects. The 'Tête de Taureau' 1943, a bull's head made from a bicycle saddle and handlebars, was just one of the works that provoked violent reactions at the Salon de la Libération in 1944 (and again at the Picasso exhibition in London, 1945). On the eve of the Salon, Picasso joined the French Communist party and never wavered in his support for their cause. During the period he spent at Antibes, 1946-7, much of his work became a hymn to fertility, with a spirited,

III Pablo Picasso
La Femme en bleu (Woman in Blue), 1944. *Oil on canvas, 130 x 96*
Musée National d'Art Moderne, Centre Georges Pompidou

dionysiac exuberance, and it was mostly work of this nature that he exhibited at the Maison de la Pensée Française, Paris, in 1948, 1949 and 1950. However his active engagement with politics, especially the peace movement, internationally symbolised by the Picasso dove, resulted in the award of the Lenin Peace Prize in 1950. 'Massacre in Corée' was perhaps his most specific political statement: a condemnation of imperialistic aspects of the Cold War that reminds us, however, with its references to the firing squads of Goya and Manet, and to Poussins's Massacre of the Innocents, of war as a constant and tragic factor of history.

Two vast murals, 'La Guerre' and 'La Paix', started in 1952 in a de-consecrated chapel in Vallauris, developed his denunciation of war in all its forms, a statement that by far transcended the petty disputes in Communist circles when his 'Portrait de Staline' was published in *Les Lettres Françaises*, just after Stalin's death in March 1953.   G.V.

right
6 Pablo Picasso
L'Ombre (The Shadow), 1953. *Oil & charcoal on canvas, 130 x 96*
Musée Picasso

GEORGES ROUAULT

b 1871, Paris, d 1958, Paris

Born during a battle in the period of the French Commune, Rouault was to be marked all his life with a heightened awareness of human destiny. He decried the miseries of social injustice, and experienced all the anxieties and the hopes of a convinced Christian. Rouault was the son of a cabinet maker, and his first apprenticeship was to a painter of stained glass. In 1891, he became a pupil at the Ecole des Beaux Arts in Elie Delaunay's studio, which was handed over to Gustave Moreau in 1892. Thus, while he was a contemporary of the future 'fauves' of the Salon d'Automne of 1905, who also worked with Moreau, Rouault fell, more than any of them, under his master's influence, and painted symbolist-inspired, religious works that he was to abandon in 1904, when his own Christian beliefs evolved under the influence of Joris-Karl Huysmans and Leon Bloy. His work became a violent denunciation of the fallen world, symbolised by judges and prostitutes and the pitiful comedy of the circus. Keeping mainly to these themes, Rouault tended to abandon gouache and watercolour after 1918, and concentrated on oils, whose dark colours, very thickly applied, suggested stained glass. His work was rich with a spirituality torn between the notions of sin and redemption, perpetually hearkening to 'the death cry of the slaughtered beast, the half open mouth which utters no sound, as in a ghastly dream'. His first exhibition was held in 1911 at the Galerie Druet, and after 1913 he became associated with the publisher Ambroise Vollard, with whom he collaborated on various luxury editions and collections of prints: *Miserere* (1922-27, published in 1948), *Les Fleurs du Mal* (1926-27), *Les Réincarnations du Pere Ubu* (1928, published in 1932), *Le Cirque de l'Etoile filante* (1934-35, published in 1938), and *Passion* (1935-36, published in 1939) which grouped together all the themes of his previous years.

He lived in isolation during the Occupation. He glorified 'Notre Jeanne' (1940-49) and decried mankind's violence in 'Homo homini lupus' (1944). Around 1946 he discovered a new serenity, with 'Véronique' (1945) and 'Sainte Jeanne d'Arc' (1951) for example, and he started using brighter colours again.

7 Georges Rouault
Homo Homini Lupus (Man is a Wolf towards Men), 1944. *Oil on paper pasted onto canvas and wood, 64 x 46*
Musée National d'Art Moderne, Centre Georges Pompidou

His eightieth birthday was celebrated in 1951 by the Centre Catholique des Intellectuels Français, and the following year a retrospective exhibition of his work was held at the Musée Nationale d'Art Moderne.   G.V.

'Far from any human consolations, I am an old servant, misunderstood, ill-favoured, foul-mouthed too.
The conscience of an artist worthy of the name is, without exaggeration, an incurable leprosy which indulges in infinite torments, but occasionally in silent joys. Shutting my eyes I sometimes seem to hear waves of
distant music. The further I withdraw, this silence becomes peopled with images, sounds, vast countries, more impenetrable than the North Pole, or the charming, intimate little thickets like one sees in the paintings of Fra

III Pablo Picasso
La Femme en bleu (Woman in Blue), 1944. *Oil on canvas, 130 x 96*
Musée National d'Art Moderne, Centre Georges Pompidou

IV Fernand Léger
Les loisirs – Hommage à Louis David (Leisure – Homage to Louis David), 1948. *Oil on canvas,*
154 x 185
Musée National d'Art Moderne, Centre Georges Pompidou

V Pierre Bonnard
L'atelier aux mimosas (The Studio with mimosas), 1939-46. *Oil on canvas, 127 x 127*
Musée National d'Art Moderne, Centre Georges Pompidou

Angelico . . . To paint joy . . . Why not? I have been so happy painting, possessed by painting, forgetting everything amid the blackest melancholy. The critics didn't notice because my subjects were tragic. But isn't the joy within the subject one paints?'

Georges Rouault: *Stella Vespertina*, René Drouin, Paris 1947.

JACQUES VILLON

b 1875, Damville, d 1963, Puteaux

From his adolescence onwards, Jacques Villon was attracted to engraving and drawing, although his father had always wanted him to learn law. He studied the necessary techniques with his grandfather, the painter and engraver Emile Nicolle from Rouen. Villon's family environment was to be of great influence throughout his career, as he exchanged ideas with his brothers Raymond Duchamp-Villon, the sculptor who died in 1918, and Marcel Duchamp the painter and seminal figure of the Dada movement. His sister, Suzanne Duchamp and his brother-in-law, Jean Crotti were also painters. The amusing illustrations he drew with great relish for several Parisian journals: *Le chat noir, La Lanterne, L'assiette au beurre*, and *Le courrier français*, and the posters and prints that he published from 1899 onwards, developed both his commercial eye, and of course, his technique. In 1910, however, Villon decided to take up painting seriously, and thanks to Raymond Duchamp-Villon, he met the artists who with him were to form the Puteaux group in 1912. This group was known as the Golden Section, and included such figures as Gleizes, Metzinger, Le Fauçonnier, La Fresnaye, Leger and Picabia. With some of these artists, Villon collaborated on the 'Maison Cubiste' project which was exhibited at the Salon d'Automne in 1912. At the same time, his work was shown at the Section d'Or exhibition at the Galerie la Boétie, and he sent several paintings to the 1913 Armory Show in New York. Conscripted into the camouflage corps during the first world war, Villon was apparently able to research into the perception of colours and forms, and his conclusions were to dominate his experimental work of the

1920s and 1930s: using certain motifs, variations on Duchamp-Villon's 'Buste de Baudelaire', 'Le Jockey' and 'Les Fenêtres, he progressively broke down form into a series of surfaces and tones.

In 1932, Villon joined the 'Abstraction-Creation' group, but while keeping to their discipline as regards the structure and colouration of his works, he returned as early as 1934 to portraiture and more realistic, figurative painting. His work was revealed to a new generation of painters at the exhibition 'Les Maîtres de l'art indépendant' in 1937, and despite his exile at La Brunie in the Lot region, he became a crucial influence on the 'Jeunes peintres de Tradition française', who exhibited seemingly abstract paintings with Resistance overtones during the Occupation. Villon was now the advocate of a rigorous and contemplative form of modernism, which he had come to analyse himself as a result of the interpretative engravings he undertook from 1922 to 1932, after the work of contemporary masters. He exhibited several times during the Occupation, notably when an important retrospective was held in 1942 at the Galerie de France, which included works by Duchamp-Villon. A new, lyrical use of colour appeared, which he developed with an increasing scope and brilliance until his death. In 1941, one of the 'Jeune peintres', Jean Bazaine, acclaimed his analysis of 'space-colour': it was 'the measure of the world'. Villon's reputation and influence grew after the war, with his frequent exhibitions at the Galerie Louis Carré in Paris and New York. In 1950 he received the Carnegie prize, and the Musée National d'Art Moderne honoured him with a major retrospective in 1951, which then went on tour outside France. G.V.

Jacques Villon has demonstrated great morale in this difficult decade of the Forties. Where many minds flinched at the onrush of world events or fellow-painters sometimes dwindled in their intensity because of advancing years, he mustered all his energies, fused them under pressure, and produced a new art where the colours were lit by a strange incandescence of the mind. And the younger French painters understood, for immediately they acknowledged this man, already well along in the sixties, as a leader of the generation still emerging.

Possibly they hailed him also because of the discipline he

communicates. Coming as did Poussin from Normandy, Villon deliberates before he executes. He measures in terms of a classical restraint and that must have come as a surprise in an era when the unrestricted impulse so often has rule. Yet that gravity merely furnished the pitch, as it were, to his music, for meanwhile the notes ascended to new levels of eloquence. At any rate, having found his level, Villon produced in his series of harvest-fields, his severe self-portraits, his country vistas and his exquisite garden-patches a new and radiant advance in French art.

Jerome Mellquist: preface to the exhibition catalogue: *Villon, Exhibition of Paintings*, 26 April – 14 May, Louis Carré Gallery, New York, 1949. (Original translation).

VI Jacques Villon
Le scribe (The Scribe), 1949. *Oil on canvas, 92 x 75*
Musée National d'Art Moderne, Centre Georges Pompidou

Aspects of Realism

BALTHUS BUFFET FAUTRIER FERNANDEZ FOUGERON GIACOMETTI GRUBER HÉLION LÉGER MASON MASSON PICASSO PIGNON RICHIER TASLITZKY

**Painting
is one of the rare weapons we are left
with to combat sordid history**

(AIMÉ CESAIRE)

Detail of cover of Salon d'Automne catalogue, 1944,
designed by Charles Walch.

The great debate of the 1930s between figurative and abstract painting started again with renewed vigour in the postwar period. The abstract tendency, with one or two exceptions, has been deliberately excluded from 'Aftermath', yet towards the end of the 1940s, it seemed to many to be the major force for change and innovation. A positive, forward-looking and well organised movement, with its own critics, its own galleries and annual exhibition, the Salon des Realités Nouvelles), it was increasingly seen to represent the avant-garde, and was violent in its denunciation of figurative painting. The situation as a whole was extremely complicated. For example, Picasso, who had embodied both modernism and a spirit of Resistance at the Salon d'Automne of 1944, remained the abstract artist par excellence in the public's eye, in spite of the intense expression of poignant reality of the Occupation, in his portraits and still lives of the period. The different aspects of realism must thus be seen developing very often within the framework of the abstraction-figuration debate. But the question of the artist's relation with reality was raised anew as a vital issue in this post-war climate, and took various forms. The relationship between the world of objects and visual perception, originally examined by the Cubists, was reinvestigated. Artists reexplored the relationship with tradition, just as André Derain had done in his later work, and after him the painters of 'réalité poétique', such as Roger de la Fresnaye and the neo-humanists of the 1930s. The relationship between art and political conviction came to the fore once more, just as in the later 1930s Paris had seen the 'engaged' painting of the 'Forces Nouvelles' group, and the work of artists who were involved in the 'Querelle du Réalisme' – prolonged debates about socialist realism held at the Maison de la Culture from 1935-6, which had a frankly Communist inspiration.

After the Liberation, the French Communist Party, or the 'parti des fusillés' as it liked to call itself, so many of its members having been shot in the war, did its utmost to recruit the most respected French intellectuals into its ranks. This led to a very polarised situation. On October 4th, 1944, Picasso became a member of the Party, and on October 5th, the poet Paul Eluard wrote

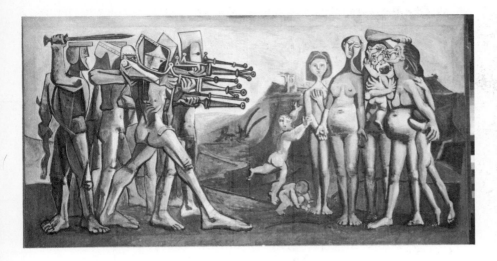

Picasso
Massacre en Corée (Massacre in Korea), 1951.
Oil on canvas 110 x 210
Musée Picasso, Paris (not in exhibition)

Picasso
La Guerre (mural) 4.8 x 10 metres, 1952.
(not in exhibition)

Picasso
La Paix (mural) 4.8 x 10 metres, 1952.
Temple de la Paix, Vallauris

(not in exhibition)

in *Humanité*, the Communist newspaper: 'We live in a period of black and white, where, when the horror recedes a little, extraordinary promises come to light on all sides, illuminating the future . . . Today I saw Pablo Picasso and Marcel Cachin embrace each other.' Fernand Léger became an active member of the Communist Party when he returned from the United States in 1945. The Front National des Arts, born as a Resistance movement, united Communist militants, 'fellow travellers' and former Resistance fighters who were artists. In December 1944 they organised an exhibition of the work of Henri Rousseau, the father-figure of naïve painting, who came to represent the alliance between the avant-garde and the ordinary Sunday painters who existed in their thousands in Paris – a situation unimaginable today. In June 1945, at the tenth Congress of the French Communist Party, Roger Garuady announced the beginnings of an *Encyclopédie de la Renaissance Française*, though the enterprise was never concluded. December 1945 saw the first number of the review *Arts de France* which was supported by numerous Communist sympathisers. It heralded this 'Renaissance' in a climate of great openess as far as the arts were concerned. Within just a few months, however, it had, together with the weekly newspaper *Les Lettres Françaises*, adopted the official position of the French Communist Party, as proclaimed by Louis Aragon in November 1946: 'I consider that the Party does hold an aesthetic doctrine, and that its name is realism'. This was confirmed at the eleventh Party Congress in June 1947 by Laurent Casanova. The following August, the Communist press published an article by the painter Guerassimov that had originally appeared in *Pravda*, the Soviet newspaper. With its emphasis on the aesthetic dictates of Zhdanov, Stalin's cultural spokesman, it started a number of violent debates focussed on Socialist realism. In spite of the references used as proofs of good faith – to the French painters of the 19th century whose politics were reflected on their work, Louis David, Honoré Daumier and Gustave Courbet, together with the Flemish primitives and the contemporaries of Laethem Saint Martin – the Social realist principles officially advocated by the French

Communist party provoked a final break with the Surrealists. *Rupture inaugurale* the manifesto issued by the 'Cause' group and signed by André Breton on June 27th 1947, was answered by Roger Vailland for the Communist Party in *Le Surréalisme contre la Révolution*. The next break was with the existentialist movement, as formulated in the polemic between the Communist review *La Nouvelle Critique* and Jean Paul Sartre's *Les Temps Modernes*. This situation fostered the reaction of the 'Surréalistes Revolutionnaires' many of whom, like Asger Jorn were founder members of the 'Cobra' movement. On the other hand, it gave rise to courageous assertions of the autonomy of art by certain militant Communists who were abstract geometric painters, such as Auguste Herbin and Jean Dewasne.

The official art of the Communist Party was upheld by certain artists who in turn received commissions from the Party and very active support from its press: André Fougeron, who won the Prix National des Arts in 1946, Boris Taslitzky, and others such as Jean Amblard, Denis Milhau or the young Gerard Singer were among the most well-known. The works of these artists, exhibited at the Salon d'Automne from 1948 onwards, culminating in violent denunciations of colonialisation and the Atlantic Pact, regularly refuelled the debate – and even provoked police intervention at the Salon of 1951. Throughout the cold war period Picasso was regularly associated with public demonstrations by the Communist Party in France and abroad – the Peace Congress at Wroclaw in August 1948 for example – but his position was in fact only marginal. Edouard Pignon on the other hand, proclaimed his solidarity with the working classes in figurative work that had nonetheless a great freedom of handling and style. In 1953, Picasso's portrait of Stalin which appeared just after the latter's death in *Les Lettres Françaises* was officially denounced by the Party, creating a scandal of such proportions that Louis Aragon, the paper's editor, was forced to issue an 'autocritique'. A few months later Aragon attacked Fougeron's anti-American canvas, the huge satirical collage 'Civilisation Atlantique' exhibited in the 1953 Salon d'Automne, the attack being due for the most part to the role Fougeron had played in the Picasso affair. The Soviet invasion of Hungary in

October 1956 put a term to Aragon's credibility as spokesman for a 'Party art, the necessary condition for a great national art', which he was still advocating as late as June 1954 at the thirteenth congress of the French Communist Party.

In November 1947, a new generation of realist painters, politically aligned to the Communists emerged at the seventh 'Salon des moins de Trente Ans'. Its position was affirmed by the manifesto of the 'Homme-Témoin' group, which was drawn up by the critic Jean Bouret: 'Painting exists to bear witness, and nothing human can remain foreign to it.' The movement broadened with the creation of the 'Salon des Peintres Témoins de leur Temps' in February 1951. Its members subscribed to a rudimentary, expressionistic type of figurative painting – the work of Bernard Lorjou is an example – but very often this went hand in hand with an attempt to create an atmosphere, a superficial version of the 'existential despair' that was so fashionable in the Quartier Latin. Bernard Buffet's paintings of this genre managed to beguile many discriminating collectors, with their very bare presentation of the symbols of poverty, wretchedness and revolt, so obviously based on the work of Soutine and Gruber.
Moreover the 'modern' style of the realist 'Témoins de leur Temps' painters encouraged an illusion of daring and taste within its frankly middle-class market.

But the horrors of war and recession were not solely the province of politically active painters. Matisse, Marquet and Bonnard (who refused to be considered as politically committed) were involved in the exhibition 'Art et Resistance' in 1946. In November 1945, Fautrier's 'Otages' appeared to André Malraux as the 'first attempt to strip the flesh off contemporary anguish to the point at which he reveals the pathos of its ideograms, and drives it, though force, into the world of the eternal today.' This sacred dimension is to be found as well in the work of Alberto Giacometti. His figures stand alone in the solitary space where man confronts death, ever-present, reductive. Whether premonitions of the concentration camps, or created after they were laid bare to the eyes of the world, these dramatic figures appear like shadows at

the furthest limits of all possible questions, the same frontier crossed by Jean-Paul Sartre, who wrote prefaces for Giacometti's exhibitions. This hieratic and spiritualised denunciation of the human drama found its striking echo in the violence of the humans and the composite, organic beings that the sculptor Germaine Richier created on her return from Zurich. These were shown in 1948 at the Galerie Maeght. The problem was no longer to bear witness to reality, but to bestow a total truthfulness on the work. Its existence in time, and its apprehension through the senses became tempered by its essence charged with the intangible. Both Francis Gruber, when he abandoned his strange and fantastic universe, and Jean Hélion, turning away from geometric abstraction, sought to translate the significant features of the visible world in all their intensity, 'Incarnation. This is the real heart of the problem' Hélion noted in 1950. The Balthus exhibition in the Galerie des Beaux Arts in 1946 embodied this attitude. His figures seemed at once to exist out of time and yet be possessed by troubling intimations of carnal desire. As the poet René Char remarked, Balthus had 'achieved the feat of rendering us *something* full, organised, capable of action within the supportable limits of human boundlessness'.
GERMAIN VIATTE

BALTHUS
(Balthus Klossowski de Rola)

b 1908, Paris

Born into a cultured and cosmopolitan family that moved in high society in the 1900s, Balthus was noticed at an early age by the German poet, Rainer Maria Rilke. He soon became fascinated by the Far East, and also immersed himself in German and English literature – Hoffman, Lewis Carroll and Emily Brontë. His series of illustrations for *Wuthering Heights* in 1933 was a glimpse into a timeless world steeped in the secret and fantastic moods of childhood, which Balthus would continue to explore. His first works appeared just when the critic Waldemar George was advocating a return to a neo-humanistic tradition, but they were nearer in some ways to the fringe of the Surrealist movement, as Balthus was very closely associated with such modern writers as Antonin Artaud and Pierre-Jean Jouve. It was Wilhelm Uhde, the champion of contemporary naive painters, who put on Balthus's first exhibition at the Galerie Pierre Loeb in 1934. Balthus, who at this time was associating with Derain, Gruber and Giacometti, now turned to the art of the past, to Piero della Francesca, Courbet and Cézanne, and tried to employ the lessons of these masters whom he so greatly admired in his own work, seeking to restore the quality of an interior vision which transcended the real. So Balthus cultivated an isolation which left him unknown to all but a small group of connoisseurs. After the war, two exhibitions at the Galerie des Arts in 1946 and 1956 revealed his work in all its silence and strangeness – an initiation that marked a significant rupture with the iconoclastic march of the avant-garde.

G.V.

'It seems that painting, weary with describing wild beasts and extracting embryonic forms, wishes to return to a sort of organic realism, which far from fleeing the poetic, the marvellous, the fable, tends more towards it, but with certain means. For playing with the unfinished and embryonic aspect of forms to create the unexpected, the extraordinary, the marvellous, seems all the same, a bit too easy. One doesn't paint schemas, but the things that exist; one doesn't stop to study the work of the inarticulate with a microscope; but the painter, fully conscious of his

8 Balthus
Jeune fille aux bras levés (Girl with Arms Raised), 1951. *Oil on canvas, 150 x 82*
Private collection

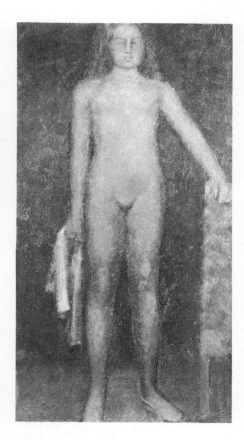

9 Balthus
Grand nu à la serviette (Large Nude with
Towel), 1952-60. *Oil on canvas, 152 x 82*
Private collection

means and his strengths, deliberately
ventures into external space, and
thence brings back objects, bodies,
forms with which he plays in a more or
less inspired manner. Balthus paints
first of all lights and forms. It's with the
light of a wall, a floor, a chair, or the
surface of someone's skin that he
invites us to enter into the mystery of a
body with a sex that becomes distinct
with all its harsh implications. A
technique of David's time, serves the
violent, modern inspiration which is
indeed the inspiration of a sick epoch,
where the conspiratorial artist only
makes use of the real for more effective
crufixions.'

Antonin Artaud, 'Exposition Balthus à la
Galerie Pierre', *Nouvelle Revue Française*,
no. 248, May 1934.

'Balthus is haunted by the world of
adolescence, by those troubled,
hesitant, delirious moments which
every adolescent has known, in the
face of a world to conquer, a world
where adults have decreed the laws
which must be broken if life is to be
breathed and lived as an adventure . . .
Balthus is not only attracted by the
'Justines', as was Sade himself, he tries
to evoke a picture of the world which

surrounds these 'Justines'. He paints a
universe in monochrome, filled with a
majestic boredom. His windows look
out onto princely courtyards, dusty,
forsaken, where one contemplates the
austere emptiness of a whole world in
itself. It is here that Balthus represents
better than any other, the ambiguity of
the actual world, where perverse
reveries and the artist's own anxiety
infuse the sinister and banal resignation
of the bourgeoisie!'

Alain Jouffroy, *Arts-Spectacles*, no. 557, 1956.

BERNARD BUFFET
b 1928, Paris
Buffet spent the first years of the
Occupation in Paris, living in extremely
reduced circumstances. He exhibited at
the Salon des Moins de Trente Ans, and
in 1948 held his first one-man show in a
small bookshop near the Sorbonne. This
was the year he shared the Prix de la
Critique with Bernard Lorjou, and in
June, he showed with Lorjou,
Rebeyrolle and other young realists in
the first exhibition of the L'Homme-
Témoin group. Jean Bouret's preface
declared 'Painting exists to bear
witness, and nothing which is human
can be foreign to it'. In 1951 Buffet
exhibited at the first Salon de Peintres
Témoins de leur Temps. After the series
'Flagellation', 'Mise en Croix' and
'Resurrection' of 1952, where 'nothing
differentiates the Son of Man, prostrate
or high on the Cross from his
executioners', Buffet painted a series of
landscapes, prompting Louis Aragon's

important articles in *Les Lettres
Françaises*, of February 1953. But in fact
these were an attempt to show the
Communist party embracing a wider
definition of realism at a time when its
own precepts were coming increasingly
under fire. Buffet's 'Horreurs de la
Guerre', (1954), again used traditional
imagery to translate the atrocities of the
moment. Yet from the forties onwards,
when his work seemed to embody the
spirit of existentialism, its intensity
became qualified by his prolific output
and the accessibility of his images of
despair.   S.W.

'What a shock – we were ravaged and
charmed at once on that first contact
with Bernard Buffet's universe!
Desolate objects – a grating, a
hurricane lamp, a broken bottle, a
spirit-stove, an iron, a coal-bucket –
bathed in an atmosphere of anguish, as
angular and elongated as the painter
with his stick-insect body, with a
triangular mask, bristly hair, perched
on a spindly stool or lying on a camp
bed, with a skinned rabbit or two dried

right
VII Balthus Klossowski de Rola
La chambre (The Room), 1947-8. *Oil on
canvas, 190 x 160*
Hirshhorn Museum, Smithsonian Institution, Washington

11 Bernard Buffet
Le Revolver (The Revolver), 1949. *Oil on
canvas, 60 x 81*
Musée d'Art Moderne de la Ville de Paris

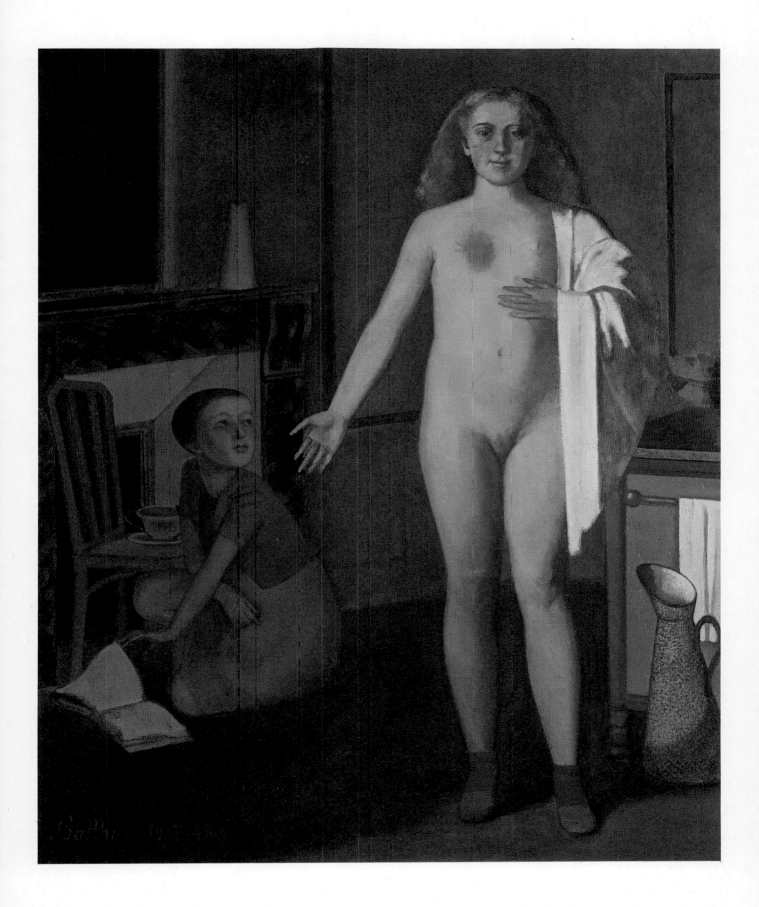

VIII Alberto Giacometti
Portrait de Jean Genet (Portrait of
Genet), 1955. *Oil on canvas, 73 x 60*
Musée National d'Art Moderne, Centre Georges
Pompidou

IX Alberto Giacometti
Homme qui chavire (Tottering Man), 1950-1.
Bronze, 30cm high
Kunsthaus, Zurich

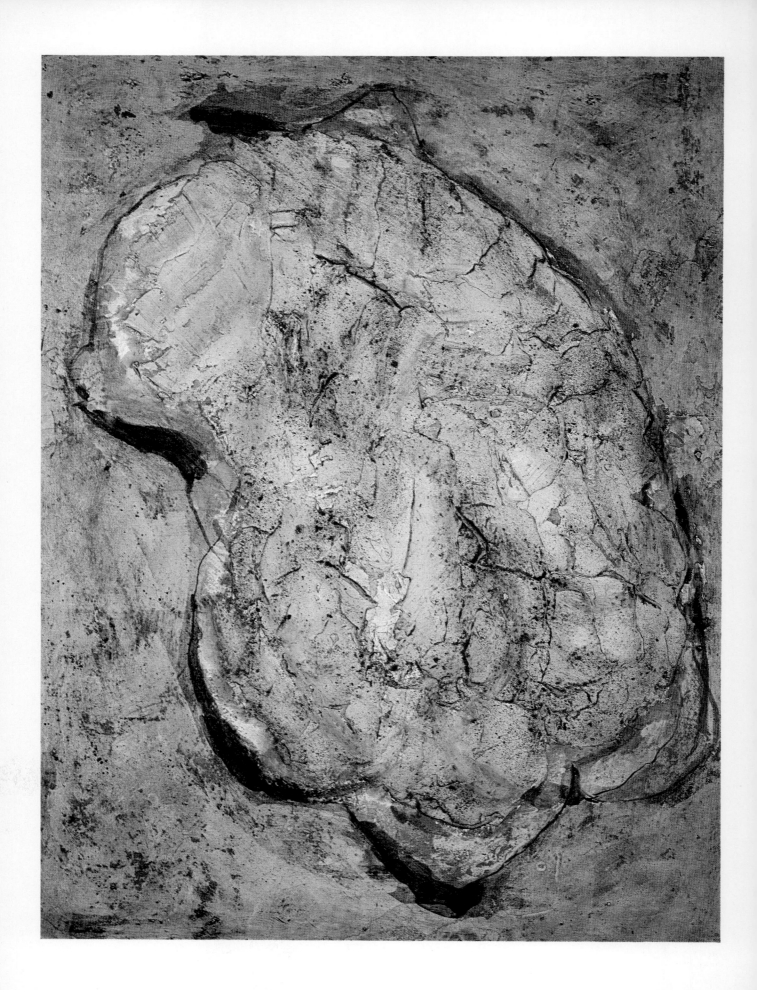

fish for company. The distress in these monochromatic compositions, the emptiness which translates all that the heart lacks, the elongation of verticals and horizontals, the nervousness of evil lines of force, lightly scratching the thin paint, all proclaim a painter fit to resume like Kafka, Kierkegaard, Sartre, the insecurity and deprivations of his childhood.'

'Soutine's sinister knives and forks, Van Gogh's old shoes and his kippers, Rouault's buffoons, and Gruber's stormy nudes certainly helped Buffet to find himself. But from his first self-portraits, his first 'Bedrooms', his 'Woman with a Hen', his 'Butcher's Shop', his 'Descent from the Cross', and his 'Net-menders', a completely original manner asserted iself, a style at once violent and frozen, cynical and caressing, naive and full of tension.'

Claude Roger-Marx, *Bernard Buffet*, introduction to the catalogue *Cent Tableaux de 1944 à 1958*.

JEAN FAUTRIER

b 1898, Paris, d 1964 Chatenay-Malabry
One of the most moving of the 'informel' artists, Jean Fautrier's initial training was in England. He studied briefly under Sickert at the Royal Academy and then at the Slade, but his real inspiration was found in the atmospheric late canvases of Turner, to whom he paid tribute in his series 'Glaciers', 1926.

The period 1935–9 when he lived as a ski-instructor in the Alps was extremely important for his conception of painting as a 'field', criss-crossed by a 'track' of sweeping curves. His first period of success was marked by the patronage of Jeanne Castel from 1925 to 1930, and his exhibitions at the Galerie Bernheim in 1927, and the Galerie de la Nouvelle Revue Française in 1933, with a preface by André Malraux.

The economic crisis of the thirties forced Fautrier to leave Paris. He returned in 1939, and met Paul Eluard, and Jean Paulhan who launched the major retrospective of works from 1915–1943 at the Galerie René Drouin. He fled with Paulhan's help to a sanatorium in the Vallée aux Loups, where most of the 'Otages' series were painted, under macabre circumstances: Fautrier was within earshot of the

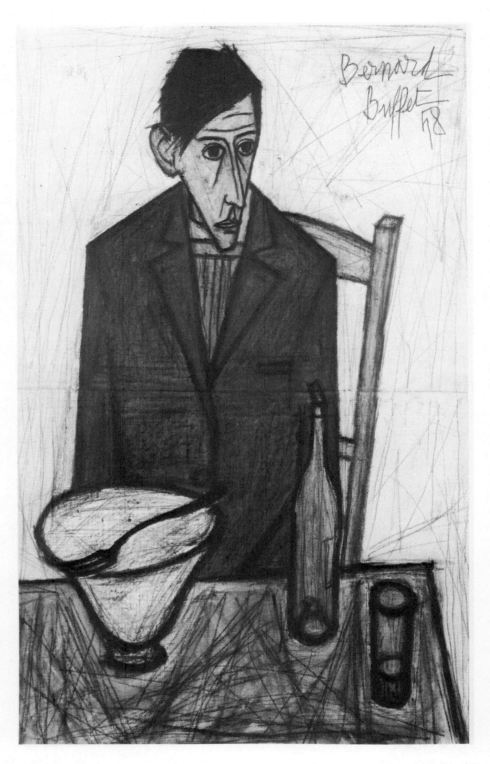

10 Bernard Buffet
Solitude – le buveur assis (Solitude – the seated drinker), 1948. *Oil on canvas, 100 x 65*
Musée d'Art Moderne de la Ville de Paris

left
X Jean Fautrier
La toute jeune fille (The Very Young Girl) 1943.
Oil on cardboard, 91 x 73
Private collection

woods where by night the Occupying forces, conducted appalling massacres. His 'Otages', exhibited at Drouin's in 1945, pay tribute to these tortured and anonymous victims – but the exquisite use of delicate and powdered colours, the open suggestion of eroticism, render them peculiarly ambivalent.

Fautrier's illustrations to Georges Bataille's *Madame Edwards* (1942), and *Alleluiah* (1947), to Robert Ganzo's *Lespugue* (1942) and André Frenaud's *La Femme de ma Vie* (1947), develop this restrained and subtle mastery of the erotic, which blossoms in 'Pièges' and 'Bergeronette' of 1946. No less than these nudes (exhibited in 1956), his 'Objets' (exhibited in 1955) and the later works which become finally more abstract, maintain the hallmarks of 'informel' painting: an external reference and a sensuality of texture that interprets Fautrier's preoccupation with metamorphosis and decay. When Fautrier first exhibited in London, at the ICA in 1958, Herbert Read stated that 'Fautrier, no less than Kandinsky, or Klee, or Pollock, is a pioneer of a movement which has transformed the whole basis and intention of the plastic arts'.

S.W.

'The Hostage which is the key to all the others is the great sculpted hostage. Rather than coming from Fautrier's paintings, these figures come from his sculpture. From his sculpture which has found, through torture, what it had sought for a long time in vain: a means of incarnation.

The art of the first Hostages is still 'rational': human faces which a simplified but directly dramatic line tends to reduce to the simplest expression — and the leaden colours which have always been those of death. But little by little, Fautrier supresses the direct suggestion of blood, the complicity of the corpse. Colours free from any rational link with torture substitute themselves for the initial ones, at the same time as a contour substitutes itself for the ravaged profiles, trying to express the drama without representing it. Nothing is left but lips, which are almost nerves, nothing but eyes which do not see. A hieroglyph of pain.

André Malraux. Preface to *Les Otages*.

12 Jean Fautrier
Grande tête tragique (Large Tragic Head), 1942. *Bronze, 33.5cm high*
Galerie Bonnier, Geneva

13 Jean Fautrier
Tête d'otage (Head of a Hostage),
1942-4. Lead, 48cm high
Musée de l'Ile de France, Sceaux

14a Jean Fautrier
La jolie fille (Pretty Girl), 1944. *Oil on
cardboard, 90 x 73*
Private collection

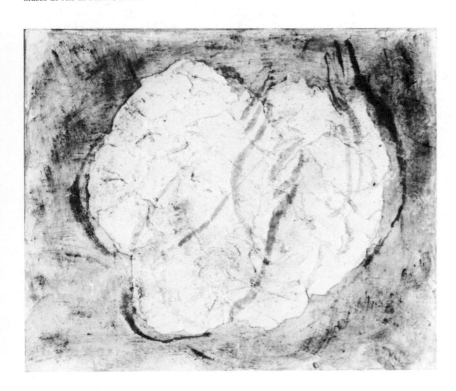

15 Jean Fautrier
Otage no 3 (Hostage no 3), 1943-5.
Oil on papier marouflé, 35 x 27
Musée de l'Ile de France, Sceaux

14 Jean Fautrier
Nu aux mains (Nude with Hands), 1942. *Oil on papier marouflé, 42 x 54*
Private collection

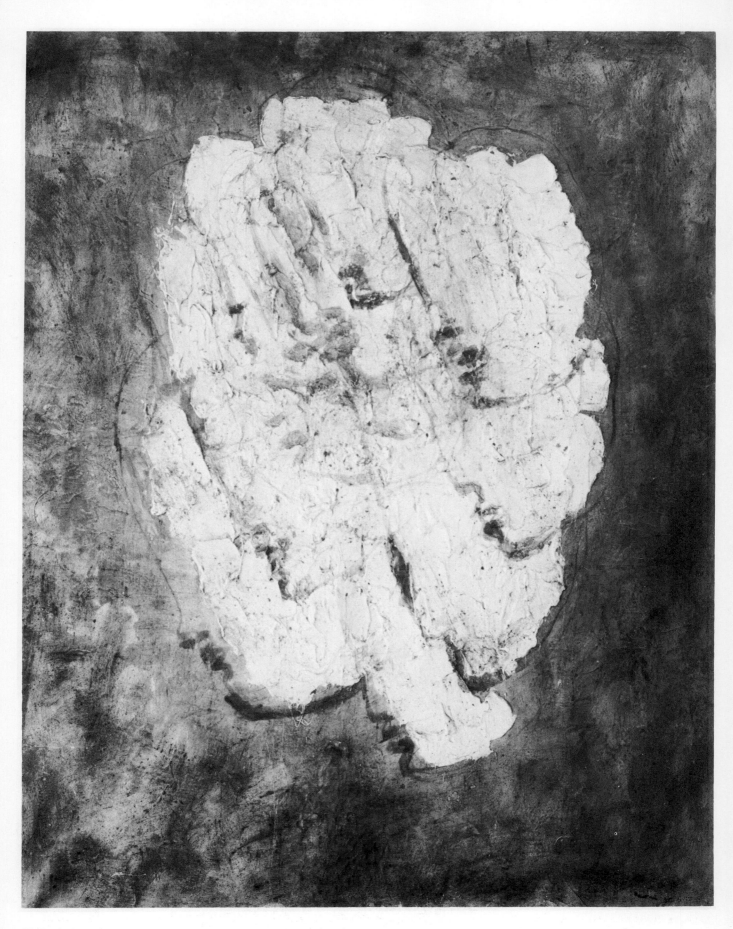

16 Jean Fautrier
Oradour, 1945. *Oil on papier marouflé, 145 x 114*
Menil Foundation Collection, Houston

LOUIS FERNANDEZ

b 1900, Oviedo, Spain, d 1973, Paris

Fernandez came to Paris in 1924, and soon became friendly with the most important artists and writers of the time: Le Corbusier, Braque, Laurens, Giacometti, Brancusi, Mondrian and Miró; André Breton, Paul Eluard, and some years later, the poet René Char. He was convinced that drawing was the most crucial element in painting, and that sculpture was the most complete form of drawing. Thus, for some years he devoted himself to sculpture, using the direct carving method on stone. When finally he took up painting again, he attempted to assimilate the lessons of abstraction, and those of Surrealism. In 1936, he painted the safety curtain, designed by Picasso, for Romain Rolland's play *Le quatorze juillet*, a piece in which the fervour of the French Revolution reflected contemporary enthusiasm for the 'Front Populaire'. Picasso's distorted figurative manner in this work and of this period soon found an echo in Fernandez's own painting. Fernandez was still at this time a theoretician at heart, preoccupied with the problems of colour, form and tradition. He published various articles on these subjects in the review *Abstraction-Création* (nos. 2-3, 1933 and 1934), and in the *Cahiers d'Art*, (nos. 1-4, 1935, and no. 1, 1936). Just before World

17 Luis Fernandez
Portrait of a young man in the Resistance (caught, questioned & executed), 1944-5.
Gouache on paper mounted on wood, 78 x 65
Menil Foundation Collection, Houston

War II, he began a series of large drawings in which the denunciation of the atrocities of the Spanish Civil War were mixed with his sexual fantasies and certain deformations stemming from his interest in anamorphoses. This violence appears again in the still-lives of slaughtered meat which he painted during the Occupation with an increasingly spare, classical technique. In these rare works, first exhibited at the Galerie Pierre in 1950, Fernandez strives to capture the light and the inner presence of beings and objects.   G.V.

'With all his inner force, Fernandez sees the model he is tackling in its physical condition and far beyond just that. Hence his tendency to avoid any steps which might lead him to cultivate an excessive attachment to the interpretation of the external appearance of objects, at the expense of evoking them . . . The result of this is also that his works are formed by the mixture of 'dead' effects and living ones. Art would know no continuation or strength without constantly new inspirations. The readjustments he brings to today's aesthetic principles are not signs of marching backwards. These readjustments are the artist himself: his aspirations towards unity in the face of a fractured world, his vision, broken in a thousand pieces, which hopes to mend itself — these serve to re-establish the right relationship between the world and the creator's irresistible impulse towards unity.'

Christian Zervos, *Cahiers d'Art*, no. 2, 1950.

ANDRÉ FOUGERON

b 1913, Paris

With his anarcho-syndicalist, working-class background, Fougeron became an enthusiastic member of the Association des Ecrivains et des Artistes Révolutionnaires at the time of the Front Populaire. He exhibited with Taslitzky and others at the Maison de la Culture in 1936, and at the Art Cruel exhibition, Galerie Billiet-Vorms in 1937, with Grosz, Gruber, Dali and Masson, where Picasso showed 'Songe et Mensonge de Franco'. Picasso and the German Expressionists were the crucial influences in these years. Fougeron joined the Communist party in late 1939, and once demobilised became prominent in the Front National des Arts, organising the printing of clandestine leaflets and *Vaincre*, a series of explicitly anti-Nazi lithographs. As secretary for the Front National des Arts, he was responsible for its policy of 'epuration' – the punishment of many artists who had collaborated by touring Germany in 1941, and associated with the German fascist sculptor Arno Breker in Occupied Paris. During this period, Fougeron had quickly become recognised as one of the most promising so-called 'young painters of the French Tradition' but despite his success he grew increasingly dissatisfied with the predictable subject-matter and the post-Cubist styles of the 'Ecole de Paris' painters. Encouraged by Louis Aragon, the brilliant writer and spokesman for the French Communist party, Fougeron radically changed his style, submitting the 'realist' 'Parisiennes au Marché' to the Salon d'Automne in 1948. His 'Hommage à Andre Houiller', scandal of the 'social realist' room at the Salon of 1949, depicted a dead Communist militant shot for flyposting anti-nuclear tracts (which Fougeron had himself designed) for the French Communist Party. Henceforth, Fougeron was popularly considered the Communist party's official painter. 'Les Juges' was one of the most controversial of the series 'Pays des Mines', exhibited in January 1950 after a period of great unrest, when the riot police had fought with striking miners. Working people were bussed from the suburbs to the Galerie Bernheim Jeune, and the paintings were seen by thousands during their prolonged tour of regional, industrial areas.

As the cold war period hardened, Fougeron opted for pure history painting: 'Marx et Engels au milieu d'un cercle de travailleurs socialistes', 1953, and finally blatant anti-Americanism: 'Civilisation Atlantique' with its references to the rearmament of Germany, the American colonisation of France, the Indo-Chinese war, etc. was slated by Aragon for personal and political reasons, and Fougeron was effectively silenced for the rest of the 50s although he continued to exhibit. In 1956 the Twentieth Party Congress of the Soviet Communist Party, where Stalin's errors and the 'cult of personality' were severely criticised, put an end to Social Realism in France.

S.W.

'Opposing ideologies confront each other on the terrain of literature and art, the exploiters and the exploited stand face to face . . . All realism which evokes the misery of the workers runs into the frozen silence or the ideological diatribes put up to defend and justify the existing order of things .

'Everywhere, in Paris, Lens, Marseilles, Saint-Etienne, Arles, in front of these paintings of vengeance, the crowds have recognised and hailed "their" painter . . . You can't separate the militant from the artist. Who would dare to maintain that Communism stops on the threshold of artistic creation? . . . A revolutionary artist cannot lag behind with retrograde formulas hostile to the people in his own field. Can you imagine a militant worker who declared himself a devotee of existentialist literature and abstract art?

XII André Fougeron
Les juges (The Judges), 1950. *Oil on canvas, 130 x 195*
Artist's collection

'. . . Here are "The Judges", three disabled miners, their flesh scorched and maimed, with arms wrenched off, collapsed vertebrae, missing eyes, a sorter with a mutilated hand, an emaciated orphan who often has to go hungry. These five accuse, relentlessly accuse those responsible for their pitiable state: State control, the ministers who pride themselves on producing coal 'at rock-bottom prices', the so-called defenders of the working class who simultaneously proclaim themselves "the loyal administrators of capitalism" . . . Here is the place of greatest desolation, of the highest courage, of the most immense hope . . .

Jean Fréville, 'Peintre de la classe ouvrière', introduction to *André Fougeron, Les Pays des Mines*, les Editions Cercle d'Art, Paris 1951.

ALBERTO GIACOMETTI

b 1901, Borgonovo, Switzerland,
d 1966, Char, Switzerland

Son of Giovanni Giacometti, cousin of Augusto Giacometti and godson of Cuno Amiet, all of whom were painters, Giacometti came to Paris in 1922 after a few months spent in Italy where he had discovered Giotto, Tintoretto and the art of ancient Egypt. His masters in Paris were Archipenko, Bourdelle and Laurens. In 1928 he started making flat sculptures, whose stylisation of the human figure showed his marked interest in primitive art, especially cycladic sculpture. In 1930 he exhibited at the Galerie Pierre Loeb and became a Surrealist, attempting to evoke fantastic images from the unconscious in his 'emotional' sculptures.

From 1935 onwards, a time when he was friendly with Balthus, Tal Coat, Gruber and Derain, he tried to find a path back to realism, and worked incessantly from the model. The profound difficulties he encountered in translating the essentials of perceived reality into sculpture drove him to work his figurines from memory — they became smaller and smaller until almost nothing remained. At this time (1940-41) he saw a great deal of Picasso and became friendly with Simone de Beauvoir and Jean-Paul Sartre (who wrote the preface for his first exhibition in New York at the Pierre Matisse Gallery in 1948). On his return from Switzerland, where he had stayed from 1942 to 1945, his paintings, drawings and sculptures seemed the very echo of the grim 'existentialist' post-war Paris.

His people and objects are apprehended dimly, as though through vertiginous spaces and distances. Isolated or in groups, static or captured in movement, sometimes reduced to a

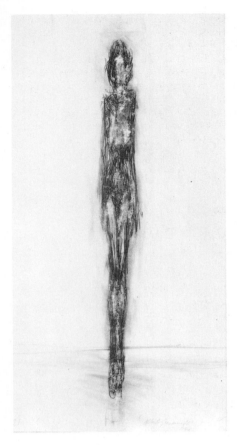

18 Alberto Giacometti
Femme debout (Standing Woman), 1946.
Pencil on paper, 53.5 x 28.5
Galerie Krugier, Geneva

crying mouth, his figures remain an anguished response to solitude and death.

G.V.

'Man . . . the human Person . . . the free Person . . . the I . . . at once executioner and victim . . . at once the hunter and the game.

Man – and man alone – reduced to a thread – in the ruinous condition, the misery of the world – who looks for himself – starting from nothing. Thin, naked, emaciated, all skin and bone. Coming and going with no reason in the crowd.

Man preoccupied with man, terrified of man. Affirming himself for the last time in a hieratic attitude of supreme elegance. The pathos of the extreme emaciation of the individual, reduced to a thread.

Man on his funeral pyre of contradictions. Not even crucified any more. Grilled. You were right, dear friend.

Man on his pavement like a sheet of burning metal from which he cannot remove his big feet.

Ah, since Greek sculpture, what do I mean, since Laurens and Maillol, man

19 Alberto Giacometti
Léonie, 1947. *Bronze, 107cm high*
Fondation Maeght, St Paul de Vence

20 Alberto Giacometti
Grand figure (Large Figure), 1947. *Bronze, 202 x 41*
Private collection

IX Alberto Giacometti
Homme qui chavire (Tottering Man), 1950-1.
Bronze, 30cm high
Kunsthaus, Zurich

has melted well enough on his funeral
pyre. It's doubtless since Nietsche and
Baudelaire that the destruction of
values has speeded up . . . They fall in
drops around him, his values, his fat, to
add fuel to his pyre!

Man not only has nothing left; there
is nothing left of him, but this I.'

Francis Ponge: 'Réflexions sur les statuettes,
figures et peintures d'Alberto Giacometti',
Cahiers d'Art, 1951.

'I don't understand very well what in art
is called an innovator. Should a work
have to be understood by future
generations? But why? And what
should that signify? That they could use
it? For what? I don't see at all. But I see
much better – although very obscurely,
that any work of art, if it aspires to the
most grandiose proportions must with
infinite patience and application, from
the first moment of its elaboration, go
back thousands of years through time,
to meet up, if possible, with the
immemorial night peopled with the
dead, who will recognise themselves in
this work. No, no, the work of art is not

21 Alberto Giacometti
Le nez (The Nose), 1947. *Bronze, 82 x 76 x 37*
Galerie Adrien Maeght, Paris

right
22 Alberto Giacometti
Portrait de la mère de l'artiste (Portrait of the
Artist's Mother). *Oil on canvas, 92 x 73*
Adrien Maeght, Paris

VIII Alberto Giacometti
Portrait de Jean Genêt, 1955. *Oil on canvas,
73 x 60*
Musée National d'Art Moderne, Centre Georges Pompidou

23 Alberto Giacometti
Diego assis (Diego Seated), 1948. *Oil on canvas*, 80.6 x 50.2
Robert & Lisa Sainsbury Collection, University of East Anglia

destined for generations who are yet children. It is offered to the innumerable peoples of the dead. Who accept it. Or reject it. But these dead of whom I speak have never been alive. Or I forgot. They were alive enough to be forgotten, and the function of their life was to make them pass beyond that tranquil shore where they wait for a sign – coming from here – which they might recognise.

While still present here, where then are these Giacometti figures I was speaking of, if not in death? Whence they escape at each summons of our eye, to draw nearer to us.'

Jean Genêt: *L'Atelier d'Alberto Giacometti*, Marc Barbezat, Décines, 1967.

FRANCIS GRUBER

b 1912, Nancy, d 1949 Boucicaut

Son of a stained-glass designer from Alsace and a Polish mother, Gruber arrived in Paris in 1916. His poor health as a child stimulated his voracious reading in literature and art history, and he painted from the age of eight onwards. Braque and Bissière, who were neighbours encouraged his precocious talents. The work of Bosch, Grünewald and Dürer strongly influenced Gruber's work of the thirties and forties. In 1933, he met Alberto and Diego Giacometti, and this friendship may well be the key to Alberto's return to realism in sculpture. Towards 1936, when he painted his 'Hommage au Travail' he was associated with politically involved artists like Boris Taslitzky, and took part in the debates about Socialist Realism which coloured the pre-war period of economic crisis. The 'Hommage à Jacques Callot' was shown in 1942 at the inaugural exhibition Hommage aux Anciens of the Galerie Friedland in Paris. While other artists honoured their formal masters, Gruber's painting was a work of resistance with a hidden message: Jacques Callot was a seventeenth century French engraver whose well-known series 'Les Horreurs de la Guerre' depicted the horrors of war in all their cruelty. Gruber had painted a huge portrait head of Jacques Callot in 1936, which was borne in the Front Populaire processions, joining the ranks of other political artists, Goya, Daumier and Courbet, for example. In 1942, however, the Callot engraving in the centre of this canvas became a symbol of the survival of art in a landscape of total destruction, passionate denunciation of war in all its forms.

In 1942, when Gruber was staying at Thommery near the forest of Fontainebleau, he discovered an ancient Bible. This prompted him to paint such dramatic biblical scenes as 'Job' (1944) and 'Judith' (1946). The text in 'Job' plays the same role as the engraving in the 'Hommage à Jacques Callot', eternalizing a scene which, despite its unreality, is a symbolic depiction of Occupied France. The quotation reads, 'Maintenant encore ma plainte est une révolte, et pourtant ma main supprime mes sanglots': 'Now, once more my cry is a revolt, and yet my

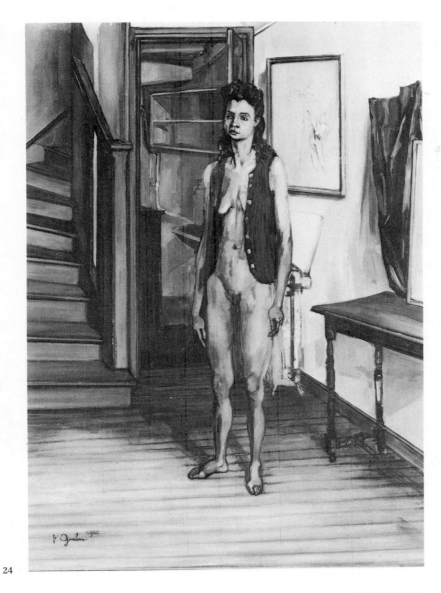

24

hand suppresses my sobs'. Gruber
joined the French Communist Party just
after the war and in 1947 was awarded
the Prix National des Arts.

Gruber's single-figure studies in
interiors during the mid-1940s affiliated
him to the 'miserabiliste' current that
found its parallel in the existentialist
novel.

Gruber spent much time in Brittany
after the war, and began to paint
delicate landscapes with a much
clearer palette shortly before his death
S.W.

. . . 'Under skies of torn clouds or
darkened with storm, he saw lost
islands arise covered with dead and
broken trees, and surrounded by rocky
and ragged shores. There wander the
innocents with empty hands. A dead
love, a bleeding foetus, lies between
them and the 'drowned woman'. It is to
be found again at the feet of 'the poet'.
Walls and roof have gone and an open
door reveals an infinite emptiness.
Later he painted with misleading
clarity his studio, the skylight with its
slender bars and the livid daylight. His
sad solitude is sometimes shared by an
emaciated nude. Sometimes it is simply
the 'coming of winter', and then

25

through the long hours of war-time occupation he is haunted by the despair and anguish of 'Job'.

'This is perhaps our own age at its most pregnant and in its deepest intimacy.

'Gruber gave more than he received: he has bequeathed his expressive and dramatic line to almost all his own generation of artists . . . Full of breaks and ruptures, torn and angular, tense and contracted, it may one day enable posterity to read our most intimate preoccupations.'

René Huyghe: Preface to the Tate Gallery retrospective, 1959 (contemporary translation)

JEAN HÉLION

b 1904, Couterne

Initially interested in science and then in architecture, Hélion turned to painting at an early age, and when he was twenty discovered modern art. In 1927, through his friendship with Torrés Garcia, he was able to develop his appreciation of Cubism. Henceforth, he would devote himself entirely to reflection on problems specific to painting: the relationship between the work of art and real experience, and the ambiguities of the visible world. An enterprising man with many contacts, he was deeply involved with many of the most important artistic movements of the century, and had many friends among artists and writers. In 1927, he founded the review *Acte*, and in 1930, when his style was developing into an uncompromising geometric abstraction, he produced with Van Doesburg and Carlsund the unique number of the review *Art Concret* and was a founder member of the group Abstraction-Création. He edited the first issue of the review of that name, and collaborated closely in the production of the next two numbers, before leaving the group in 1939. In 1931, Hélion had met Tatlin in Moscow, and Gorky in the USA, and the following year he spent some time in America with Alexander Calder. He returned to the USA in 1936, 1937, 1938, and from 1942 to 1945 spent most of his time in New York. During this period his work changed radically, from geometric neoplasticism towards a figurative mode that was the result of an aesthetic and moral crisis: an interrogation of the relationship between the visible world and its significations in the context of social and political crisis which preceded the

27 Jean Hélion
Mannequinerie (Tailor's Dummies), 1944
Pen, indian ink and watercolour on paper, 20 x 25
Musée National d'Art Moderne, Centre Georges Pompidou

war. He reintroduced volume into his painting of geometric rhythms, then areas of highlight and shadow 'Figure Tombée' 1939 still predominantly non-figurative, shows his interest in the expressive potential of instable volumes in space, while 'Au Cycliste' of the same year introduces emblematic figures from everyday life reminiscent of the work of Fernand Léger. Hélion returned to France in 1945, and exhibited his recent work in 1947 at the Galerie Renou et Colle. In 1951, the Hanover Gallery in London gave a retrospective of his works from 1947 to 1951. Hélion's ambition to find a figurative incarnation of the 'signs' of painting beyond abstraction is summarised in the painting 'A Rebours' of 1947, and in the series of paintings that followed: 'Nus', 'Citrouilleries', 'Journaleries', and the 'Mannequineries'. Around 1952, Hélion developed a more searching and scrupulously detailed approach to reality, similar to the attitudes of Gruber and Giacometti, before evolving a freer and more allusive style towards the end of the 1950s.   G.V.

'Was I just speaking of David? We're right in the Middle Ages. Nature, as we have looked at it since the eighteenth century, doesn't exist any more.

There's no more question of imitating it. Now we must paint from knowledge, not from experience; and paint objects conceived in the mind, not observed. In conceptual painting, hell and paradise at once, chasing away all other exterior worlds, are brought back into everyday life. But I must emphasise at the same time: they aren't separated, and that's what's in it which makes it modern. Good and evil find themselves intimately mixed. It's a realism of the absurd.'

Francis Ponge: 'Hélion', *Cahiers d'Art*, no. 2. (The text is dated 10 January 1951.)

26 Jean Hélion
La fille-Temple (The Girl-Temple), 1949.
Charcoal on paper, 100 x 65
Musée Nationale d'Art Moderne, Centre Georges Pompidou

28 Jean Hélion
A rebours (Topsy-turvy), 1947. *Oil on canvas. 113 x 145*
Musée National d'Art Moderne, Centre Georges Pompidou

29 Jean Hélion
Grande mannequinerie (Large Tailor's Dummies), 1951. *Oil on canvas, 130 x 162*
Musée d'Art Moderne de la Ville de Paris

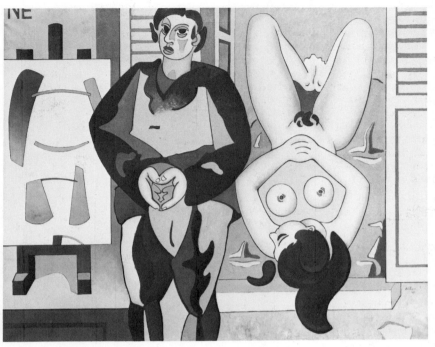

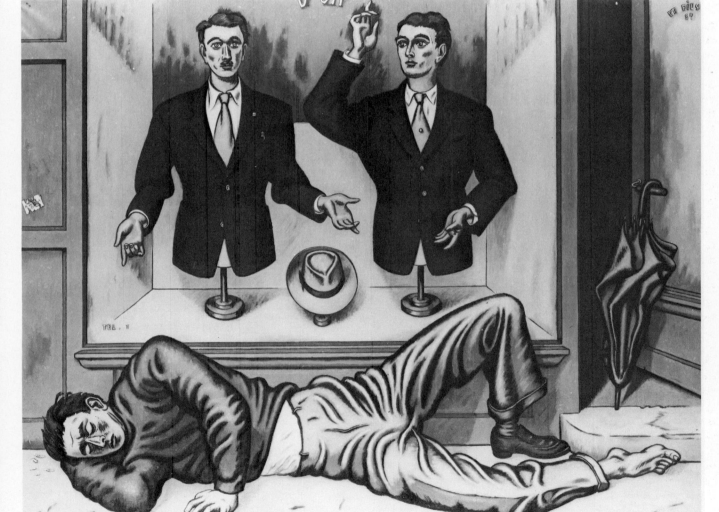

31

FERNAND LEGER

(see page 35)

'When I designed 'Les Constructeurs', I didn't make a single artistic compromise. It was while driving along in my car every evening on the way to Chevreuse that the idea came to me. There was a factory being built there in the fields. I saw the men balancing high up on the iron scaffolding. I saw man like a tiny gnat, seemingly lost in his own inventions, with the sky above him. I wanted to portray that: the contrast between man and his inventions, between the worker and all that architecture in metal. That concrete, those bits of iron, those bolts and rivets and the clouds too, I placed technically where they ought to be, but they make a game of contrasts with the beams. Not a single concession to sentiment, even if my figures are more varied and more individualised . . . Anecdote dates fast.' . . .

'I took 'Les Constructeurs' to the Renault factories and they were hung on the walls of the canteen. At noon the men arrived. They looked at the paintings while they were eating. There were some who laughed, "Look at them, how could those blokes work with hands like that?" Altogether they were making judgements by comparisons. They thought my canvases were funny, they didn't understand a thing. As for me, I just listened to them, and sadly downed my soup. Eight days later I went back to eat in the canteen. The atmosphere had changed. The men weren't laughing any more, they weren't bothering about the paintings and yet quite a few of them while they were eating would glance up, stare for a second at my pictures and then look back into their food. Who knows, were the paintings intriguing them? And when I was ready to leave, up came a man and said to me: "You're the painter, aren't you? You'll see, my mates are going to notice when they've taken your pictures away, when they've got a blank wall in front of them, they're going to see what your colours really mean." That pleased me, that did! . . .

Fernand Léger, *Fernand Léger*, Musée des Arts Décoratifs, Paris, 1956.

33

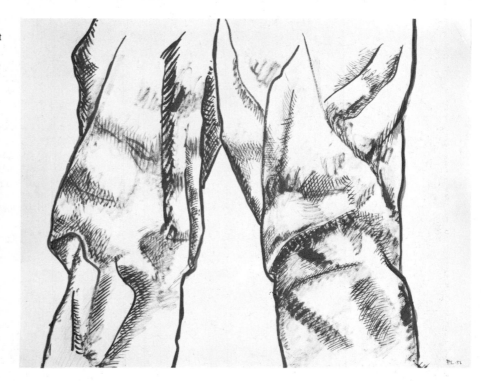

31 Fernand Léger
Etude pour les constructeurs (Study for the Builders), 1950. *Gouache, 78 x 54*
Musée Fernand Léger, Biot

31a Fernand Léger
Composition pour les Constructeurs (Composition for the Builders)
1950. *Oil on canvas, 162 x 115.*
Galerie Adrien Maeght, Paris

32 Fernand Léger
Etude de jambes (Study of Legs), 1951. *Indian ink, 50 x 64*
Galerie Louise Leiris, Paris

33 Fernand Léger
Etude pour les constructeurs – l'ouvrier à la lampe (Study for the Builders – worker with a lamp), 1951. *Indian ink on paper, 75.5 x 54*
Musée Fernand Léger, Biot

34 Fernand Léger
Les mains – à la memoire de Maiakovski (Hands – in memory of Mayakovsky), 1951. *Oil on canvas, 130 x 89*
Private collection

XI Francis Gruber
Job, 1944. *Oil on canvas, 162 x 130*
Tate Gallery, London

XII André Fougeron
Les juges (The Judges), 1950. *Oil on canvas, 130 x 195*
Artist's collection

RAYMOND MASON

b 1922, Birmingham

Raymond Mason studied initially at the
College of Arts and Crafts in
Birmingham and after a time at the
Royal College of Art in London in 1942,
went to the Ruskin School of Fine Arts,
Oxford, where he spent his evenings on
fire duty in the Ashmolean Museum and
was deeply impressed by its classical
sculpture collection. Back at London at
the Slade he finally turned from
painting to sculpture. In 1946 he moved
to Paris with a scholarship to the Ecole
des Beaux-Arts, and in 1947 participated
in the group show Les Mains Eblouies
at the Galerie Maeght. Mason had first
drawn street scenes during his
childhood in Birmingham, and later in
London. However, in Paris, where he
had no studio, he was literally forced to
work out-of-doors in the streets in the
late 1940s and early 1950s. The 'framed'
effect of 'Le Tramway de Barcelone', the
sense of perspective and the
architectural effect relate Mason's work
back to Italian Quattrocento painting.

Mason cites Balthus, Bacon and
Giacometti as the artists he most
admires: yet the sense of claustrophobia
produced by the vertical relief
sculptures is the antithesis to the
impersonality and panic of Giacometti's
open squares peopled with minuscule
figures hurrying to and fro. The contrast
summarises the alienation and the
solitude of the twentieth century 'man
in a crowd'.

In 1948 Mason exhibited at the Salon
de Mai, where he continues to send his
work annually. Recognised above all for
his reliefs, especially the street scenes,
Raymond Mason lives and works in
Paris.   S.W.

ANDRÉ MASSON

b 1896, Balagny

André Masson was only eleven years old
when he was enrolled at the Académie
Royale des Beaux-Arts in Brussels. His
family were living in Belgium at the
time. Although his education there was
completely traditional, he gradually got
to know modern art, and thanks to the
support of the poet Emile Verhaeren, he
was finally allowed to become a pupil at
the Ecole des Beaux-Arts in Paris in 1912.
He had met the painter Paul Signac at
Verhaeren's Sunday meetings and was
able to establish through this
friendship a 'living' link with
Impressionism, whose all-important

35 Raymond Mason
Le tramway de Barcelone (Barcelona Tram), 1953. *Bronze, 80 x 125 x 24*
Galerie Claude Bernand, Paris

emphasis on light was crucial for
much of his later work. In 1914 he
went briefly to study art in Italy. On
his way back he stopped for a time in
Switzerland, where he read Nietzsche.
It was a personal revelation. At about
the same time he discovered the
world of the Marquis de Sade.
However, World War I brought him
into brutal contact with reality and
when he was very seriously wounded,
face to face with the prospect of
death. Back in Paris he continued to
paint, and he eventually signed a
contract with D.H. Kahnweiler, after
which, in the winter of 1921, he took
a studio very near Miró in the Rue
Blomet. In this lively quarter he met
many artists and writers who were
part of the circles surrounding Michel
Leiris, Georges Limbour, and Roland
Tual. He shared their passionate
curiosity about the German Romantics,
Sade and Lautréamont. In 1923 he
met André Breton, who brought his
picture 'Les quatre Elements', and
Antonin Artaud, who published an
article about his painting 'Homme' in
La Revolution Surréaliste in 1923.
'Homme' was shown the same year in
the Surrealists' first exhibition at the
Galerie Pierre with 'L'Armure', an
emblemmatic composition based on
the female body, which was purchased
by the writer Georges Bataille.
Masson's experiments with automatic
drawing led him to abandon the
Cubist structure of his 'interior

images' for a freer, more gestural
approach. He next started shaking
sand onto wet paint surfaces, forming
images of aggression and conflict
associated with his increasingly
violent use of sexual symbolism, as
may be seen in the illustrations to
Sade's *Justine* (1928), or his series
'Massacres' (1930–4), for example. His
themes, increasingly drawn from
classical myth, were curiously
prophetic in their condemnation of
the brutalities that were to take place
during the Spanish Civil War and
World War II. In 1936, Masson
contributed to Georges Bataille's
review *Acéphale*, and designed the
décor for Jean-Louis Barrault's
production of Cervantes' play
Numance in the following year. In
1939 he illustrated the cover of
Minotaure, in which André Breton
praised the violent eroticism of
Masson's art. Two years later Masson
fled to the USA, where his influence
was soon very apparent among the
young generation of Americans who
were developing 'action painting' in
the mid 1940s. He featured in the
exhibition War and the Artist at the
Pierre Matisse Gallery, New York, in
1943, and in 1944 painted 'Liberation',
a very large work which was shown
after his return to Paris in 1945, at Art
et Résistance, an exhibition which
was seen in London, New York and
Moscow after its initial showing in
Paris. The Galerie Louise Leiris

36 André Masson
La Résistance (Resistance), 1944.
Oil on canvas, 176 x 139.
Galerie Louise Leiris, Paris

37 Pablo Picasso
Femme enceinte (Pregnant Woman), 1950)59.
Bronze, 110
Musée Picasso, Paris

showed work from Masson's American period in 1945, and in 1946, he did the décor for Sartre's play *Morts sans Sepulture*, having met Sartre for the first time in the USA. In 1949, Masson's illustrations for André Malraux's book *Les Conquérants* were shown at the Galerie La Hune. Masson, who was very concerned at the time about the relationship between art and the public, withdrew in 1947 to Aix-en-Provence, where his own work underwent a crisis, and he found himself 'rediscovering' Impressionist technique, while thanks to his long-standing friendship with Georges Duthuit, he renewed his interest in the Far East and Zen Buddhism. The style he evolved at this time was gradually abandoned after 1955, when he returned to gestural painting.

G.V.

'What do you think an artist is? An imbecile who only has eyes if he's a painter, ears if he's a musician, or a lyre in every chamber of his heart if he's a poet, or even, if he's a boxer only muscles? On the contrary, he is at the same time a political being, constantly alert to the horrifying, passionate, or pleasing events in the world, shaping himself completely to their image. How is it possible to be uninterested in other men, and what cold nonchalance could permit you to detach yourself from the life they supply in such abundance? No, painting is not made to decorate

38 Pablo Picasso
Dessin pour la Guerre et la Paix (Drawing for 'War' and 'Peace'), 1952. *Pencil on paper, 25 x 35*

apartments. It's an offensive and defensive weapon against the enemy.'

Simone Téry, 'Picasso n'est pas officier dans l'armée française', *Les Lettres Françaises*, 24 March 1945.

'Picasso's dove flies over the world. The State Department threatens it with poisoned arrows, the Fascists of Greece and Yugoslavia with their blood-red hands. The assassin MacArthur throws napalm bombs on the heroic people of Korea. The satraps who govern Colombia and Chile want to bar its entry into their land. In vain, Picasso's dove flies over the world, very white, luminous, bringing soft words of hope to mothers everywhere, and waking the masses with the beating of its wings, reminding them they are men, sons of the people, and that we do not wish them to go to their deaths.

Pablo Neruda, on the occasion of the award of the Lenin Peace Prize which he shared with Picasso, at the second World Peace Congress, Warsaw, 22 November, 1950.

EDOUARD PIGNON

b 1905, Bully les Mines

The son of a miner who was a militant member of the Socialist Party, Pignon broke away from his origins to go to Paris in 1927, where he worked in the Renault and Citroën car factories, and attended evening classes in painting and sculpture. In 1931 he became a militant, and joined the Association d'Ecrivains et d'Artistes Revolutionnaires, where he met leading left-wing intellectuals, such as Louis Aragon and André Malraux, and a host of painters including Léger, Hélion, Gruber and Taslitzky. He met Picasso in 1937 and was deeply impressed by 'Guernica'. During the Occupation, Pignon was active in the Front National, and contributed two lithographs to the Resistance album 'Vaincre'. His involvement in the exhibition at the Galerie Braun in May 1941 was crucial:

39 Edouard Pignon
Le mineur (Miner), 1952.
Charcoal on paper, 63 x 48
Musée National d'Art Moderne,
Centre Georges Pompidou.

these 'Vingt jeunes Peintres de Tradition
Française', whose brilliant, semi-abstract
canvases were a deliberate provocation
to the occupying Nazis, were a new
generation of post-Cubists, who under
the aegis of Braque, Bonnard and Villon,
formed the core of the future Ecole de
Paris. Pignon's contracts with Louis
Carré and then the Galerie de France
cleared the way for a successful Parisian
career. But despite the 'Collioure' series
of 1945–6 (see the 'Catalane au fond
bleu'), and the grey-blue-rose marine
series begun in Ostend in 1946, his
position became increasingly
ambiguous as a communist.

Pignon deliberately kept aloof from
the furore provoked by the growth of
'Social Realism' at the Salons d'Automne
of 1948 and 1949. The second 'Ouvrier
Mort' exhibited at the Salon de Mai in
1952, was Pignon's test-piece. Although
for him it reinterpreted the theme of
1936, it must be seen in context with the
numerous studies of 'dead workers',
(notably Fougeron's 'Hommage à
Houllier') produced by the major and
minor 'realist' painters of the early 1950s.

Pignon's relationship with Picasso at
this period bears consideration: They
spent much time together at Vallauris,
and in August 1952 held a joint
exhibition of pottery at the Maison de la
Pensée Française in Paris, where
Pignon exhibited again in 1954.
Undoubtedly Pignon drew much formal
and emotional strength from this
association, but one speculates to what
extent for Picasso, too, this direct
contact with a convinced and generally
militant Communist was significant at
an ambiguous stage in his own work:
the period of the evolution of 'La Guerre
et La Paix'.   S.W.

**... 'Already in 1936, with the technique
I had then, I had chosen this theme for
a first canvas. The idea came from a
childhood memory, a gas explosion. I
was six at the time of the Clarence mine
disaster, but I always remembered the
violent image of the men they brought
up, burned and screaming, the
mourning women pressed to the
railings. This canvas turned a
childhood memory into a painting, but
it also represented all my youth in the
mines. They call it 'L'Ouvrier Mort', but
its real name at the beginning, in my
head, was 'Solidarité'...**

E. Pignon, in *Edouard Pignon: 50 Peintures
de 1936 à 1962.*

40 Edouard Pignon
La Catalane (The Catalan
Woman), 1946. *Oil on
canvas, 162 x 96*
Musée Nationale d'Art Moderne,
Centre Georges Pompidou

41 Edouard Pignon
L'ouvrier mort (Dead Worker), 1951.
*Charcoal on paper mounted on
canvas, 105 x 75*
Musée National d'Art Moderne, Centre Georges Pompidou

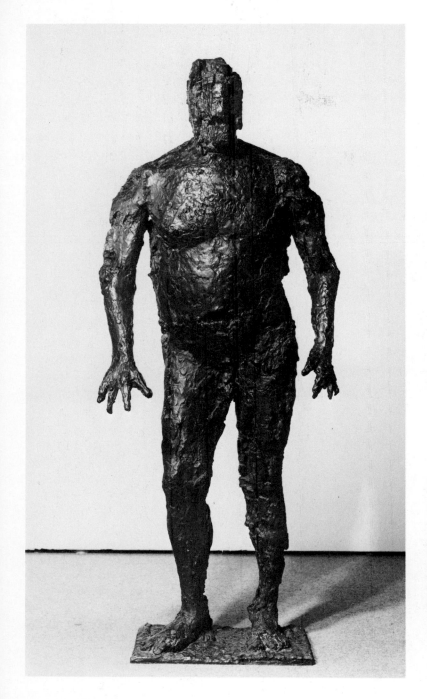

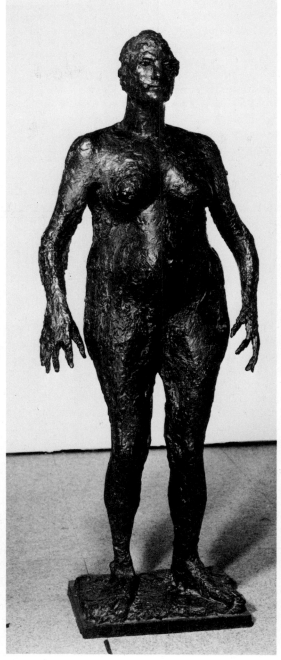

42 Germaine Richier
L'Orage (The Storm), 1947-8. *Bronze, 200 x 80 x 51*
Musée National d'Art Moderne, Centre Georges Pompidou.

43 Germaine Richier
L'Ouragane (The Hurricane), 1949 *Bronze, 179 x 67 x 50*
Musée National d'Art Moderne, Centre Georges Pompidou

GERMAINE RICHIER

b 1904, Grans, d 1959, Montpellier

Germaine Richier spent her childhood in Provence, and began her professional training as a sculptor with one of Rodin's former pupils, Guignes, who was the director of the Ecole des Beaux-Arts in Montpellier. She went to Paris in 1925, and worked for four years under Antoine Bourdelle. Her work remained completely classical until the war: she won the Prix Blumenthal in 1936 and an honorary diploma at the Exposition Internationale of 1937. Once Paris was occupied Richier left, and spent the rest of the war in the south of France and Switzerland, where in 1945 she exhibited with Marino Marini and Fritz Wotruba at the Kunstmuseum in Basle. Her work of the post-war period, portraying creatures from a disturbing universe of strange, half-metamorphosed figures, was first shown at the Galerie Maeght in Paris in 1948. 'L'Araignée' (1946), 'La Mante' (1946), 'L'Orage' (1947–8) and 'L'Ouragane' (1948–9) translated in imaginary terms the secret violence of nature which she had observed as a child in Provence; yet at the same time they could be seen to interpret clearly contemporary doubts and fears. Man's spiritual struggles contrast with the most basic aspects of animal and vegetable life as Germaine Richier

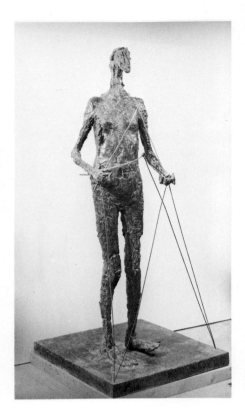

44 Germaine Richier
Le Diabolo, (The Diabolo Player), 1950.
Bronze, 160 x 49 x 60
Musée National d'Art Moderne, Centre Georges Pompidou

combines the emphatically brutal
nature of her material with elements
from popular legend. Her 'Christ',
commissioned for Le Corbusier's
church at Assy in 1950 represented the
Redeemer as an appallingly tortured,
suffering human figure, and created
such a scandal that the ecclesiastical
authorities removed it from the
sanctuary. The Musée National d'Art
Moderne presented a retrospective
exhibition of her work in 1956, and up to
her death in 1959, Germaine Richier
continued to add to her 'bestiary' of
anthropomorphic creatures, in which
the actual material of her sculpture
seemed to assert itself with increasing
insistence.   G.V.

**'At a higher level comes the theme of
death, idea and representation, and on
this note one should end. There is not, in
truth, a sculptor who does not make us
think of death (for all that a number of
sculptors, to their cost, have not given a
thought to it themselves). This is well
known to Richier, for whom the
intimidating art of sculpture holds no
mysteries, and she flinches from none
of the consequences of her craft. She
spares the bronze — from the time the**

**work is clay to the moment when it is all
put together — neither privation nor
torture nor the ultimate agony. She is
not afraid of going as far as the corpse,
carrion, even putrefaction. Some of
her creatures, the gentle ones, submit
to death as to a caress; others storm,
and will only perish in a splendid
battle; the ones which are wicked,
which are killers, carry their own end
about inside them, and their own
gesture or air condemns them: one
would say that they were already in a
world beyond, like larvae that will be
dead at the moment of their birth. Then
there are those that are haggard,
thundering giants, and I'll be hanged if
you can see nursing fathers in them . . .'**

André Pieyre de Mandiargues, Preface to the
Germaine Richier exhibition, The
Hanover Gallery, London 1955.

BORIS TASLITZKY

b 1911, Paris

Taslitzky's Russian emigré father was
killed in World War I, and Taslitzky
lived in relative poverty with his
working mother, from whom he was
often separated for long periods.
However, he resolved to become a
painter and went to drawing classes in
the Boulevard Montparnasse, and to
Léger's Académie Moderne in the Rue
Notre Dame des Champs, while at the
same time he made copies in the
Louvre, where Géricault and Delacroix
were his favourites. He was apprenticed
for a period to Francis Gruber's father, a
stained-glass maker, and became close
friends with Gruber, at the time a
veritable child prodigy. Together they
took part in the Front Populaire
processions of 1934, in which 'the
museum was carried on the street'.
Taslitzky carried Gruber's 'Jacques
Callot', Gruber his friend's 'Daumier'.
Taslitzky was the secretary of the
Union des Peintres et Sculpteurs de la
Maison de la Culture, which issued its
own *Journal*, and he was fully involved
in the exhibitions and the exhilarating
meetings of the Association des
Ecrivains et des Artistes
Révolutionnaires, where speakers like
Louis Aragon (*Pour un Réalisme
Socialiste*, 1935) and André Malraux
took the chair. From the start,
Taslitzky's work was politically
involved. 'Les Grèves de Juin 1936'
shows a strike meeting, while 'La
Télégramme' (1938) recalls the
assassination of the poet Garcia Llorca
during the Spanish Civil War.

45 Boris Taslitzky
Le Délegué (The Delegate), 1947. *Oil on
canvas, 197 x 114*
Artist's collection

By this time Taslitzky was a dedicated
Communist. In November 1941 he was
arrested, and six months later was sent
to St Sulplice La Pointe, where in secret
he painted large murals on the chapel
walls, portraying courage and victory.
When finally he was sent to
Buchenwald, he made a number of very
moving clandestine drawings, which
resulted in the imposing canvas, Le
Petit Camp de Buchenwald which was
purchased by the Musée National d'Art
Moderne. Taslitzky exhibited his work
relating to Buchenwald in 'Art et
Résistance' at the Musée National d'Art
Moderne in February 1946, and at his
one-man show, 'Témoignage', in June of
the same year. With Jean Amblard
Taslitzky went to the northern
industrial region of the Pas-de-Calais in
1946 to record the lives of miners and
produced sketches that lead to the
painting 'Les Délégués', 1948, showing
four miners standing in a defiant row,
which related to the serious strikes and
unrest during the winter of 1947–8. In
April 1950 he supervised the team of
mural painters who decorated the walls
of the market halls at Gennevilliers for

the twelfth congress of the French Communist party, himself painting a huge portrait of Stalin. 'La Mort de Danielle Casanova' showing the death at Auschwitz of the wife of Laurent Casanova, a party leader, was exhibited the same month at L'Art et la Paix (Art and Peace) in Lyons. In 1951, at the Salon d'Automne, two of the seven canvases taken down by the police were Taslitzky's: one showed striking dockers at Port de Bouc, the other was a portrait of Henri Martin. Both were protests about the Indo-Chinese war. Taslitzky and the young artist Mireille Miailhe were the first to undertake a documentary project in Algeria in 1952. The exhibition Algérie 52, describing the lamentable social and political conditions they found there, opened in January 1953, almost two years before armed French intervention in Algeria.

S.W.

'In capitalist society there is no free art. The writer and artist depend on the power of money which controls the market of thought and marks up talent like values on the Stock Exchange. We, however, wish to free the artist from the servitude which degrades him, which dries up his inspiration. It's the capitalists who marshal writers into brigades, who give them orders, impose certain tasks. It's they who limit artists to an art without content and without subject matter.'

Maurice Thorez: Speech to the 12th Congress of the French Communist Party, Gennevilliers, April 1950.

'Drawing here is not 'free': it must bear witness to reality . . . for the first time this notion, crucial to our times, "the constant struggle of colonial peoples against imperialism for independence and liberty", finds its reflection in painting. It's this, "the work of truth and brotherhood" that the 25,000 dockers in Algiers hail and salute. It's this which embarrasses those who have so much to fear from that struggle, as a simple dispatch dated January 5th would have sufficed to teach us: "By order of the Minister of the Interior, the police forces proceeded at 1.30 pm today with the removal of the pole supporting the poster for the exhibition Algérie 52." There's much to see, then in these drawings and canvases, a chronicle of the misery and the daily struggle of the whole Algerian people. Here are the agricultural workers, tilling their fatherland which has been taken from them, and here they are militating for better salaries. Here are the women, old at thirty, and here they are again in a meeting held for peace. Misery? Here are the children who are taught at school (if they go to school at all, for only 10% of the muslim children are "scholarised") that "France is our mother country" . . .

But the essential remains: "the work of brotherhood". We're here in front of our brothers who share with us the same certitude in the same future. It's this, which sheds the particular light on Boris Taslitzky's portraits, drawn or painted.

Anon: 'Quelques aspects d'une exposition Algerie 52': corrected proof for La Nouvelle Critique in the possession of Taslitzky.

Primitivism and Art Brut

ALOÏSE ANONYMOUS CRÉPIN FORESTIER GILL MÜLLER WILSON WÖLFLI

APPEL ATLAN BRASSAÏ BISSIÈRE BRAUNER CHAISSAC CONSTANT CORNEILLE DOUCET DUBUFFET ETIENNE-MARTIN GILBERT JORN KEMENY LAPICQUE MIRO PICASSO REBEYROLLE

Real art is always lurking where you don't expect it. Where nobody's thinking about it or mentions its name.
(DUBUFFET)

Primitivism and Art Brut

In April 1946, the writer and poet Jean Paulhan published an article of great charm in the *Cahiers de la Pléiade*: 'Guide d'un petit voyage en Suisse au mois de juillet 1945'. After years of makeshift and privation, he had travelled to this innocent and prosperous country, he said, in the company of a painter called 'Limérique' (Jean Dubuffet) who was 'obsessed with the idea of an immediate, "unpractised" art – an "art brut" whose rudiments could be found among prisoners and the insane', and which was rife in 'the mental asylums of the region'. Dubuffet was at the time finding works for his Art Brut collection and he was compiling the references to those works of the 'homme du commun' which were still extant, and which would be exhibited on the basement floor of the Galerie René Drouin from 1949 onwards. Since the time of the poet Arthur Rimbaud, artists and writers had often travelled in search of the bizarre and the innocent. These explorations were at once justified on purely formal grounds, and were nostalgic ventures into a lost continent, that went hand in hand with the development of modern art. Fauvism, Cubism and Surrealism in their turn appealed to the primitive as an inspiration and a justification for their experiments. But 'primitives' could also be discovered in the streets of contemporary Paris: the banquet offered to the Douanier Rousseau in 1908 was the first homage artists paid to the 'Maîtres Populaires de la Réalité', the title of an exhibition held at the Galerie Royale in 1937, the year of the Exposition Internationale, concurrent, symbolically enough, with the 'Maîtres de l'Art Indépendant', a magnificent exhibition of contemporary masters at the Petit Palais. In the preface to this exhibition, the critic Maximilien Gauthier noted, as Dubuffet would do later: 'Art is not the exclusive domain of a few initiates. It is a common asset, barred to no one. You enter without a key, sometimes even without knowing it, led by instinct'.

Dubuffet
'Georges arrive demain' *(message; indian ink & gouache on newsprint)* 1944.

Dubuffet
Cover for projected album of gouche drawings about the Metro.

A statement which was particularly apt for those times of the French Popular Front, when naive art appeared to certain artists as the best answer to the problem of realism. It came up again in the same context as the basis for the survey 'L'art et le public' published in *Les Lettres Françaises* of April 1946. But it is well known that Jean Dubuffet challenged the naive, regarding it as a perverted attempt to ape 'cultural art', despite its continued celebration in Wilhelm Uhde's *Cinq Maitres Primitifs* (1949) and the contemporary works in French by Anatole Jakovsky on the same subject. Dubuffet opted for the art of those completely cut off from society, the outcasts and the mentally sick. The development of these theories, their sources and their influences on the artistic climate of post war Paris are excellently mapped out in Henry-Claude Cousseau's article, 'The Search for New Origins'.

The refusal of 'culture' that these theories entail undoubtedly became more entrenched during the Occupation, with the dispersion of the population, and the psychological isolation and material need that was the general lot. Chaissac in the Vendée, Bissière in the Lot region, and Victor Brauner in the Alps constructed their individual mythologies in solitude, discovering in their own fashion the benefits of deprivation, and the materials that presented themselves by chance for their work. Here the search for origins became often one and the same as the recourse to tradition. The interest in Romanesque art, so evident in Paris just before the war was enlarged by the taste for prehistoric cave painting, reawakened in 1940 by the discovery of the sources of French art at Lascaux.

While the Academy and the Institute were often linked with the reactionary aesthetics of the Vichy Government, the truth was to be found on the walls of Paris: their graffiti, their proclamations, and their messages. Jean Dubuffet's 'Messages' created in June 1944, mark his true point of departure as an artist. Dubuffet at this moment abandoned the Romanesque style of his 'bonshommes' and started incorporating informal, ephemeral, trivial elements, waste and humble materials, and writing into his work. Gaston Chaissac's role in this evolution will undoubtedly be assessed

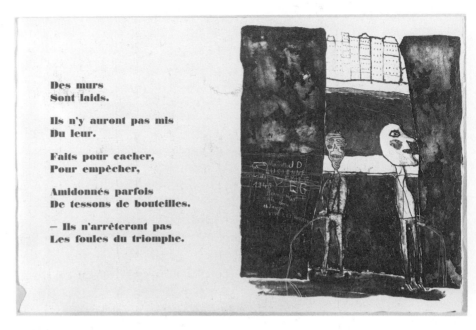

Dubuffet
'Des murs sont laids' (Sheet 8 from *Les Murs*).

one day, and there is no doubt as to the importance of their correspondence from 1944 onwards.

Whatever its sources, Dubuffet's work took on quite another dimension as he became involved in the methodical and relentless exploration of his chosen path. He retraced the nervous system of a reality torn to pieces; he extracted the particular detail in all its force from the amorphous and the general. As early as 1944 he wrote to Jean Paulhan: 'My system depends in fact upon the identical character of all men; for me there is only a single man in the universe, whose name is Man, and if all painters signed their works with this name: picture painted by a man, see how pointless any questioning would appear. My system applied to the arts implies, you are well aware, a whole series of consequences, and I pursue these consequences to their most extreme conclusion'. The recourse to matter itself as fertile soil for the imagination enabled Dubuffet to associate the brutality of everyday life with the most abstract mental speculation. The lithographs he made in 1944 to accompany Francis Ponge's text *Matière et Mémoire*, and his 'Murs' series of 1945, designed to go with Eugène Guillevic's poems on the 'walls' theme, preceded the alchemical transformations of the common and vulgar in the brutal metamorphoses of

the 'Mirobolus, Macadam et Cie' series exhibited at the Galerie René Drouin in 1946. Dubuffet succumbed to some of these 'sirens with intoxicating invitations' whom he had catalogued in the preface to René de Solier's Court traité des graffiti' (*Cahiers de la Pléiade*, April 1946): '1. She of the bizarre and of excess in the search for the bizarre. 8. She who heaps abuse on logical reasoning. 10. She of abstractions, intellectualism, cerebral attitudes. 21. She of ethnography. 26. She of despair and of the absurd.'

Dubuffet's research was echoed in the various enterprises long since undertaken by members of the Cobra group which was founded in Paris in 1948. Coming from various horizons, converts to Surrealism since before the war or marked by its influence, tempted for a moment by revolutionary modes of practice, they sought in their review, their group exhibitions and individually for an original, lively art, rooted in popular, national cultures and animated by the unconscious. They felt they had to escape 'prefabricated painting which transforms the painter's hand into a pistol, . . . platonic painting which transforms the painter's genitals into a question mark, . . . cultivated painting which transforms the painter into a gilder of coats of arms: those of the bourgeoisie . . . scientific painting which wants to preserve the skeleton

Atlan
Letter from prison, with drawings.

established around 1945 and 1946 between Dubuffet, Lapicque and Atlan for example. Atlan's exhibition at the Galerie Maeght in 1947 was a great success. His North African origins, his training as a philosopher, his encounter with the mentally ill at the St Anne hospital in Paris, where he stayed to escape the Gestapo, and the instinctive, ritual violence of his painting – all made him a rather privileged contributor to the aesthetic modes of the period.

The importance of the work of Miro and Picasso as regards spontaneity, popular traditions and everyday materials in modern art has never been underestimated. It is interesting that these two artists, quite apart from their influence on the younger generation, each contributed to the reawakened interest in primitivism. For Miro, the new experiments would be in the field of ceramics, which he created from 1944 to 1946 in his studio at Artigas, exhibiting his results in 1948 at the Galerie Maeght. These plaques, made at first from ceramic rejects, were covered with anonymous lines and marks and seem to be subject to the antique rites of earth and fire, as though they were apparitions from an immemorial past. Miro here meets up with the timeless character of Dubuffet's 'archetypes'. 'A profoundly individual gesture', Miro said, 'is anonymous. In its anonymity it gives way to the universal, I'm convinced: the more localised a thing is, the more it is universal.' (Joan Miro, *Je travaille comme un jardinier*, 1958, compiled and edited by Y. Taillander, XXème siècle, Paris, 1964.)

The figurines of clay that Picasso modelled during the Occupation contained explicit references to archaic Greek art, a source that became manifestly central in his work from 1947 onwards at Vallauris. Close to the fetishes of propitiatory magic in his 'maternity' figures, the archaic reference is developed in 'La Femme à la Pousette', where Picasso's method is to associate his reflections upon the structure of the visible world with a choice of found objects assembled according to a previously determined plan. This double approach, both intellectual and instinctive, is apparent in the work of many artists, through modes of discursive thought and in writing. It was characteristic of the most original developments of postwar art in France.

GERMAIN VIATTE

before the body is born . . . ironic painting which wants to express the organic joys of the universe well enough . . . but is a bit ashamed, and cuts the aesthetic spirit with an elegant little intellectual penknife' (Christian Dotremont, preface to the exhibition 'Appel, Constant, Corneille' Galerie Colette Allendy Paris 1949). Here there was a refusal to be aligned with any tendency, a liberty in graphic style and a brilliance of colour that is to be found again in the work of Charles Lapicque. He was an independent painter, linked for a moment with the 'Jeunes peintres de Tradition Française', who in no way renounced culture, but developed the capriciously intertwining lines of his 'personnages' using rocks and mystic Breton Calvaries as a starting point.

Certain stylistic influences doubtless had their origin in the contacts

ALOÏSE (Aloise Corbaz)

b 1886, Lausanne, Switzerland,
d 1964, La Rosière, Switzerland

Aloïse worked as a governess in Leipzig, Berlin and Potsdam before returning to Switzerland in 1913. She became a religious fanatic, producing inspired writings, and was diagnosed as a schizophrenic and hospitalised in 1918. She was infatuated with the German Kaiser, Wilhelm II, and manifested her frustrated romantic yearnings in brilliantly coloured, compartmentalised large-scale drawings. Full-bodied, theatrical women with flowing hair and huge opaque eyes are seen flanked by men in military uniform. Her ladies were called 'Mary Stuart', 'Anne Boleyn', 'Andromache', 'Ophelia' and so on. Jean

Dubuffet stated: 'I believe that Aloïse's tapestry with its thousand segments may be considered the one truly splendid manifestation in painting of the strictly feminine pulsation'. In Dubuffet's exhibition of 1949, L'Art Brut préféré aux Arts Culturel, Aloïse showed thirteen works. Two were tempera paintings; the rest were executed in coloured crayons and had very poetic titles: 'O Colombe immolée sur l'autel', 'Cléopatre, fille de la lune' and 'Train nénuphar dans mes bras'. Aloïse's output was most prolific, especially from 1941 up to her death in 1964.   S.W.

'Then until I die I shall always recognize the crusader fanaticism of His Majesty because one does not know whom one

has in one's arms except by means of telepathy unless it be that of his reporter Wolf always half-asleep at night one feels absolutely penetrated kissed enveloped as if one were in a bridal bed still seeing the vision of bodies which touch yours one cannot express it in any other way . . .'

Aloïse extract from a letter reproduced in Roger Cardinal, *Outsider Art*, Studio Vista, London 1972.

ANONYMOUS

These works from the collection of the Centre d'étude de l'expression at the Hôpital St Anne in Paris are exhibited anonymously, just as was the case at the Exposition d'oeuvres executés par les malades mentaux in 1946. On that

XIII Aloïse
La loge (The Box), no date. *Coloured pencil on paper, 40 x 27*
Private collection

47 Anonymous
La Sultane d'Orient (Oriental Sultana), no date. *Indian ink and watercolour on card, 66 66 x 50*
Centre d'étude de l'expression, Hôpital St Anne, Paris

48

49

50

occasion 141 untitled works were shown, often with elaborate case histories. 36 additional works were contributed by Dr Gaston Ferdiere, the case histories being summarized as 'manic', 'schizophrenic', 'persecution complex' and so on. (The artist Artaud was under Ferdiére's supervision at this time.) The catalogue was illustrated with two works from Prinzhorn's *Bildnerei der Geisteskranken*, 1922 Dubuffet's Art Brut exhibition contained 16 completely anonymous works among the 200 numbered exhibits, but generally artist's names were cited, though abbreviations were sometimes used: Forestier appeared as Auguste For and Muller as Henrich Anton, for example. S.W.

FLEURY-JOSEPH CRÉPIN

b 1875, Hénin Lietard, d 1948, Montigny en Gohelle

Crépin left school at fourteen, and worked in his father's plumbing and roof-mending business. He was extremely musical: he composed for the clarinet, and conducted a miners' brass band and the Hénin-Liétard trumpet society. In 1930 he met Victor Simon, a friend and follower of Augustin Lesage, who was himself a medium and a painter. Crépin was able to meet Lesage, and joined the Spiritualist circle at Arras. In 1931 he started making a reputation as a water-diviner and healer. When he was sixty-three he suddenly felt impelled, while copying out some music, to doodle some designs in the margins of his work. This led to the creation of exercise books full of motifs, which he enlarged, working in colour on big sheets of paper. In 1939 he turned to oils. Crépin's technique was meticulous: he built up his hieratic, temple-like structures using his design

48 Anonymous
Ni dieux, ni maîtres, ni fleurs, ni couronnes (No Gods, No Masters, No Flowers, No Crowns), no date. *Oil on paper, 27 x 36*
Centre d'étude de l'expression, Hôpital St Anne, Paris

49 Anonymous
Combat du Giaour et du Rache (Battle between Giaour and Raschid), no date. *Indian ink, coloured ink, watercolour and pencil on card, 50 x 65*
Centre d'étude de l'expression, Hôpital St Anne, Paris

50 Anonymous
Ciment Poliet chausson (Heads on a Chessboard), no date. *Gouache on card*
Centre d'étude de l'expression, Hôpital St Anne, Paris

XIV Joseph Crépin
No. 11, 1945. *Oil on canvas, 49.5 x 65*
Private collection

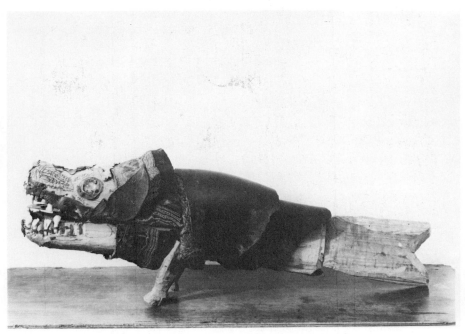

book of motifs and cross-ruled paper, always keeping to a system of obsessive bilaterial symmetry. During World War II he painted by night, listening to concerts on the radio or to his daughter playing the violin. He received a prophecy from a spirit voice that when he had painted three hundred pictures the war would end. It was fulfilled on 7 May 1945. His last development, the 'Tableaux Merveilleux' used luminous globules of paint mixed with varnish, resembling tiny beads, to enrich his already ornate surfaces. Nine such paintings, dating from 1939 to 1947 were shown after his death at the exhibition L'Art Brut préféré aux Arts Culturels in 1949. S.W.

AUGUSTE FORESTIER

b 1887, d 1958

From the age of twenty-seven until his death, Auguste Forestier lived in the Hôpital de St Alban, apart from brief escapes during which he indulged in his mania for train rides. In the hospital corridor he arranged a rudimentary studio-workshop for himself. With odd bits of wood, remnants of leather and cloth, rubbish from floor sweepings and even kitchen waste, Forestier created superb and bizarre objects, that from their method of construction are more properly called 'assemblages' than sculptures. The 'Monstre marin' ailé was illustrated in the catalogue of l'Art Brut préféré aux Arts Culturels, 1949, and with it nine other sculpted wood pieces were shown including two clothed dolls – a king and a general – a boat with a thirteen-man crew, a sword with a rubber teat, and the 'profile of a hairy man with a rabbit on his hat'. S.W.

51 Auguste Forestier
Monstre marin ailé (Winged Seamonster), no date. *Composite object – wood, leather, teeth, 20 x 90*
Gaston Ferdière

52 Auguste Forestier
Un bateau (Boat), no date. *Composite object – wood, paper, metal, 120 x 25*
Gaston Ferdière

53 Madge Gill
Peace, Christ,
The Founder of World
Peace. *Ink on calico, 476 x 148*
East Ham Library, London

54 Madge Gill
Untitled, no date. *Gouache
and ink on paper*
East Ham Library, London

MADGE GILL

b 1882, Walthamstow, d 1961 East Ham,
London

An illegitimate child, Madge Gill was
put into a Dr Barnado's home at the age
of nine, and was later transported to
Canada to work on a farm. Returning to
London in 1903, she married and had
four children, two of whom died
tragically, while Madge herself lost her
left eye after a serious illness. It was at
this time that she became seriously
involved in spiritualism. From 1919
onwards she produced hundreds of ink
drawings, sometimes coloured, on
huge rolls of untreated calico. She
worked these like scrolls, claiming
inspiration from 'Myrninerest', her
spirit guide, and never saw the full
extent of a drawing until it was hung on
a gallery wall. She exhibited annually
from 1932 onwards at the Whitechapel
Gallery's show for amateur artists – as
many as thirteen panels each 2½ metres
high were displayed in 1940, for
example. In *Myrninerest, the Spheres*,
a broadsheet written by her son Laurie

XIII Aloïse
La loge (The Box), no date. *Coloured pencil
on paper, 40 x 27*
Private collection

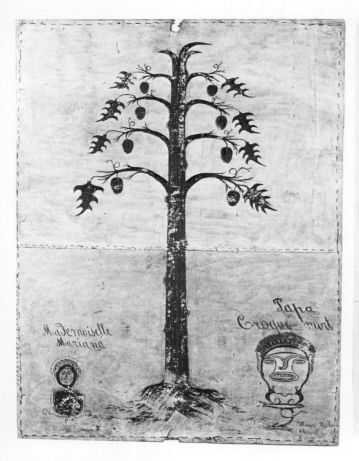

55 Heinrich Anton Muller
Mademoiselle Mariane – papa croque mort (Daddy the Mute), no date. *Gouache and pencil on paper, 78 x 59*
Musée des Beaux-Arts, Bern

56 Scottie Wilson
Composition rose (Pink Composition), no date. *Indian ink and coloured pencil, 56 x 37*
Thomas le Guillou, Galerie Messine, Paris

in 1926, the full extent of Madge's activities was revealed: 'Spiritual or Inspirational drawings, Writings, Speaking, Singing, Inspired Piano-Playing, making knitted woollen clothes and weaving silk mats in beautifully blended colours'. Madge Gill did not figure in Dubuffet's exhibition of 1949.
S.W.

'The world is delivered from its impunities that caused it. Life ebbs and flows. Today we are here. Tomorrow may perhaps never come. Man also has his limits. A time of order is approaching. The trumpets will ring out.'

Madge Gill, inspired writing, dated 5 March 1944

top
XIV Joseph Crépin
No. 11, 1945. *Oil on canvas, 49.5 x 65*
Private collection

bottom
XIV Madge Gill
Timeless, Mars, Jupiter and Saturn in conjunction. *Gouache and ink on paper, 19.3 x 23.7*
East Ham Library, London

HEINRICH ANTON MÜLLER

b 1865, Bottingen, Switzerland, d 1930, Switzerland

Muller suffered a mental breakdown when, in 1903, his ingenious invention for pruning grapevines was exploited and commercialised by neighbours. In 1906 he entered a psychiatric hospital, where he began to suffer from hallucinations and delusions of grandeur. He constructed highly elaborate perpetual motion machines, and painted wild and aggressive compositions featuring animals, people, trees and bicycles, in combinations of crayons, chalk, watercolour and gouache on thick wrapping paper. Two illustrations of works by 'Heinrich Anton' appear in the catalogue of the 1949 exhibition L'Art Brut préféré aux Arts Culturels. S.W.

SCOTTIE WILSON

b 1890, Glasgow, d 1972, London

Scottie Wilson came from a very poor family and had no formal education. He was for much of his childhood fascinated by zoos and circuses. He joined the army at sixteen and after service in India and South Africa fought in France during World War I. He then worked in fairs and circuses, and was over forty when he first began to draw, while running a junk shop in Toronto, Canada. His early images are very intense, and portray the struggle of creative and destructive forces within totemic structures, but his later work becomes more serene, with a marked bilateral symmetry and a characteristic use of sinewy cross-hatchings. Scottie returned to Britain in 1945, and started to exhibit in an old bus, stubbornly resisting all forms of commercial exploitation. Five drawings in coloured inks were shown in Dubuffet's exhibition L'Art Brut préféré aux Arts Culturels. S.W.

57 Adolf Wölfli
La comète de Saint Adolf (St Adolf's Comet),
1946. *Coloured pencil on paper, 53 x 43*
Fondation Adolf Wölfli, Musée des Beaux-Arts, Bern

ADOLF WÖLFLI

b 1864, Bern, Switzerland, d 1930, Bern
An orphan, Wölfli grew up to become a
farmhand, and in 1895, after several
unhappy love affairs and imprisonment
for child-molesting, he was committed
to the Waldau psychiatric clinic in
Bern . He was a violent patient, and
from 1897 onwards spent most of his
time in solitary confinement filling his
cell with piles of his work. His strange,
symmetrical drawings, dense with a
'horror vacui', incorporate aerial
perspectives, strange symbolic poems,

numbers and even musical notations.
They relate the fantastic adventures of
his alter-ego, a child divinity, Saint
Adolf II. As early as 1921, Dr W.
Morgenthaler published a book on
Wölfli, *Ein Geistenkranker als
Künstler* (A mentally ill patient as
artist), the year before Hans Prinzhorn's
definitive *Bilderei des Geisteskranken*
(Pictures by the mentally ill) appeared
in Berlin. Dubuffet saw Wölfli's work at
the Waldau clinic in 1945, and exhibited
five compositions, including 'Symboles
et partition musicale' at L'Art Brut
préféré aux Arts Culturels.   S.W.

KAREL APPEL

b 1921, Amsterdam

After studying at the Académie des Beaux-Arts in Amsterdam, Appel had his first one-man show at Gröningen in 1946. In Paris in 1948 he was one of the founder members of the Cobra group, and he helped to organise the exhibition of Cobra artists and other members of the experimental avant-garde at the Stedelijk Museum. At the time he was making sculptures of a Dadaist type — 'assemblages' of discarded bits and pieces; he then went on to reliefs made of odd pieces of wood, sawn off at random and violently coloured, inspired by children's drawings. He went to live in Paris in 1950, and the same year participated in the Cobra exhibition organised at Galerie 73 by Michel Ragon to celebrate the publication of his book: *Expression et non-figuration, problèmes et tendances de l'art d'aujourd'hui*. Appel's work changed at that time, finally becoming very expressionistic, with a loose handling of drips and trickles and torrential colours from

which crude human and animal silhouettes would emerge. In 1951 Appel joined the exhibition Cinq Peintres at the Galerie Pierre, and then showed work at Signifiants de l' Informel organised by Michel Tapié at the Studio Fachetti. After a journey to New York where he was influenced by Action Painting, his work became increasingly dynamic, full of movement which tends to dissolve form.   G.V.

JEAN-MICHEL ATLAN

b 1913, Constantine, Algeria,
d 1960, Paris

Atlan went to Paris at the age of seventeen and graduated in philosophy at the Sorbonne. He earned his living as a history and philosophy teacher and began to write poetry.

Arrested for Resistance activity in 1941, he managed to escape deportation by pretending to be insane, and subsequently spent the rest of the war in the St Anne mental hospital in Paris where he began painting seriously [and

kept up an almost daily correspondence with his wife Denise]. *Le Sang Profond*, a book of illustrated poems, was published on his release in 1944.

In his first 'manifesto' of 1945 he stated: 'The essential task for young painters is to substitute, for a vision of reality, the authenticity and reality of vision' (*Continuity*, 1945, no. 2). His painting was rich in animal imagery, similar to that of the Cobra painters, whose work of this period would be exhibited later in Paris, but Atlan's frequent Old Testament subjects, like 'Le lion de Judah', 'Jericho', 'Salome', 'Dalila', gave his work a wider relevance, relating it to his Jewish background. At the Salon des Surindépendants of 1945, and later at the Galerie Maeght, his work was associated with that of such artists as Hartung, Poliakoff, Schneider and Soulages. In 1948 and 1949, he exhibited with Pignon in Copenhagen, and contributed to the review *Cobra* in 1950.

Atlan, a Communist sympathiser, illustrated in 1949 Saint-Just's *Pour la défense de Robespierre*. His violent forms recalled flames, spears and teeth:

58 Karel Appel
Femme et oiseau (Woman and Bird), 1953. *Oil on canvas, 79 x 130*
Musée National d'Art Moderne, Centre Georges Pompidou

XIX Karel Appel
Enfants interrogeant (Questioning Children), 1948. *Assemblage: oil on wood in two pieces, 87 x 60* J.W.N. Segaas, Galerie Nova Spectra, The Hague

59

60

61

an abstract response to a political subject. His opinion of contemporary social realism in 1953 was that 'not a single valuable work has come out of that pseudo-revolutionary aesthetic' (*Preuves*, Paris, July 1953, no. 29). In contrast, as we see in the 'Miroirs d'Asie', he was interested in the magical and the erotic.

From 1948 to 1955 he suffered a period of neglect but became increasingly popular again after 1953. He died in Paris in 1960.   S.W.

'I feel close to the "hasidim", the moslem dervishes, the buddhist dancers, the voodoo rites of Africa and America. The need for rhythms characterizes my painting. Its forms are dance-like, warrior-like, you can always find the theme of battle or war in them, the erotic fury of lovers, or the dance.'

Letters to Michel Ragon, in *Atlan*, Musée National d'Art Moderne.

ROGER BISSIÈRE

b 1888, Villereal, d 1964, Boisierettes

Influenced by Cubism and his friendship with Braque, Bissière was one of the first to promote the values of a 'return to order', recognising in the 'esprit nouveau' the classical rigour of Seurat, Corot, Ingres and Raphael. From 1925 to 1938 he taught at the Académie Ranson, significantly shaping the careers of numerous artists of the post-war generation without, however, finding his own style. He took part in the preparation of the Exposition International of 1937, and from then on his work underwent a

59 Jean Michel Atlan
Paysage (Landscape), 1944. *Oil on canvas, 38 x 55*
Alexander & Stella Margulies, London

60 Jean Michel Atlan
Peinture (Painting), 1951. *Oil on canvas, 81 x 100*
Musée National d'Art Moderne, Centre Georges Pompidou

61 Jean Michel Atlan
Les Miroirs de l'Asie (Mirrors of Asia), 1953-4. *Oil on canvas, 195 x 130*
Musée National d'Art Moderne, Centre Georges Pompidou

62 Roger Bissière
La Vénus noire (Black Venus), 1945. *Oil on canvas, 100 x 81*
Galerie Jeanne Bucher, Paris

XXIII Roger Bissière
Le Soleil (The Sun), 1946. *Appliqué and patchwork, 170 x 245*
Musée National d'Art Moderne, Centre Georges Pompidou

62

63 Roger Bissière
La Vénus blanche (White Venus), 1948. *Oil on canvas, 110 x 76*
Galerie Jeanne Bucher, Paris

profound transformation, with the influence of Romanesque art and Mathis Grünewald's Isenheim altarpiece. From 1938 to 1945, he lived in a provincial isolation which protected him from the artistic speculations of the Parisian milieu. Instead, he was led to investigate popular art, finding therein the authenticity of the 'French tradition' much mooted at the time. From 1938 onwards, his spirited resistance to fashions and formulas asserted itself – first in sculptures created from old agricultural machinery, then after 1945, in a series of primitivistic piecework tapestries. These were presented together with several graffiti-laden paintings at the Galerie René Drouin in 1947. Pursuing his solitary path, counter to any contemporary stereotypes, Bissière painted a series of 'untitled images' exhibited at the Galerie Jeanne Bucher in 1951 and 1952. They marked his return to painting with an enthusiasm, a serenity and a humility which perfectly suited him and which led him on to illustrate St Francis of Assisi's *Cantique à notre Frère Soleil* in 1954.   G.V.

'Ah! Modern Painting, ancient painting, mural painting, oil painting, fresco, the Spanish, the Dutch, the Italians and the French, and all the swings and roundabouts for museum curators or pupils of the Ecole du Louvre – as if I could give a damn! I don't go into a museum or an exhibition to look at paintings, but to meet people. But how rare real people are! You're more likely to meet conjurors, so elegant, so at their ease. They've got nothing in their hands, nothing in their pockets, and every time their act works. 'Chacun son goût'. Personally, I prefer those who make a blunder from time to time. Especially those who don't always do the same thing. Who try a new turn every day, unknown, dangerous, risking their neck every time. Those who can't catch sight of a door without wanting to see what's behind it, even if behind it there's a booby trap.'

Roger Bissière, 'Defense d'Afficher' in 'Les Problèmes de la Peinture', *Confluences*, Paris, 1945.

'It's a theatre of sacred puppets, schematic as graffiti or a Polynesian drawing, leading you into the delirium of Kashmir, among the gods and the fetishes, as in the friezes of some pagan Parthenon. There you meet the dishevelled angels and the great barbarous dolls covered with childish daubs, but hallowed because of their size and magnified by the composition. They mix poetry, humour and majesty with a sense of the hieratic, an impalpable mystery which touches on an animal enigma, which is disturbing, fascinating, seductive.

Alexandre Vialatte, *Tableaux de chiffons et sorcelleries plastique.* Text written for the exhibition *Bissière* at the Galerie René Drouin in 1947, reproduced in *Bissière*, Musée des Arts Decoratifs, Paris 1966.

BRASSAI (Gyula Halasz)

b 1899 Brasso, Rumania (now Hungary)

Brassai spent two years at the Academy of Fine Arts in Budapest, and then went to Berlin, before his arrival in Paris and his decision to devote himself almost exclusively to photography. He became friends with Henry Miller, who called him the 'eye of Paris', for his records of the brilliant nightlife of the cafés, the backstreets, the prostitutes and the poverty immortalised in his *Secret Paris of the 1930s*. In 1932 he met Picasso who was living in the Rue la Boétie, and photographed his sculptures for *Minotaure* in 1933. From this period onwards he recorded the conversations they had together.

His photographs of graffiti, begun in the early thirties and continued throughout the Occupation, are equally the record of a 'secret Paris': the clandestine messages of children and lovers and the political slogans became all the more poignant in wartime, as holes created by bullets and shrapnel were transformed into skulls and crossbones, eyes, breasts and sexes. Many artists besides Picasso were attracted to graffiti. As important as the primitive signs themselves was the record of the 'life' of the wall as changing and eroding matter, which provided a parallel to the researches of the 'informel' and 'matière' painters specifically Fautrier and Jean Dubuffet. From 1944 onwards, the magazine *Harper's Bazaar* not only commissioned Brassai's brilliant portraits of such figures as Braque, Giacometti, Jean Genêt and Germaine Richier, but sent him on photographic missions throughout the world in the late forties and fifties.

Brassai's activity as a graphic artist started at the age of 22, and in 1945 his drawings were exhibited at the Galerie Renou et Colle. Thirty drawings were chosen to illustrate a poem by Jacques

64 Brassaï
Graffiti, no date. *Photograph.*
Artist's collection

Prévert in 1946. He has recently begun
making sculpture and tapestry. s.w.

'. . . The wall gives its voice to that part
of man which, without it, would be
condemned to silence . . . The
remainder of a primitive existence of
which the wall may be one of the most
faithful mirrors. Graffiti is our state of
civilisation, our primitive art. . .'
'Since I began photographing graffiti,
contemporary art has given rise to an
event of historic significance, perhaps
as important as the Cubist movement,
that of the realisation of the wall by the
greater number of our artists. . .Art –
and correlatively the history of art –
has returned to its origins, to the art of
all ages, and above all to archaic arts, to
instinctive gestures, to primordial
marks. Graffiti reach the heart of the
burning problems of our age. It is also
understandable why most of them
remind us of the lost civilisations –
Peruvian, pre-Columbian, Mexican, or
even more ancient cultures – and at the
same time remind us also of the works
of Picasso, Klee, Rouault.
'The world of the graffiti sums up the
whole of life in three leading themes:
birth, love, death. Birth: the image of
man, spelt and identified for the first
time. Love: under its two aspects,
carnal and romantic. Death:
decomposition, annihilation and
adventure. Animism, always present,
calls up not only warriors, heroes,
animals, but also devils, wizards,
fauns, phallic gods, monsters,
half-brute, half-human creatures. This
strange universe of signs, figures,
symbols and even spells and witchcraft
– of which many traces can be
discovered – still persists today under
the electric sky of our cities.'

Brassai: *Language of the Wall.*

65 Brassaï
La mort (Death), no date.
Photograph
Artist's collection

66 Brassaï
Le roi soleil (The Sun King), 1952.
Photograph
Artist's collection

GASTON CHAISSAC

b 1910 Avalon, d 1964 La Roche sur Yonne

Chaissac was a nervous, sickly child; slow at school and already 'different' from other children. In 1923, he started work as a kitchen boy, and took up various other jobs: he was an ironmonger, a saddler, a stable boy, and in 1931 he became a cobbler, as his father had been before him. He went to Paris for the first time in 1934, and living in considerable poverty in the Quartier Mouffetard, began creating objects using scraps of old leather. The following year he returned to Villepourçon. His second trip to Paris in 1937 was to be a revelation. He stayed with his brother in the same building as the painter Otto Freundlich and his companion Jeannine Kosnick Kloss.

With their encouragement, Chaissac started to paint and draw and went to Freundlich's academy 'Le Mur'. 'Un peintre nous est né' – 'A painter is born to us' said Freundlich.

Chaissac's early work was tentative and childish, but gradually a fascinating vocabulary emerged based on shapes that were quite consciously related to prehistoric forms. 'Bête, oiseaux et serpents' of 1938, relates these forms in an already highly conceptualised space, where the animal and vegetable worlds interpenetrate in a primitive universe. Chaissac's use of dark contours both divides objects and spaces and unifies them in rhythmic sequences. This would seem to be related to Freundlich's chequered, abstract work of the same period. Freundlich's use of colour juxtapositions encouraged

Chaissac to experiment, but his own development, notably in the collages of the 1950s far surpassed that of his early master, and Chaissac must be seen as one of the most audacious colourists of his time.

As early as 1938 he held his first exhibition at the Galerie Garbo in Paris, attracting the attention of Marie Cuttoli, Gleizes and Robert Delaunay. Having contracted tuberculosis, he spent much time between 1938 and 1939 in various clinics and at the Clairvivre sanatorium in the Dordogne he met his future wife Camille Guibert. In St. Rémy de Provence in 1942 Chaissac met many more artists, but in October moved to the Vendée and began a very rural existence.

In spite of the difficulties of the Occupation and the tragic deportation

67 Brassai

L'amour (Love), no date.
Photograph
Artist's collection

68 Gaston Chaissac

La chambre (Room), no date. *Gouache on card, 50 x 65*
Annie Raison

XVII Gaston Chaissac
Composition, 1945-6. *Oil on wood,*
209 x 110
Galerie Messine, Paris

69 Gaston Chaissac
Sans titre (Untitled), no date. *Oils on paper*
mounted on plywood, 63 x 48
Annie Raison

70 Gaston Chaissac
Sans titre (Untitled), 1948. *Gouache on*
cardboard, 49 x 64
Annie Raison

of Freundlich, Jeannine Kosnick ensured that Chaissac showed in various exhibitions, particularly the Salon des Indépendants of 1944. Here the writer Raymond Queneau, already familiar with Chaissac's work, suggested that Jean Dubuffet and Jean Paulhan begin a corespondence with him.

Chaissac thus became appropriated as an Art Brut artist, despite his quite sophisticated involvement with modern art, and it was Dubuffet who wrote the preface to the catalogue of his first important exhibition at the Galerie de l'Arc-en-Ciel in 1947 – with the usual elaborate whimsy. André Breton, Camille Bryen and Louis Cattiaux also began corresponding with Chaissac. This was the period, 1947–8, in which the influence of Picasso became apparent in his work. Chaissac goes as far as parody in 'La Chambre', 1948, with its tiny 'Picasso' on the wall. In 1948, Chaissac moved to Ste-Florence, an even more isolated community, dominated by a very hostile and backward clergyman. In utter isolation, Chaissac started his brilliant collages, the paintings on stones and old iron, the murals, and his curious letters filled with drawings and writing in patterns, addressed to the highest and the lowest of society. He was astonishingly prolific at this time. He exhibited three works 'L'Art Brut préferé aux Arts Culturels' including 'La Dame de Moire', a piece of sculpted coal resembling a prehistoric 'Venus', such as the 'Dame de Lespugue', which inspired artists such as Jean Fautrier and Roger Bissière during the same period.

Chaissac read widely, contributed to provincial reviews and was perfectly aware of contemporary developments, many of which were ignored in Paris. Through certain contacts he was even in touch with Belgium, and may have had an influence on the Cobra movement. In 1951 *Hippobosque au bocage* was published by Gallimard, and from 1953 onwards, Chaissac made regular contributions to *La Nouvelle N.R.F.* In 1956 Chaissac visited Dubuffet in Vence, but shortly afterwards all contact between them ceased. Chaissac began to receive critical recognition as significantly more than a mere Art Brut artist in 1961, only three years before his death.   S.W.

71 Gaston Chaissac
La binette (The Hoe), no date. *Painted object,* *26 x 16* Annie Raison

'My state is pretty much like that of a man in solitary confinement. My soul is imprisoned in a suffering body which can't fulfil my desires, and there's no hope of escape. I was made for action. I would have liked to do all sorts of jobs, live in all sorts of places and write down what I saw, and I'm reduced to daubing on bits of paper. It makes me desperately sad, and nothing can stop it. I try to hide it, and manage not to show myself as I really am because I've given up trying to be understood for a long time.'

Gaston Chaissac, 'Lettre à Mlle C,' in *Cahiers de la Pléiade*, Paris, winter number, 1948.

XVIII Gaston Chaissac
Figure dans un panier (Face in a Basket), no date. *Ripolin on wicker and cardboard,* *60 x 45*
Musée de l'Abbaye Sainte Croix, Les Sables d'Olonne

'Here there are no precious materials, no more clichés or artistic prejudices. Forms and rhythms spring directly from his vision with no intervening processes. Spontaneously. No ornament or preparation. A continuous burst. Discontinuous rather. Because once the image has been fixed, he leaves it there and goes straight on to another. With no transition, no apparent connection. If at the time he only sees a head and a hand, the hand will grow straight out of the head. This disturbs the spectator who hasn't been warned, who wants to say it's mad. Not as mad as all that though, is Chaissac. Far from it.

... 'Chaissac "illuminates" stone, roots, bricks and old junk of every kind, like the monks who used to illuminate parchment.

'Spurts of enamel, or even those dreadful colours gold and silver which no respectable artist would use are all he needs to create the faces which appear on the local slate. A knotty root set off by a beard of garlic leaves repeats or recreates these same faces ... And what faces! Serious, stately, barbarous, eternal, charged with a life which scarcely seems to resemble ours at all. But as he works so fast, these faces always seem to be a little bit awry. Another trap for the distinguished critics and the knowledgeable connoisseurs of the 'Fynarts'. From there it's only one step to mixing up Chaissac with the naive painters. Nothing's further from the truth. What the naive painters create as a result of painstaking application, immense attention to detail, and innumerable hours of laborious handywork, Chaissac can get with no trouble, at a single stroke, thanks to the purity of his vision and his freshness of colour. Yes, it's a question of talent: you've either got it or you haven't. He paints like the birds sing, and like naive artists paint birds singing, that's the sole reason for the confusion. Then, as he lives in the Vendée and is a cobbler and ex-stable boy by trade, all that goes into the picture too.'

Anatole Jakovsky: *Gaston Chaissac, l'homme-orchestre.*

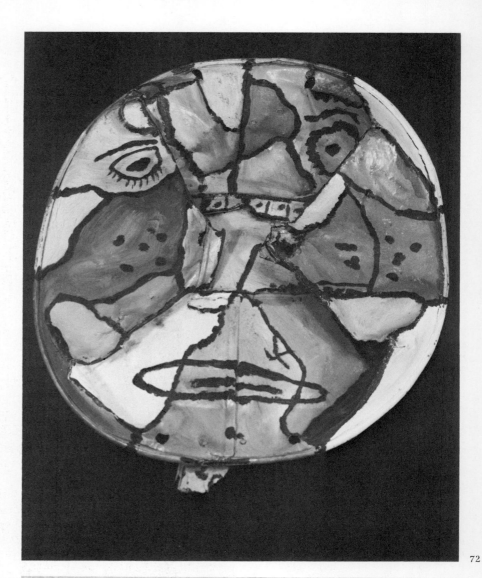

72

72 Gaston Chaissac
Bassine ecrasée (Crushed Pan), no date. *Painted object, 48 x 41*
Annie Raison

73 Gaston Chaissac
Sans titre (Untitled), no date. *Oil on paper mounted on plywood, 49 x 60*
Annie Raison

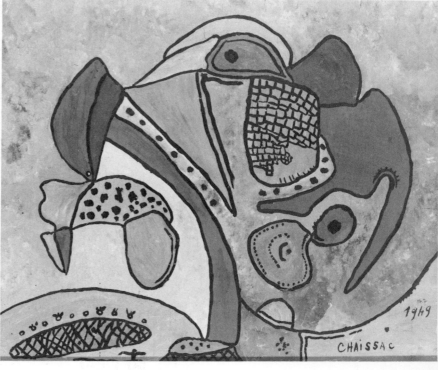

73

'I searched for harmonies as hard as I could, with my ignorance of drawing and my palette full of colours which generally didn't go together. There was no question of lessons: I was completely broke, and didn't have a grant. But I often used to see myself as one of the younger brothers of old times, whose schooling was vastly neglected but who picked things up from the education the elder brother had received. And as I could only draw things in a stilted way with my summary technique, I used to accentuate my clumsiness sometimes, as I'd realised that the worse my drawing was, the less it had that stiff look of the apprentice draughtsman about it. You're elegant in your own way, and it's not just because I'm poor and it's more practical that I always wear workers' clothes, but because I choose to. I often chose my friends among the farmhands for the same reasons; besides, to break with my origins would have been very bad manners.

'And Benjamin Peret was certainly more perceptive: he goes so far as to see me as a 'popular dandy'. That provides part of the answer for the people who think that a cobbler doesn't express himself as I do.

'They say I'm mad, but it doesn't seem to me that they think I'm a poor, irresponsible fellow, because they don't just think I'm pathetic, but that I ought to be blamed for it too.

'I'm in the middle of painting a picture on the back of another one. And making multicoloured masks out of old tools. So early this morning I had a good session hammering away with a big hammer. These poor remains of a basin, which burst where it had been soldered – I thought for a moment I'd sew the bits together with wire to get it all of a piece again, but after thinking a while, I nailed the pieces onto a plank of wood. I prefer painting on canvas than on the wrinkly bottoms of my old basins. It's easier.'

Gaston Chaissac, extracts from letters to his friends, in Gilles Ehrmann, *Les inspirés et leurs demeures* (Preface by André Breton and Benjamin Peret), Le Temps, Paris 1962.

CONSTANT (Constant Anton Nieuwenheuys)

b 1920, Amsterdam

On his first visit to Paris in 1946 Constant met Asger Jorn, and immediately sympathised both with his utopian political convictions and with his interest in primitive societies. In July 1948, with Karel Appel and Corneille, he created the experimental

74 Gaston Chaissac
Sans titre (Untitled), 1954. *Collage, 84 x 59.5*
Annie Raison

group, whose manifesto was to be the review *Reflex*. The same year he participated in the conference at the Centre de documentation sur l'art d'avant-garde organised in Paris by the Surréalistes Révolutionnaires whose members included Christian Dotremont, Edouard Jaguer, Noel Arnaud and René Passeron. He was in addition one of the dissidents who created the Cobra group, and was involved with the review *Cobra* until 1950. He came to live in Paris in 1950. The drawings of 'L'imagination

effrayante', and his paintings at the same time were filled with the horror of war: a primitive and fantastic animal symbolism is associated with the recurring theme of the broken wheel.

After a period in London he returned to Amsterdam in 1953, and became increasingly interested in spatial problems. That same year he published *Pour un colorisme spatial* with Aldo van Eyck. In 1956, his researches into nomadic environments gave rise to the projects 'New Babylon' and the 'Déclaration d'Amsterdam', published

in no. 2 of the review *L'Internationale
Situationniste*. After making contact
with E.G. Debord, he became attached
to this group and its attempts to define a
possible framework for coherent
collective action as creative artists. G.V.

CORNEILLE
(Cornelis Beverloo)

b 1922, Liège, Belgium

In 1940 Corneille went to live in
Amsterdam but his studies at the
Académie des Beaux Arts were
brusquely interrupted by the German
Occupation, and he had to discover
modern art completely on his own. A
prolonged stay in Budapest in 1947
marked the moment when he found his
personal style: paintings which evoked
ruined cities peopled with phantoms.
He was one of the original founders of
the groups Reflex and Cobra in 1948,
sharing with his friends a vitalism and

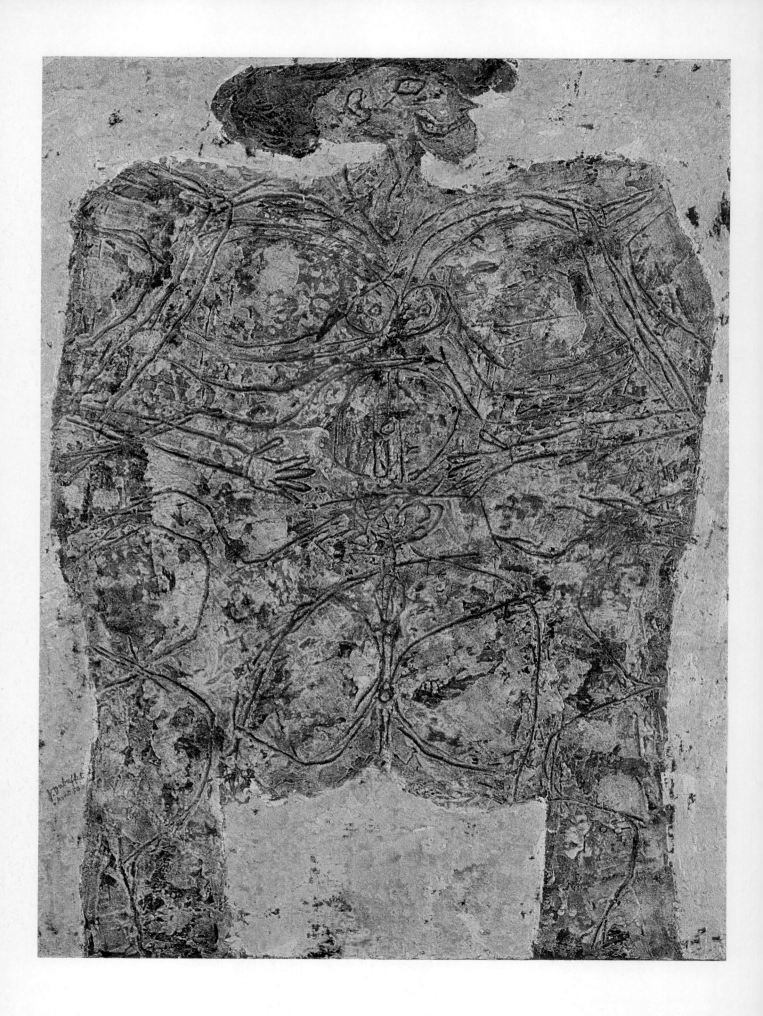

left
XVI Jean Dubuffet
Le Metafisyx, 1950. *Oil on canvas,
116 x 89*
Musée National d'Art Moderne, Centre Georges
Pompidou

XVII Gaston Chaissac
Composition, 1945-6. *Oil on wood,
209 x 110*
Galerie Messine, Paris

belief in instinct which saw itself in reaction to the classic geometric abstraction of the De Stijl movement. He settled in Paris in 1950, but made frequent voyages to North America and to the Sahara in 1948, 1949 and 1952. His graphic style, deliberately reduced and infantile, describes a universe of mythical beings. From 1952 onwards, Corneille progressively abandoned figurative presences, opting for sensuous, spontaneously generated natural rhythms. It was in the 1960s that he was to return to legendary archetypes and the magic bestiary of the Cobra years.　　　　　　　G.V.

'The artist paints the rock on which he sits, the pebbles his foot has just struck, the thorns which scratch him and bar his way, the air he breathes, the water he drinks. He paints the trees and the sky, the desert sands, the flight of birds, according to the rhythms of his organs, the circulation of his thoughts, the unfolding succession of his dreams. There's no more need to sing of Being, to attempt to grasp the Absolute – one must bare real sentiments and reactions, a way of living . . . For Corneille there was never a question of avoiding the real (nor of copying it, which would have no sense): the problem has always been to search within himself and to reveal it through painting, in existential, environmental terms.'

Jean-Louis Ferrier in *Corneille*, Galerie Ariel, Paris 1961.

JACQUES DOUCET

b 1924, Boulogne sur Seine

In 1948 the movement 'Surréalistes Révolutionnaires' held an exhibition Prise de Terre at the Galerie René Breteau, where Jacques Doucet showed works, influenced by Klee and Miro, which evoked graffiti and children's drawings. As early as 1947 he had established contacts with Corneille and his Dutch contemporaries, contributing afterwards to the review *Reflex* published by the 'experimental group' that Constant formed in Amsterdam in July 1948. Doucet was the only Frenchman to sign the Cobra manifesto at the end of the same year. With the Cobra artists he shared an enthusiasm

XVIII Gaston Chaissac
Figure dans un panier (Face in a Basket), no date. *Ripolin on wicker and cardboard, 60 x 45*
Musée de l'Abbaye Sainte Croix, Les Sables d'Olonne

for archaic forms and a violent treatment of paint in splashes and trickles. In March 1949 he took part in their exhibition La fin et les Moyens at the Galerie des Beaux-Arts, Brussels, in the scandalous International Exhibition of Experimental Art at the Stedelijk Museum, Amsterdam in November 1949, and he was present at the group's last exhibition at the Palais des Beaux-Arts in Liège in 1951. Doucet exhibited at the Galerie Colette Allendy in Paris from 1948 to 1953 and was invited to participate in Les Mains éblouies in 1949 at the Galerie Maeght, while from 1948 onwards he showed at the Salon de Mai, and was at the Salons d'Octobre of 1952 and 1953.　　　　　　　G.V.

'In all times and in all places, graffiti have been charged with an exceptionally liberating form of energy. In the cell where the Nazis had locked him up, I suppose that Jacques Doucet realised this through a direct experience: the sordid magic carved in the prison walls impregnated his art with all its strength — a prisoner, in truth, must bear witness, for to witness is to exist, and exist fully. Man gathers his forces the moment he is hunted down. Painting, writing is created to counter death. The work of a desperate individual is not full of anguish: it is a way out, a crack in the system of despair which surrounds him. If it is not exactly happy, it reaches towards happiness. Jacques Doucet resurrecting for us "The green paradise of children's loves" gives us confidence, these days when man, fully able to assume his condition as a child, can at last be himself in his maturity.'

Jean Laude, *Jacques Doucet*.

77 Jacques Doucet
Sans titre (Untitled), 1949. *Oil and sand on wood, 60 x 73*
Private collection

78 Jean Dubuffet
Jazz Band (Dirty Style Blues), 1944. *Oil on canvas, 97 x 130*
Madeleine Malraux

JEAN DUBUFFET

b 1901, Le Havre

Fascinated by painting at a very early age, Dubuffet met Suzanne Valadon, Raoul Dufy and Elie Lascaux as early as 1919. A long period divided between business and travelling, during which time he encountered a number of writers and artists, including Max Jacob, Fernand Léger and Céline preceded his own artistic activity. In Switzerland, thanks to his friendships with the painter René Auberjonois and the writer Charles Albert Cingria, and his contacts with certain doctors concerned with the artistic expressions of the mentally ill, Dubuffet became very involved with forms of art considered marginal by society. He tried several times to give up his

business concerns: from 1933-7, for example, he became interested in making marionettes. It was only in 1942 that he finally succeeded in devoting himself totally to art, embarking on his astonishing series of 'Travaux'.

In his search for contact with the common man, Dubuffet's very calculated approach soon appeared to be a radical and subversive challenge to culture itself and to the conditions of the production and diffusion of art. Refusing to comply with any facile techniques, and emphasising above all spontaneous primitive elements, he in fact exalted the real by reducing it to schemas and archetypes, while he re-endowed his materials with their original special qualities.

With Jean Paulhan's backing, Jean Dubuffet met René Drouin and had an

exhibition of his 'hautes pâtes' called 'Mirobolus, Macadam & Cie' in 1946. Then in 1947, he showed his 'Portraits' series: 'Plus beaux qu'ils veulent, beaux malgré eux'. These portraits assembled the whole of the post-war Parisian avant-garde. Dubuffet's great affinity with contemporary writers appears in a number of books, particularly those he made in collaboration with Francis Ponge, Eugène Guillevic and Jean Paulhan, as well as his own polemical and theoretical writings. His experimental texts written in phonetic code are especially interesting and amusing: *Ler dla canpane* 1948, ('Country Air'), *Anvouaige par in nimbesil avec de zimage*, 1949, ('A voyage by an imbecile with images') and *La bonfam a beber*, 1950 ('The woman has a baby').

During his several trips to North Africa in 1947, 1948 and 1949, Dubuffet found in the desert his ideal 'tabula rasa', the bare starting point of all art. This gave rise to the 'Corps des Dames' series and the landscapes 'Paysages du mental', exhibited at the Pierre Matisse Gallery, New York, in 1951 and 1952.

It was from 1945 onwards that Dubuffet started collecting Art Brut ('uncultured' art), with the patronage of the members of the Compagnie de l'Art brut, André Breton, Jean Paulhan, Charles Ratton, Henri Pierre Roché, and Michel Tapié. Then, in 1949, Dubuffet published *L'Art Brut préféré aux arts culturels*. Various Art Brut exhibitions were held in 1947 and 1951 in the basement of the Galerie Drouin, then in a small annexe to the *Nouvelle Revue Française* offices. The collection is housed today in the Château de Beaulieu in Lausanne.   G.V.

'Real art is always lurking where you don't expect it. Where nobody's thinking about it or mentions its name. Art loathes being recognized and greeted by name. It hurries off straight away. Art is a somebody who adores being incognito. As soon as you discover him, point a finger in his direction and he escapes, leaving his place to a figure with a laurel wreath, who carries a big signboard on his back marked 'Art', whom everyone immediately toasts with champagne, and whom the conference people lead from town to town with a ring in his nose. That one's the fake Mr Art. He's the one the public know, because he's the one with the wreath and the signboard. There's no danger that the real Mr Art will go and squash himself between signboards! So nobody recognises him. He walks around everywhere, everyone's met him on his path, and has bumped into him twenty times a day on the street corner, but no one has an inkling that 'that' could be the Mr Art that everyone says such nice things about. Because he doesn't look like that at all. You understand of course, it's the fake Mr Art who has the right air, and it's the real one who doesn't look the part! That means you get it wrong! Lots of people get it wrong!'

Jean Dubuffet: *'L'Art Brut préféré aux Arts Culturels'* from the catalogue of the exhibition at the Galerie René Drouin, 1949.

'In the forty or fifty pictures I painted between April 1950 and February 1951 there was good reason not to take the drawing seriously. It was always outrageously crude and careless, enclosing the figure of the nude woman in a way which, taken literally, would suggest abominably obese, deformed creatures. My intention was that the drawing should deny the figure any particular shape; that on the contrary, it should prevent the figure from assuming this or that particular form, that it should keep it on the level of a general concept, of something immaterial. It amused me (and I believe this propensity to be almost constant in all my paintings) to juxtapose brutally in these female bodies the most general and the most particular, the most subjective and the most objective, the metaphysical and the grotesquely trivial. As far as I believe, one finds itself considerably reinforced by the presence of the other. This same tendency gives rise to apparently illogical relationships between textures suggesting human flesh (to the extent of offending one's sense of decency a bit sometimes, but that seems very effective too, to me), and other textures which have nothing more to do with anything human but instead suggest earth, or all sorts of things like bark, rocks, botanical or geographical phenomena. I must admit I experience a certain pleasure in jumbling up facts like this which belong to completely different spheres. It seems to me that it provokes all sorts of transformations and polarisations which throw objects into an unusual light, and can give them new and unknown meanings.'

Jean Dubuffet, in Georges Limbour: *L'Art Brut de Jean Dubuffet. Tableau bon levain à vous de cuire la pâte*, Pierre Matisse Gallery, New York 1953.

'It's true that during my treatment of various 'matières' and the way I apply them, I've found myself suggesting certain materials, not so much those with a 'noble' reputation, like marble or exotic woods, but instead very ordinary ones with no value at all like coal, asphalt, or even mud, all the accidental patternings which rain makes on

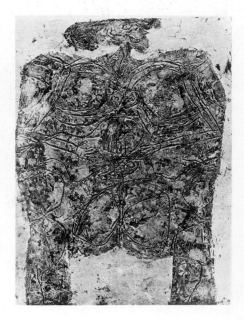

XV Jean Dubuffet
Dhôtel nuance d'abricot (Portrait of Dhôtel in apricot shades), 1947. *Oil on canvas, 116 x 89*
Musée National d'Art Moderne, Centre Georges Pompidou, bought with the help of the Scaler Foundation

XVI Jean Dubuffet
Le Metafisyx, 1950. *Oil on canvas, 116 x 89*
Musée National d'Art Moderne, Centre Georges Pompidou

79 Jean Dubuffet
Le caviste (The Cellar Man), 1946.
Oil on canvas, 46 x 38
Private collection

80 Jean Dubuffet
Pierre Matisse – portrait obscur (Pierre Matisse – obscure portrait),
1947. *Oil on canvas, 130 x 97*
Pierre Matisse

81 Jean Dubuffet
Paysage vineux (Wine coloured landscape), 1944. *Oil on canvas,*
124.5 x 96
Florence Resnais

common soils, or the traces of age on the crudest objects, rusty old iron, flaking walls, and all sorts of dirt and decay associated with scrap and rubbish. Perhaps some things will lead people to conclude that there are objectionable propensities on show here, and they'll complain about all the dirty objects. I would ask them to think about this instead: in the name of what – except perhaps the coefficient of rarety – does man bedeck himself with necklaces of shells, and not spiders' webs, with foxs' fur and not their guts, in the name of what, I'd like to know? Mud, rubbish and dirt are man's companions all his life; shouldn't they be precious to him, and isn't one doing man a service to remind him of their beauty? Think how little children look into streams, and find a thousand wonders in the rubble on the river-bed.'

Jean Dubuffet 'Réhabilitation de la boue',
Juin, no 12, May 7, 1946.

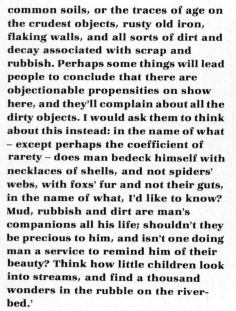

XXII Etienne-Martin
"La Julie". *Painted wood, 47 x 22 x 21*
Musée National d'Art Moderne, Centre Georges Pompidou

ETIENNE-MARTIN

b 1913, Loriol

Etienne-Martin trained initially at the Académie de Beaux-Arts in Lyons and after 1934 in Paris at the Académie Ranson under Charles Malfray. He met Marcel Duchamp at this time. In 1936, with Stahly, Manessier and Le Moal, he joined the Témoinages group, based in Lyons. With the collector Marcel Michaud at its head, the group proposed to 'give back to Man his eternal nature which is the absolute'. They were seeking to recapture the primitive spiritual qualities which inspired the French Romanesque and medieval periods. After the outbreak of war, Etienne-Martin was imprisoned in Germany. Then, in 1942, he became a member of the 'Oppède' artists' community, which had been founded by the architect Bernard Zehrfuss. He lived at Dieulefit from 1943 to 1944. With Henri-Pierre Roché, the writer, collector and friend of Marcel

82 Etienne-Martin
Le grand couple (Large Couple), 1946. *Wood, 220 x 63 x 53*
Musée National d'Art Moderne, Centre Georges Pompidou

Duchamp and Wols, Etienne-Martin made a monumental sculpture of a virgin in a sand quarry, which of course rapidly eroded. From 1944 to 1947, he lived with Stahly and Manessier at Montagna and created several large sculptures in wood. These were shown in 1946 at the Galerie René Drouin, at an exhibition organised by Michel Tapié. 'Le Dragon', 'Le Grand Couple' and 'La Grand Nuit Ouvrante' were three of these works. Back in Paris in 1947, he met Jean Dubuffet and Henri Michaux, and became one of the community which had established itself around the figure of Gurdjieff. In 1949, Etienne-Martin moved into a studio in the Rue du Pot de Fer. This developed gradually into an esoteric environment which reflected the spirit of his work. His sculpture was wilfully archaic, with its use of massive structures and rough materials, particularly wood and twisted roots, while an ephemeral quality was suggested with the rags and pieces of cloth, such as we see in the 'Passementeries'. The themes and elements to which he constantly reverted from the late 1930s onwards, conjure up places and people from his own past. 'La Demeure' recalls memories of his childhood home: 'Le Couple' is the symbol of desire, of union, of confrontation. The theme of night, in 'Nuits' suggests the dark, unconscious world of man, while that of play as in 'Jeux' shows how form emerges from the textures and shapes of the materials themselves. It is here that Etienne-Martin shares the spirit of 'un art autre', 'other art', as Michel Tapié baptised the work of his chosen 'informel' artists. But this was only one aspect of his creation, which as a whole constitutes a sort of great work in the esoteric sense, unifying matter with the realms of the spirit.   G.V.

84 Etienne-Martin
Passementerie I, 1949. *Textile assemblage,*
30 x 20
Musée National de l'Art Moderne, Centre Georges Pompidou

83 Etienne-Martin
Passementerie II, 1949. *Textile assemblage,*
60cm long

Musée National de l'Art Moderne, Centre Georges Pompidou

85 Etienne-Martin
Passementerie III, 1949. *Textile assemblage, 30cm long.*
Musée National de l'Art Moderne, Centre Georges Pompidou

STEPHEN GILBERT

b 1910, Fife, Scotland

From 1929–1932, Gilbert who quickly decided to abandon architectural studies in favour of painting, studied at the Slade School, London, under Henry Tonks. His first visit to Paris lasted from 1938 to 1939. The war years he spent with his wife, Jocelyn Chewett, a sculptor, in the countryside just outside Dublin, where he met the White Stag group of refugee painters from England, including Rakoczi, Hall and Nichols; and Mainie Jellat and Evie Hearn, both pupils of Albert Gleizes. Here, between 1943 and 1944, in isolation and completely on his own initiative, Gilbert broke with all his academic training, and began to produce monstrous heads, strange beasts, skull and crossbone imagery, which found astonishing confirmation when he became the sole English member of the Cobra group in 1948.

Gilbert himself suggests that 'contact with Celtic art similar to the original art of Denmark might well have been an unconscious influence'. In 1946, he settled permanently in Paris, but it was not until 1948 that his work was noticed by Asger Jorn at the Salon des Indépendants. He was invited to join the Cobra group, and at Jorn's insistence travelled up by train through the bombed-out cityscapes of Germany to Copenhagen for the Cobra conferences at Fredericksholmshytten. There he spent a month with Jorn and Dotremont, and completed a mural on the wall of the house which some of the Cobra artists were decorating. He participated in the first exhibition of Cobra at the Stedelijk Museum, Amsterdam, where he met Constant, who was to remain a close friend for many years. In 1949, however, Gilbert was the first of the Cobra artists to turn to abstract painting, which

resulted in a break with Jorn, although most of the group eventually followed suit. He exhibited from 1950 to 1956 at the Salon des Réalités Nouvelles, and in 1954 turned to metal polychrome constructions. He has continued to work as a sculptor in metal and has achieved international recognition, notably with a Gulbenkian award in 1962, at the Biennale de Tokyo in 1965, and with his monumental constructions in London.

S.W.

'He employs the most 'fantastic' means that exist, the most terribly 'real'. To proclaim man's torn, divided being to the world, his universe creates a legion of substitutes: insect-birds, insect-puppets, voracious butterflies, death's-head moths, sphinxes, harpies. . . And these massacred figures of total perdition emerge from chaos to demonstrate the full extent of our aberration and the 'urgent necessity to

86 Stephen Gilbert
Sans titre (Untitled), 1943. *Oil on canvas, 55 x 46*
Artist's collection

XIX Karel Appel
Enfants interrogeant (Questioning Children), 1948. *Assemblage: oil on wood in two pieces, 87 x 60*
L.W.N. Segaas, Galerie Nova Spectra, The Hague

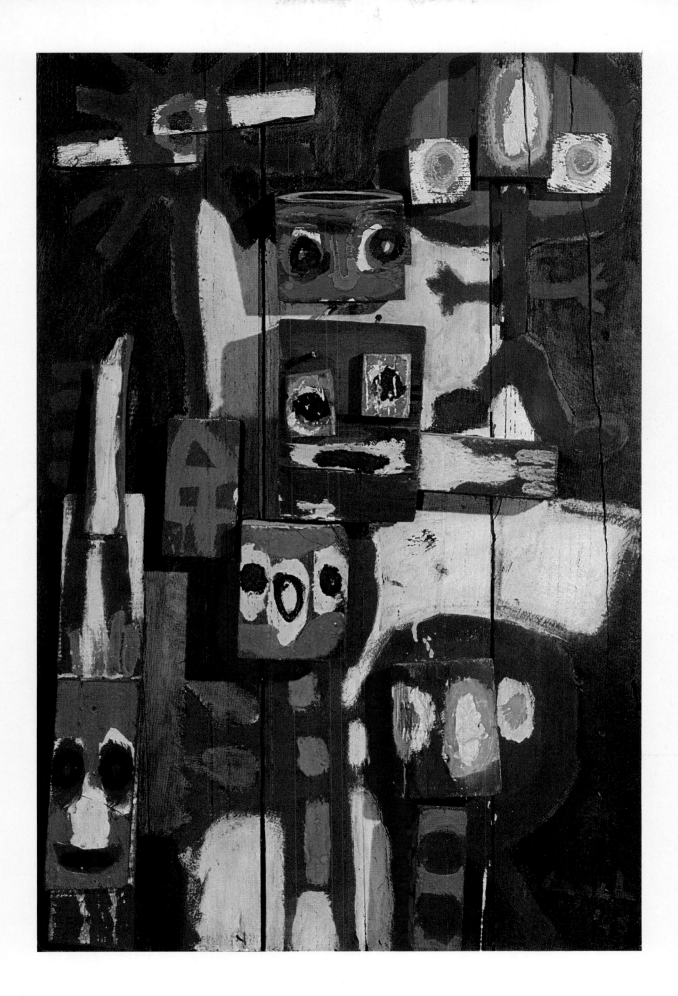

left
XX Constant
L'animal sorcier (The Animal-Sorcerer), 1949. *Oil on canvas,*
120 x 90
Musée National d'Art Moderne, Centre Georges Pompidou

XXI Asger Jorn
Sans titre (Untitled), 1947. *Oil on canvas, 101 x 81*
Private collection

awake'. If Gilbert prefers the colours of
fear, it's because he does not feel the
moment has come to paint the world
pink, or to spread his wings. With
certain earth-colours, 'burnt' or blood-
red, certain ochres, he chooses to
express the particular air of
devastation, of extermination which
surrounds us.'

Edouard Jaguer, *Gilbert*.

87 Stephen Gilbert
Sans titre (Untitled), 1948.
Oil on canvas, 72 x 53.5
Artist's collection

88 Stephen Gilbert
Sans titre (Untitled), 1949.
Oil on canvas, 65 x 53.
Artist's collection

XXII Etienne-Martin
"La Julie". *Painted wood, 47 x 22 x 21*
Musée National d'Art Moderne, Centre Georges Pompidou

ASGER JORN

b 1914, Vejnum, Denmark, d 1973,
Aarhus, Denmark

As early as 1929, Asger Jorn went to live
with his family in Silkeborg, Jutland.
Today the museum there is partly
reserved for his works. After making
contact with the Danish artists known
as the Linien group, he went to Paris in
1936, frequenting Fernand Léger's
studio. At the Exposition International
of 1937 he created a monumental fresco
for Le Corbusier's Pavillon des Temps
Nouveaux, taking a child's drawing as
his starting-point. The work of Klee and
Miró was a passionate discovery at the
time. He returned to Denmark in 1938,
and exhibited several times in
Copenhagen with the group Høst,
which flourished from 1941 to 1944,
publishing the review *Helhesten*. He
produced a series of engravings entitled
'Occupations' (1939-1945). Returning to
France in 1947, he collaborated with
Pierre Wemaere in the production of
several tapestries. He attached himself
to the international movement of the
Surréalistes révolutionnaires, and

XXI Asger Jorn
Sans titre (Untitled), 1947. *Oil on canvas,*
101 x 81
Private collection

89 Asger Jorn
Mati, 1950-1. *Oil on wood, 152 x 96*
Haags Gemeentemuseum, Holland

soon refused to recognise any political or aesthetic dogma, signing the manifesto 'La cause était entendue . . .' and founding the Cobra group in Paris. His concern was to restore culture to its popular and authentic origins, and he promoted the sense of play and sensual expression versus 'cultured' or 'scientific' forms of painting. Jorn and the Cobra group were open to every type of experimentation which gave rise to archaic, totemic, instinctive forms, these forms being 'conceived as language'. Between 1950 and 1951 he lived at Suresnes near Paris, then after Cobra was dissolved in 1951 he went back to Silkeborg and with Christian Dotremont rested for a while at the sanatorium there. Henceforth, he divided his time between Denmark, Italy and France, playing a vital role in the development of both the Bauhaus Imaginist and the International Situationist movements after 1954. G.V.

'To state and attempt to resolve the problem for its part, a materialist art must put art back on a foundation of the senses. We say "put back" with reason, for we believe that the origins of art are instinctive and thus materialist. It is the metaphysical aspects of classicism which have managed to spiritualise and intellectualise art. And it's miserable today to see the materialists in all good faith marching along on their heads – with a realism and a naturalism which are opposed to reality and to nature, which are based on 'illusion'. True realism, materialist realism, lies in the search for the expression of forms faithful to their content.

But there's no content detached from human interest. True realism, materialist realism, renouncing the idealist equation of subjectivity with individualism as described by Marx, seeks the forms of reality that are 'common the the senses of all men'.

Thus, the red flag is an expression of revolution which immediately strikes the senses, the senses of 'all men', a synthesis of the reality and the vested needs of revolution, a common link and not an allegory, outside the range of the senses or a symbol for 'flag manufacturers'. We can identify ourselves only accidentally with a poor woman buying a fish.'*

Asger Jorn: 'Les formes conçues comme langage', *Cobra* no. 2, 1949.

* This last phase refers to André Fougeron's first 'Social Realist' canvas 'Parisiennes au Marché'. [Translator's note]

90 Zoltan Kemeny
Ténèbres (Shadows), 1947. *Pavatex and earth relief, 121 x 79*
Musée National d'Art Moderne, Centre Georges Pompidou

ZOLTAN KEMENY

b 1907, Banica, Hungary,
d 1965, Zurich, Switzerland

Kemeny spent his childhood in a small Transylvanian village, and was interested in painting from his earliest years: at the age of ten he began working for a sign painter whose style was very naive and simple. From fourteen to eighteen he worked as a carpenter, after completing an apprenticeship. Then in 1924 he went to Budapest, studying architecture at the School of Applied Arts until 1927, when he became a pupil at the School of Fine Arts. That same year he toured the Hungarian countryside, in order to study peasant art and folklore, and finally discovered modern art through

91 Zoltan Kemeny
Les bourgeois de toutes les villes (All the Towns' Bourgeois), 1950. *Iron and rags on a
wood and earth base, 38 x 39.5 x 26*
Musée National d'Art Moderne, Centre Georges Pompidou

his teacher, the painter Vaszary.

In 1930, Kemeny emigrated to Paris.
He married in 1933, and was forced to
take up a variety of jobs during the next
ten years in order to survive. In 1942 he
set himself up in Zurich as a fashion
designer and returned to painting
based on folklore and peasant motifs
which he exhibited for the first time at
the Galerie des Eaux Vives in Zurich in
1945. 1946 was the year of his first
exhibition in Paris, at the Galerie
Kleber. This brought together the works
of popular inspiration, alongside much
more violent paintings, which showed

the influence of Jean Dubuffet, whose
exhibition of 'Hautes Pâtes' at the
Galerie Drouin had made a sensation in
May of the same year. In fact, Zoltan
Kemeny and his wife Madeleine were
very friendly with Dubuffet at the time,
and Kemeny's works of 1948, especially
the series of the 'Jardinier vu par ses
amis' were stamped with the Art Brut
aesthetic, through the deliberate
association of the most incongruous
materials. Using this method, he
achieved an extreme of
anthropomorphic violence in the
collages, reliefs and objects of 1950,

which expressly employed the most
ephemeral and impoverished of
materials such as earth, old rags, rusty
pieces of iron. After attempting to
introduce light into his reliefs in 1951,
Kemeny sought to translate rhythms
and spaces from the world of science
into three dimensions. The 'Images en
relief' exhibited in 1954 at the Galerie
Fachetti in Paris heralded the discovery
of his personal style, which took the
form of increasingly ambitious metal
reliefs until his death in 1965.   G.V.

CHARLES LAPICQUE

b 1898, Thieze

Lapicque was educated from 1909
onwards in Paris, and after serving in
World War I, entered the Ecole Centrale
in 1919, where he had to draw
machinery and architecture with
projections and perspectives. His first
oil paintings were figurative landscapes
and marine subjects but in about 1925
he became influenced by Cubist
abstraction and enjoyed the patronage
of Jeanne Bucher, who in 1929 put on
his first exhibition. From 1931 to 1943 he
worked as a laboratory technician in the
Science Faculty of the Sorbonne, and
here, during the 1930s, he made many
scientific investigations into the
composition and contrasting values of
colour, publishing his discussions in
learned journals. In 1939, in his 'Christ
aux Epines' he devised the blue
armature against a rosy background
which inverted the normal red/blue,
earth/sky disposition of colours, and
which had great influence on painters
such as Jean Bazaine. Although his
work was typically post-Cubist, subjects
such as 'Jeanne d'Arc' (1940) and the
'Libération de Paris' (1944) had
obviously more than formal
implications. Exhibitions which
followed at the Galerie Jeanne Bucher,
the Galerie Friedland and the Galerie
Louis Carré established Lapicque as an
important painter of the new Ecole de
Paris. His fascination with marine
landscape and wave movement
developed into abstract representations
of interlocking bodies, and finally the
'Danse Macabres' of 1948, where
Lapicque's preoccupation with
transparency and contour is translated
by frenzied anatomies, that are
uncharacteristically aggressive, for he
reverted to drawings of the sea,
harbours, horses and so on immediately
afterwards. Lapicque's graphic work is
essential to the conception of his
paintings: the écriture, or 'writing', of
coloured lines over flat planes, that we
see in the 'Duc de Nemours', has a
Fauvist precedent. Lapicque continued
to be one of the most successful Ecole de
Paris painters throughout the 1950s.
S.W.

93 Charles Lapicque
Danse Macabre II (Dance of Death II), 1948.
Pen and indian ink on paper, 22 x 17
Musée National d'Art Moderne, Centre Georges Pompidou

92 Charles Lapicque
Danse Macabre III (Dance of Death III), 1948.
Pen and indian ink on paper, 22 x 17

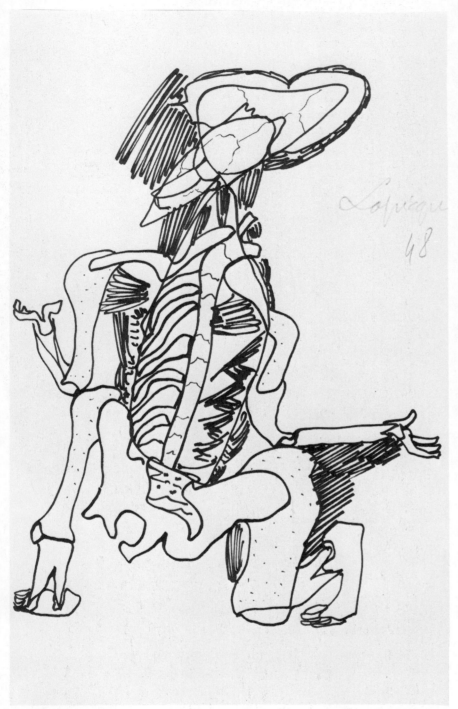

94 Charles Lapicque
Danse macabre I (Dance of Death I), 1948. *Pen
and indian ink on paper, 22 x 17*
Musée National d'Art Moderne, Centre Georges Pompidou

95 Charles Lapicque
Le Duc de Nemours (The Duke of Nemours),
1950. *Oil on canvas, 129 x 97*
Musée National d'Art Moderne, Centre Georges Pompidou

**'1948 saw me passionately involved
with anatomy. Untiringly, I drew bones
and muscles, not to mention the rest,
which I poked and stirred with as much
solicitude as a horseman at a bullfight
putting back the insides of a
disembowelled horse. All this, of
course, plunged me into a rather
morose state of mind, which one day
changed unexpectedly into revolt and
contempt for the objects I was using as
models. Right in the middle of the
methodical work programme I had
mapped out for myself, an unforeseen
development arose with an irresistible
spontaneity. Beneath my pen dipped
in indian ink I saw the birth of a
whole population, far less classical
than one could have expected from
their initial premises. I had the
audacity to class them in a file under
the following generic title: "the
anatomy lesson".'**

Charles Lapicque, 'Apprentissage et
Spontaneité 1956, reprinted in *Dessins de
Lapicque.*

110

JOAN MIRO
b Barcelona 1893

Influenced very early on by the ancient cultural traditions and crafts of Catalonia and Majorca, Joan Miró studied first with the painter Francesco Gali and then at the Free Academy of San Lluch. From 1915 onwards his vivid paintings isolated and juxtaposed various elements of reality. Thus, in 1921-2 he created 'The Farm', an allusive and poetic elaboration of these principles, which rejected perspective in favour of a dreamlike, limitless space punctuated with signs. Coming to Paris in 1919, Miró shared in the activities of the Surrealist group whose writers and painters frequented his studio in the Rue Blomet. In 1928, he created a series of 'Dutch Interiors' which parodied the scrupulous objectivity of the seventeenth-century Dutch painters, but at the same time he started a series of 'papiers-collés' and collage-objects which were followed in 1929 by his first constructions. These were exhibited in 1931 with sculpture objects at the Galerie Pierre. Creating poetic metaphors from these ensembles of crude materials, dilapidated odds and ends, Miró went beyond the Dadaist phase, and the Surrealist infatuation with Lautréamont's paradox: 'as beautiful as the chance encounter on a dissecting table of a sewing machine and an umbrella' and his new objects of 1932 manifested a great interest in the irrational and the instinctive. His liking for rough materials can be seen equally in the paintings of 1936, done on paper coated with tar and sand, and those of 1939 painted on sacking. After completing the series of 'Constellations', begun at Varengeville in 1940, Miró returned to Spain, and from 1944 onwards collaborated with the ceramic artist Joseph Llorens Artigas. Miró covered ceramic rejects with infantile drawings of pin-men which reasserted his interest in graffiti. This was the start of a prolific period of ceramic work and sculpture. In 1947 he exhibited this work with his paintings at the Pierre Matisse Gallery, New York, and then in 1948, 1950 and 1953 at the Galerie

98 a & b Joan Miro
Plaque double-face (Double sided plaque), 1945. *Ceramic, 15 x 13*
Pierre Matisse Gallery, New York

Maeght in Paris. His paintings at the time alternated between laborious and time-consuming pieces, and others, violent and spontaneous, where the artist's unconscious instincts found expression.   G.V.

'This lyrico-magical projection of himself which superimposes a mythic reality on the perception of the world, turns normal actions into surprising visions, and country fields into fields of dream. With a sort of humour full of tenderness, Miró disguises the modern world, abolishing its vilent contra-dictions – only emphasised by "common sense" – between the visible, and what remains indecipherable for minds dull with reasoning. He neutralises their forces by reversing appearances. His works are the peremptory demon-stration that – if art is to be at all didactic – the ephemeral aspect of a ridiculous world and its projection into an imaginary realm are not separated in the way that logical prejudice would have us believe. It must be recognised that this vanishing of the real and its reconstitution in the form of signs proceeds without peril for Miró, who ceaselessly hesitates on the vertiginous borders of reality. These transmutations, though counter to rational physics, do not force him to lose his personality, and in no way diminish his astonishing faculty for steering from the conscious to the unconscious. With Miró, feelings are always the basis and the substance of his work. He cannot conceive of the world except as a function of his own being and each time, at the end of his numerous adventures, he rediscovers the shadow of himself. Miró's every drawing, painting or even sculpture is the converging point for his state of mind, and demonstrates his clear desire to determine the state of his subconscious.'

Christian Zervos, 'Remarques sur les Oeuvres récentes de Miró', *Cahiers d'art* 1949, no. 1.

97 a & b Joan Miro
Plaque double-face (Double sided plaque), 1946. *Ceramic, 19 x 26.5*
Pierre Matisse Gallery, New York

XXIII Roger Bissière
Le Soleil (The Sun), 1946. *Appliqué and patchwork, 170 x 245*
Musée National d'Art Moderne, Centre Georges Pompidou

PABLO PICASSO

(see page 38)

'Raphael's image of a woman is only a sign. A woman by Raphael is not a woman, it's a sign that in his spirit and ours represents a woman. If this woman is decorated with an aureole and if she has a child on her knee, then she is a Virgin. All that's only a sign. We understand that this sign represents a woman because it can't represent a horse or a tree. I'll show you something odd, apropos.'

Picasso leaves a moment, and returns with an object in iron: a statuette representing a woman in some archaic civilisation, or perhaps Negro, but a very modern conception. A flat head, long centre of the circle a smaller circle pierced with holes which could be breasts, and below, two legs which support the whole.

'What would you call it? I'd call it the Venus of the Gas Company.'

'Why?'

'Because the object I'm showing you isn't a statuette, it's a simple part of my gas meter. You'd probably find the same in your kitchen.'

'I admit I was fooled.'

'Why fooled? This object could very well be the sign of a woman, and the lines and volumes are harmonious. It sufficed to discover them.'

Andre Warnod, 'En peinture tout n'est que signe, nous dit Picasso', *Arts*, no. 22, 1945, from *Picasso, 50 Years of His Art*, Museum of Modern Art, New York, 1946.

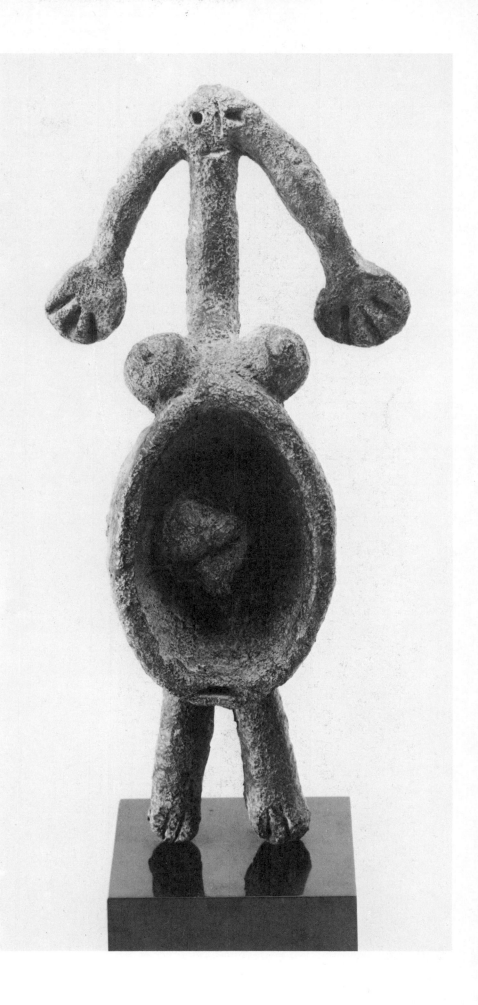

98 Pablo Picasso
La petite femme enceinte (Small Pregnant Woman), 1948. *Bronze, 32 x 9 x 7*
Musée Picasso, Paris

left
XXIV Joan Miro
Peinture (Painting), 1953. *Oil on canvas, 195 x 131*
Galerie Maeght, Paris

left
99 Pablo Picasso
Personnage (Person), 1948. *Bronze, 18 x 14 x 7*
Musée Picasso, Paris

100 Pablo Picasso
Femme à la poussette (Woman with
Pushchair), 1950. *Bronze, 203 x 145 x 61*
Musée Picasso, Paris

PAUL REBEYROLLE

b 1926, Eymontiers

Arriving in Paris in 1944, to live in the artists' community of La Ruche, Rebeyrolle was greatly impressed with the Picasso exhibition at the Salon d'Automne of 1944, (the Salon de la Libération), and subsequently by the Soutine retrospective at the Galerie de France in 1945. Van Gogh was also to have a marked influence after the important exhibition of his work at the Orangerie in 1947. The very violent expressionism of Rebeyrolle's first paintings, such as 'Les Paysans Tireurs de Langues', gave way in the later forties to an almost caricatural realism, in paintings often of very large dimensions. While referring back to Courbet these showed the influence of Rebeyrolle's contemporary Bernard Lorjou.

In 1948, Rebeyrolle participated in the exhibition l'Homme-témoin with Lorjou, De Gallard, Mottet and Thompson, and became one of the leading lights of the Salon des moins de trente ans, an exhibition for painters under thirty which had started during the Occupation. Rebeyrolle was anxious to promote a socially and politically meaningful art, reacting against the avant-garde of the time. In 1950 he received the Prix de la Jeune Peinture which led to a quarrel among the jurors. He exhibited in 1951 at the Galerie Drouant-David, and in 1954 at the Marlborough Gallery in London. G.V.

101 Paul Rebeyrolle
Les paysans tireurs de lange (Peasants Sticking their Tongues out),
1945. *Oil on canvas, 100 x 73*
Private collection

The Frontiers of Identity

ARTAUD BELLMER BRAUNER BRYEN FRANCIS HARTUNG KLOSSOWSKI LAM MATHIEU MATTA MICHAUX PICABIA RIOPELLE SERPAN DE STAEL VAN VELDE VIEIRA DA SILVA WOLS

The desire to find a complete expression of man's being, stripped of all cultural pretentions had been a feature of modern art since Surrealism, and later again, when artists looked back to the 'tabula rasa' of primitivism. It became especially acute when the relationship between painting and writing was involved. The painter's relationship to writing was answered by the artistic expressions of certain writers, who, having drawn and painted in secret for a long time, suddenly granted this type of work a public and important position.

For Antonin Artaud, Henri Michaux and, in another vein, Pierre Klossowski or Jacques Audiberti in particular, drawing seemed to be a spontaneous and fantastic formulation of the universe of their inmost selves. This could be seen as a 'transgression' of man's relationship with himself and others as a social being. Henri Michaux's *Ici Poddema* of 1946 reveals the writer's visionary world of terrifying homunculi, the phantoms that appear again in the fluid, womb-like world of the large washes and the watercolours that were exhibited at the Galerie René Drouin in 1948 and 1949. Artaud discovered a spiritual kinship with Van Gogh, and found that for the outcast, the 'man that society didn't want to listen to, that society prevented from uttering

unbearable truths', drawing as much as spoken language, could be a direct means of revealing the urgent and uncompromisingly expressive features of the body, together with its relationship to the sacred. Here the link between the erotic and the sacred appears again, just as before the war the members of the Collège de Sociologie had investigated the same questions in their review *Acéphale*. Georges Bataille, a founder member of the Collège, chose Fautrier and Hans Bellmer as illustrators for his writings in the 1940s; and work of this nature, together with the constant reference to the Marquis of Sade, were crucial to the understanding of the latest developments of Surrealism, as presented at the Exposition Internationale du Surréalisme, Galerie Maeght, 1947.

The erotic appeared to underlie everything, as the path to initiation and the vector of 'permanent insurrection' (Maurice Nadeau). André Breton's formula in *L'Amour fou*, 1937 – 'convulsive beauty will be erotic and veiled, explosive and fixed, magic and contingent, or it will not exist' – was pursued in the Surrealist exhibition: a series of altars accorded an important place to magic, occult and primitive forces and the exaltation of the erotic. Three artists embodied these new directions: Wifredo Lam, Victor Brauner

and Roberto Matta. Lam's work reflected his actual experience – the fusion of a primitive universe with Western culture; Victor Brauner, whose drawings of the Occupation period were strange, experimental 'exorcisms' using a wax relief process, later explored the more disturbing elements of the unconscious in his paintings of 1951-2; Matta continued Marcel Duchamp's pictorial alchemy of 'passage', inventing new spatial dimensions. The work of the young Iaroslav Serpan, a painter, writer and biologist also shown at the Galerie Maeght exhibition, was equally preoccupied with organic metamorphoses, and his proliferations of 'cellular' form, which bring to mind certain stereotypes of psychotic art are no less significant than his gestural, 'informel' painting which he had developed at a very early stage in his career. Challenging Surrealism, Francis Picabia was a sympathetic and paradoxical figure for newcomers to the movement. His presence was illuminating and extremely influential during these years. Abandoning the deliberately kitsch imagery of the war years, Picabia continued his satirical reflections on painting, going beyond what was for him the sterile and suspect game of 'isms' to flirt with an abstraction which 'might be a means of

I'm waiting for an art that's ungrateful, ugly, crude, as painful as giving birth, because it's a question of birth, not games any longer, here as elsewhere.

(PIERRE LOEB)

Two installation photos from the Exposition Internationale du Surrealisme, 1947. *Top* Victor Brauner: L'Oiseau secretaire *below* works by Tanguy, Lam, Martins.

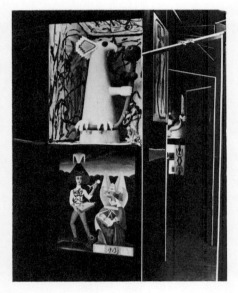

exchange for our sensibilities in their purest state, which might express the truest part of our interior being' (*Journal des Arts*, November 1945). Picabia was a deadly serious hedonist who experimented by mingling genres and jumbling up chronologies at whim, and who also loved to go back to the primitive magic of cave paintings and African masks. With Picabia's backing, a new abstract painting began to make its mark everywhere, finding its sources in the pre-1914 'psychological abstractions' of Picabia himself, and in Kandinsky's 'improvisations'. The many aspects of this abstract movement are represented in 'Aftermath' by the few artists who

most strikingly express an 'incarnation' in sign and gesture within their works. It must be remembered that many of the abstract painters, including some of the most important, Serge Poliakoff or Pierre Soulages for example, favoured a manifestly formalist approach which excludes their work from the context of this exhibition. But Nicolas de Staël, whose 'La Vie Dure' is present here, was considered by Guy Dumur at the time the consummately 'ontological painter'. His violent physical engagement with the canvas during the years 1944-8 reflected the dramas of everyday life – and at times an encounter with death. Samuel Beckett discussed the painting of Bram Van Velde as an expression of failure and of the difficulty of existence, in the articles he wrote for the exhibitions of 1946 and 1948. In no way does Van Velde's painting symbolise a moment or a state of mind, rather it becomes in itself a dramatic space where the attempt to reconstruct a broken, individual universe is played out in all its pathos. Vieira da Silva, remote from the war symbolised by 'Désastre', the title of one of her paintings of 1942, tried desperately to achieve a reconciliation between figurative suggestions of the real world and its events, and an abstract space, entramelled in all directions by a network of perspectives, which give a dizzying impression of time and movement. In the 'Partie d'échecs' life is played out in a labrynthine, uncontrollable, all-devouring space, which became completely abstract much later, after her exhibition at Pierre Loeb's gallery in 1949. Hans Hartungs' 'tachiste' painting of the late 1930s was premonitory of the post war developments of 'abstraction lyrique'. In 1947 his exhibition at the Galerie Lydia Conti recalled the progression of his work from 1935 to the present in a series of thirteen paintings. Georges Mathieu recognised him as a pioneer of the painting of gesture, and invited Hartung to participate in his exhibition 'L'Imaginaire' at the Galerie du Luxembourg in December 1947. Hartung communicated the reflection of internal energy as movement in his painting, but soon his practice of enlarging drawings and his instinctive sense of composition showed a very formal intelligence of work, qualifying its spontaneity.

It was ultimately Wols who would

most radically redefine the existential nature of the relationship between painter and the painting. His first exhibition at the Galerie René Drouin in December 1945 was the revelation of a solitary being whose drawings evoked visions of the unconscious, their patterning arranged, according to Henri-Pierre Roché, 'in a crisis'. The forty paintings exhibited from May to June 1947 at the Galerie Drouin gave this 'existential crisis' quite another dimension: that of the absolute physical engagement of the body in the painting. Jean-Paul Sartre recognised Wols as the existential painter par excellence. Here, Sartre joins the Merleau-Ponty of *Phénoménologie de la Perception*, 1945, who defined the body as 'our anchorage in the world.' This trance of the instincts was closely paralleled at the time in the work of Camille Bryen, who also featured in the L'Imaginaire' exhibition. Jean José Marchand, who wrote the preface, made a distinction between 'the two distinct forces (behind humanism) one towards art, the other towards the expression of the Individual ('pure form' and 'pure essence'), making the connection between this new subjectivity and the work of Van Gogh. Reference to Van Gogh was a constant theme in the post-war years, and is particularly illuminating in the case of Jean-Paul Riopelle and the Canadian 'automatistes' who showed at 'L'Imaginaire'. For Riopelle, who also exhibited at the Exposition Internationale du Surréalisme in 1947, painting was again a question of symbiosis into his work. The work thus became a link between living human energies and the forces of nature as a whole. This image of seething life finds its contrast and counterpart in the paintings of Sam Francis. These express the 'fullness of the void' and the oriental tradition which he seemed to embody and reanimate. The painting became a mirror of the painter and of the universe. As Georges Duthuit wrote in 1953 'By going to the very heart of his emotions rather than simply attempting to transcribe the facts that give rise to them, the painter rediscovers the precious fundamental harmony which links us with those facts, enabling us to bridge the gulf between our interior universe and that which surrounds us'.
GERMAIN VIATTE

antonin artaud

24 Juin 1947

ANTONIN ARTAUD

b 1896, Marseilles, d 1948, Ivry

Antonin Artaud, celebrated as the inventor of the 'Theatre of Cruelty', was at an early age subject to deep depression. The year 1915 saw both his first recorded self-portrait and his first visit to a sanatorium. Demobilised after only nine months' service in World War I,

he was finally put into the care of Dr Dardel, near Neuchâtel in Switzerland, for two years. It was there that Artaud began to draw seriously and he continued this activity on his return to Paris in 1920, where he became the patient of Dr Edouard Toulouse. Several drawings of this period, often quite humorous, still exist. Artaud then became an actor at the Théâtre de l'Oeuvre. In 1923 he undertook portraits in oils at the request of Yvonne Gilles, a young woman who exhibited regularly at the Salon d'Automne, and whom he had met in 1917. But the experiment with portraits was a failure. Artaud began to write prolifically, and in 1924 joined the Surrealist movement.

In 1927, breaking with the Surrealists for political reasons, he created the 'Théâtre de Alfred Jarry', and was responsible for the décor of nearly all its productions. Artaud's 'Theatre of Cruelty', whose manifesto was published in 1932, foundered in 1935 with the complete failure of *Les Cenci* based on Shelley and Stendhal. Abandoning the theatre, Artaud visited Mexico, in search of a primitive tribe, the Tarahumaras, 'There is no art . . . and the world is in a perpetual exultation,' he said of their solar rites, in which the spectacle of cruelty became a religious act.

After a bizarre voyage to Ireland his equilibrium became increasingly precarious. He was sent to various mental hospitals, finally ending up at Rodez, under the supervision of Gaston Ferdière, who had established one of the earliest collections of psychotic art. Ferdière took a keen interest in his new patient – inevitably playing the role of Dr Gachet to Artaud's Van Gogh.

Artaud began the 'Cahiers de Rodez' in school exercise books in February 1945. By June the first drawings

103 Antonin Artaud
L'exécration du père-mère (Detestation of the Father/Mother), 1946. *Graphite, pastel and watercolour on paper, 64 x 49*
Musée National d'Art Moderne, Centre Georges Pompidou

left
102 Antonin Artaud
Autoportrait (Self Portrait), 1947. *Pencil on paper, 55 x 45*
Private collection

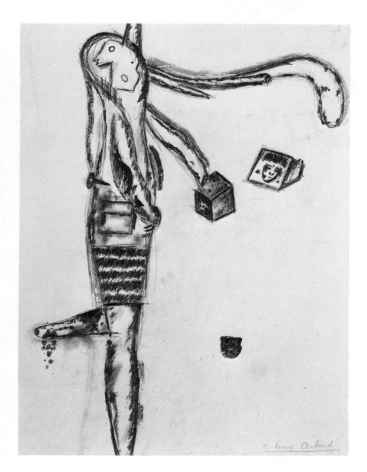

104 Antonin Artaud
Sans titre (Untitled), no date. *Pencil and pastel on paper, 65 x 50*
Bernard Noel

105 Antonin Artaud
Sans titre (Untitled), 1946. *Pencil on paper, 64 x 47*
Private collection   ?

appeared in the margins of his text. Gradually marks evolved into geometric forms; finally the drawings and writings become indissoluble. A certain vocabulary emerged: coffins, gibbets, nails, bones, breasts. Apart from the notebooks, Artaud created a number of large drawings from about 1945 onwards, symbolic allegories scattered with phrases and syllables partly invented – the graphic equivalent of glossolalia 'speaking with tongues'.

After leaving Rodez in 1946 Artaud reverted to his previous bohemian existence in Paris. Paradoxically, this was the period of his major portraits and much of his best writing, notably *Van Gogh, ou le Suicidé de la Société*, inspired by the Van Gogh exhibition at the Orangeries in January 1947. The same year, 1947, Artaud prefaced his own exhibition 'Portraits et dessins' at the Galerie Pierre Loeb with the following words: '. . . The human face is an empty force, a field of death . . . the human face bears in effect a kind of perpetual death on its countenance. It

is precisely up to the painter to save this face by restoring its personal features . . .'   S.W.

'. . . On a large sheet of white paper he had drawn the abstract outlines of a face, and in these barely sketched traits, where he had placed black blotches, apparitions of the future, with no mirror for reflection, I saw him create his double, as though in a crucible at the price of nameless torture and cruelty. He worked with rage, broke crayon after crayon, enduring the throes of his own exorcism. Amid cries and the most feverish poems which ever emanated from the spleen of a tortured being, he cursed and cast spells on a nation of obstinate worms; when, suddenly taking on reality, his face appeared.

It was the ghastly lucidity of Artaud's creation of himself, the horrible mask of all enslaved horizons, thrown out to challenge the feeble means and mediocre technique of the painters of reality (those who look at themselves in mirrors). And when the face had become a symbolic identity with his own face, when its dark image was

displayed before him, the tragic destiny of the actor was fulfilled . . . With the creative rage which made him burst the bolts of reality and all the locks of the surreal, I have seen him blindly put out the eyes of his own image. For that was what being a visionary was to him: to look with the pupils's blackness at the reality of the other side of things.'

Jean Dequeker, *'Birth of the image'*, from 'Antonin Artaud ou la Santé des Poètes', *La Tour de Feu* no. 63-4, 1959

right
106 Antonin Artaud
Portrait d'Arthur Adamov, 1947. *Graphite and red chalk on paper, 62.5 x 48*
Florence Loeb

123

Antonin Artaud
mai 1947

124

XXV Antonin Artaud
Portrait de Minouche Pastier, 1947. *Graphite
and coloured pencil on paper, 60 x 46*
Private collection

HANS BELLMER

b 1902 Kattowitz, Germany (now Poland),
d 1975 Paris

Born in a mining village on the German–
Polish border, Bellmer worked in a
steelworks and as a coalminer until
1923, when he went to the Berlin
Polytechnic to study pure mathematics
and technical drawing. There he read
Marx, Lenin, Zola and Baudelaire, and
his contacts with George Grosz, Rudolf
Schlichter and the photographer John
Heartfield were important, not only
artistically but for their anti-
establishment ideas.

   Bellmer spent the winter of 1924–5 in
Paris, and discovered the work of Seurat
and Jules Pascin. Returning to Berlin,
which was plunged into economic
crisis, he met Lotti Pritzel, who
designed heavily decorated wax dolls in
the style of Aubrey Beardsley. In 1928 he
married, and very soon his provocative
adolescent niece joined the household.
When in 1932 Bellmer's mother sent
him a box of broken dolls and old toys,
he suddenly had the idea of creating an
'artificial girl', a lifesize Surrealist doll
that not only embodied many
suppressed incestuous desires, but that
he saw as a subversive act and a gesture
of defiance against the German Fascist
state. It was the year, incidentally, of his
discovery of Grünewald's Colmar
crucifixion, and his profound study of
early German art – Altdorfer, Hans
Baldung Grien, and the art of the Wars

108 Antonin Artaud
Autoportrait (Self Portrait), no date. *Pencil on
paper, 38 x 28*
Private collection

left
107 Antonin Artaud
Portrait de Mania Germain. *Pencil on paper,
62 x 48*
Albert Loeb

'. . . And what is an authentic madman?
A man who has preferred to go mad in
the sense that society understands it,
rather than forfeit a certain superior
idea of human honour.

   This is how society has had strangled
in her asylums all those she has wanted
to get rid of or protect herself against
those who have refused to become her
accomplices to certain lofty
obscenities.

   For a madman is also a man society
does not want to hear, whom it wants to
prevent from uttering unbearable
truths . . .

Antonin Artaud *Van Gogh*, Paris, 1947

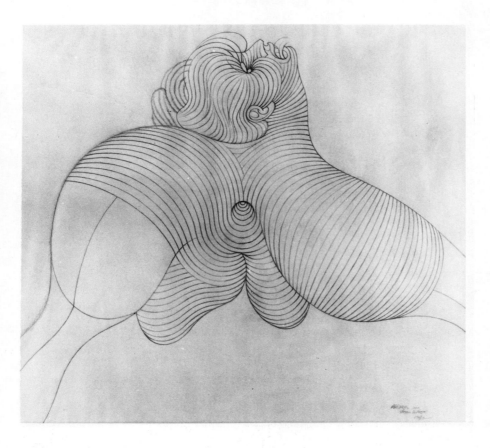

109 Hans Bellmer
Céphalopode, 1947. *Graphite on tracing paper, 52 x 60*
Galerie André-Francois Petit, Paris

what was desired, but the delicacy of Bellmer's drawings redeems them from all hint of obscenity. S.W.

'What do you want me to call you when the inside of your mouth ceases to resemble a word, when your breasts are on their knees behind your fingers and when your feet open to hide your armpit, your beautiful face on fire . . . Your dress must make the image of your thighs coincide with your breasts, printed on the material in three colours. The legs well spread out then to right and left along the padded sleeves, and the white stockings long gloves striped with pink, will encourage your fingers to be the little boot twice over . . . Its heel would be the corset for your thumb, and the red points would be the index finger.

Your shoulders have the contours of your hips: on the back of the dress, reversed, is your front view, naked, so that naturally between your buttocks the vertical line rises which separates the breasts on the image.

The right foot repeats itself several times in your hair, but with arbitrary dimensions, because your black hair, the colour of pitch with vaseline highlights, is arranged in irregular coils. Each one resembles your right foot and merges in the depths of your hair, in certain places where a glance is hidden . . .'

. . . 'As soon as I am still under the pleated skirt of all your fingers, and weary from unweaving the garlands with which you have surrounded the somnolence of your always unborn fruit, then you will breathe into me your perfume and your feverish passion, so that in radiant light, my sex may emerge from the inside of your sex.'

Interanatomical Dreams II.
Hans Bellmer: *La Petite Anatomie de l'Inconscient Physique ou l'Anatomie de l'Image*, 1941–45.

of Religion, with its Last Judgements and Temptations, deeply impregnated with a sense of sin, a fear of the devil and the tortures of the Inquisition.
Bellmer sent photographs of the doll – first published in *Die Puppe* (1934) – to the Surrealist review *Minotaure* in Paris, which eagerly accepted his work, and *La Poupée* appeared in full in 1936 thanks to Editions Gallimard.
Bellmer's discovery of highly articulated wooden dolls, with a central swivelling joint, said to be from the school of Dürer, enabled him to create still more subtle and perverse schemas. Photographs of this second doll were published with Paul Eluard's text in 1949, as *Les Jeux de la Poupée*.

In 1938, Bellmer's wife died, and he had no hesitation in fleeing Nazi Germany to join the Surrealist group in Paris. When in 1940 he was interned, he found himself in the same camp as Max Ernst, in a former brickworks near Aix. Bricks became a dominant motif in his drawings at the time. There he started writing *La Petite Anatomie de l'Inconscient Physique, ou l'Anatomie de l'Image*, first published in 1957. It was

a manifesto of his beliefs in the erotic, where the notion of the anagram provides an analogy for the bodily distortions and displacements that evoke desire. In 1941, Bellmer buried his German passport in a sewer at Castres. After the Liberation he became intensely active again, painting, writing and illustrating, including sixty-four etchings for *Lord Auch, Histoire de l'Oeil* by Georges Bataille, and the illustrations to the Marquis de Sade's *Justine* published in 1950. He showed work in the Exposition Internationale du Surréalisme at the Galerie Maeght in 1947. In 1953 he met Unica Zürn, his future companion and the subject of many works. His portraits of Arp, Breton, Tzara, Camus, Bachelard, Matta, Ernst and Lam were exhibited in 1955, at the Galerie J.J. Pauvert. This was also the year that he made engravings after the de Sade drawings of 1946, though *A Sade* was not published until 1961.

'C'est une fille, c'est mon désir' (Paul Eluard, *Jeux de la Poupée*). For Bellmer, as for Sade, eroticism meant both the objectification and appropriation of

VICTOR BRAUNER

b 1903, Piatra Neamtz, Roumania,
d 1966, Paris

His father's passionate interest in spiritualism meant that Brauner as a child was present at many séances, first in Roumania, and after 1912 in Vienna where his family had settled. In 1921 he spent a brief period at the School of Fine Arts in Bucharest, where his first exhibition was held in 1924 at the Galerie Mozart. The same year, Brauner founded a review *75 HP* with the poet

Ilarie Voronca, in which he published his manifesto 'Pictopoésie', and an article on 'Le Surrationalisme'. From 1928 to 1931 he worked with the Dadaist and Surrealist review *UNU*, which published most of his drawings and paintings. Settling in Paris in 1930, he met Brancusi, who introduced him to photography, and Yves Tanguy, through whom he was to meet the major Surrealists. His 'Autoportrait à l'oeil énucléé' was painted at this time. His first one-man show at the Galerie Pierre Loeb in 1934 had a catalogue preface by André Breton. This was the year of 'Force de Concentration de M.K.' and 'L'Etrange Cas de M.K.', Ubuesque departures from his normal Surrealist style, where in strange landscapes the theme of the eye was becoming more obsessive. He returned to Bucharest briefly in 1935 but, back in Paris in 1938, he lost his left eye in a brawl at Oscar Dominguez' studio. It was to be 'the most painful and important fact of my life'. This period of 'lycanthropic', 'somnambulesque', 'chimeresque' paintings, full of alchemical and erotic imagery, stopped abruptly at the onset of war. Brauner fled to Perpignan and then to the Pyrenees, managing to keep contact with the Surrealist group at Marseilles. In 1942 he found himself living with his wife and the sculptor Michel Herz in the Alps, and without any painting materials to hand he began his 'dessins à la bougie', inspired by stone textures and painted with coffee or walnut stain on relief drawings done in simple candle wax. These were followed in 1943 by oil paintings on canvas primed with melted wax. 'L'Homme Idéal' includes paper collage as another feature. It was the period of objects of enchantment and exorcism, like the strange ithyphallic sculpture 'Nombre', or the 'Portrait de Novalis', both of 1943. His love of alchemy, magic, the Tarot and the Cabbala led him to see reality as double, if not multiple, as in the 'Conglomeros' series, 1941–45. Returning to Paris in 1945, Brauner

110

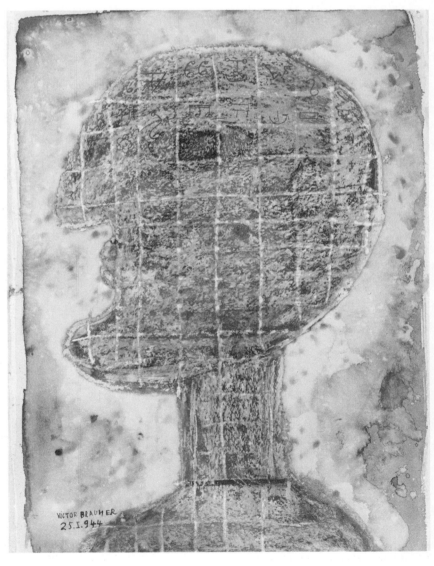

110 Victor Brauner
L'Ampuse, 1943. *Grey, wash, wax, pen and indian ink on paper, 50 x 64.5*
Musée National d'Art Moderne, Centre Georges Pompidou

111 Victor Brauner
Sans titre (Untitled), 1944. *Walnut stain and candle on paper, 64.5 x 50*
Musée National d'Art Moderne, Centre Georges Pompidou, gift of Mme Victor Brauner

111

painted 'Lion, Lumière, Liberté', seven canvases conceived as a single work, which were exhibited on the premises of the Cahiers d'Art in 1947. A small one-man show at the Galerie Pierre Loeb in 1946 preceded Brauner's participation in the Exposition Internationale du Surréalisme at the Galerie Maeght the following year. His texts in the catalogue, two 'self-coronations', the first signed 'Victor Brauner' and the second 'Emperor of the kingdom of personal myth, signed Rotziv Renubarb', are high points of his esoteric form of megalomania.

After a serious illness and convalescence in Switzerland, where he read Dr. Séchehàye's *La Réalisation symbolique*, he returned to Paris for his first major exhibition at the Galerie René Drouin in 1948. He had signed the manifesto *Rupture Inaugurale* in 1947, which dissociated the Surrealists from the French Communist party, and now ceased to associate with the group as a whole, though Roberto Matta's influence became increasingly apparent in Brauner's own painting. The aggression and the 'lines of force' in 'Endotête, pénétrations psychologiques' (1951) are typical. Yet this style existed alongside static, two-dimensional works, reminiscent of hieroglyphs or Aztec codices like 'La Pluie', 1950. The autobiographical series of 'Victors' or 'Onomatamanie' was started in 1949. In 1954 Brauner was shown at the Venice Biennale, and he was chosen again to represent France with a complete room of his works in 1966, the year of his death.   S.W.

'In the course of my walks along the banks of the Durance River and the torrent at Cellier de Roussel in the Alps, I was attracted by the stones which one finds there in great numbers. These stones were remarkable to me in that patterns of white lines were incised on the surface. Immediately I wanted to master the beauty of this effect, and I began to experiment in search of its secret. Thus the idea of wax came to me, and now I am convinced that it is the best medium for expressing the secret of drawings, the marriage of black and white on a surface.'

112 Victor Brauner
L'Homme idéal (The Ideal Man), 1943. *Pen on paper stuck down on wood, waxed, 36.5 x 16*
Musée National d'Art Moderne, Centre Georges Pompidou

XXV Antonin Artaud
Portrait de Minouche Pastier, 1947. *Graphite and coloured pencil on paper, 60 x 46*
Private collection

antonin artaud
22 mai 1947

'*The Process*: I rub candlewax freely and with some force on a sheet of white paper. Then I cover the waxed surface with a thin wash of Chinese ink. When the ink has dried, I draw or more literally scratch in the design using a pointed instrument. Then again I cover the surface with an ink wash, and when that has dried I scrape away all the excess wax. *The result*: a drawing and mysterious quality. . . The formula reveals the origins of all synthetic formulae; we discover the core which contains the motive principles of the universal essence of 'All in All'; we rediscover the extremes and that which lies between them. The formula invokes the true center of cosmic radiation. It is Science's principal key.'

Victor Brauner, 'My Drawings in Wax' in *Victor Brauner*, Julian Levy Gallery, New York 1947

'Fragments of an instant
our feelings find themselves in the unreal
beings, things, spaces are in another world.
We have strayed beyond
the limits of the obviously real.
The space of the unreal is the space of panic.'

Victor Brauner, 1952, in Sarane Alexandrian, *Victor Brauner*

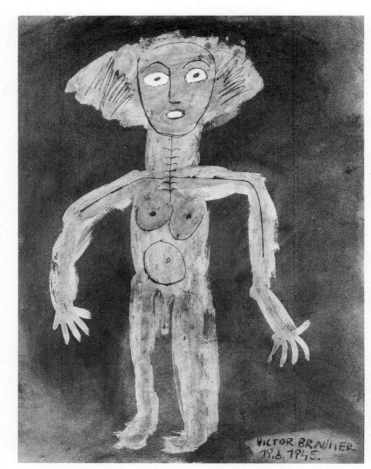

113

CAMILLE BRYEN

b 1907, Nantes, d 1977, Paris

A poet, painter and illustrator, Camille Bryen was considered one of the most radical intellectuals in post-war Paris. He had come to Paris in 1926, and in 1927 published the first collection of his poems, *Opoponiax*, but it was not until 1934 that he exhibited a series of 'automatic' drawings, inspired by Surrealism, but with a ferocity and instinctive character that were closer to

113 Victor Brauner
Sans titre (Untitled), 1945. *Grey wash and wax on paper, 65 x 50*
Musée National d'Art Moderne, Centre Georges Pompidou, gift of Mme Victor Brauner

114 Victor Brauner
Endotête, 1951. *Oil on canvas, 73 x 50*
Musée National d'Art Moderne, Centre Georges Pompidou

XXVI Henri Michaux
Sans titre (Untitled), 1945. *Watercolour and ink on paper, 65 x 50*
Musée National d'Art Moderne, Centre Georges Pompidou

114

115 Camille Bryen
Aquarelle no 296 (Watercolour no 296), 1949. *Pen and indian inks on paper, 50 x 32*
Musée National d'Art Moderne, Centre Georges Pompidou

116 Camille Bryen
Aquarelle no 307 (Watercolour no 307), 1949. *Pen, indian ink, gouache and watercolour on paper, 49 x 32*
Musée National d'Art Moderne, Centre Georges Pompidou

graffiti, and evocative of Art Brut . From then onwards, art for Bryen was pure action, a revelation of being liberated from any signification, refusing all 'expression'. In 'L'aventure des objets' (1937) Bryen presented his 'objets à fonctionnement' – object with functions, that had taken him two years to create, associating disparate elements according to an internal logic which demonstrated the workings of the unconscious. 'It was a matter of making one's own life a weapon of liberation', Bryen declared. He was close to a Dadaist position both in his painting and his personal conduct. In 1943 in fact, Bryen was undoubtedly the sole person to mention the 'éspirt Dada' during the Occupation in a public lecture in Lyons, and in 1945 he vehemently opposed the 'Lettrist' group when Iliazd, the poet and editor, gave a lecture called 'Après nous le Lettrisme': Bryen recalled the

anteriority of futurist and Dadaist experiments with the letter as an autonomous creative element.
Then in 1949, his paintings were shown in the Galerie des Deux Iles, with a catalogue preface by the poet Jacques Audiberti. He collaborated with Audiberti in 1952 to publish *L'Ouvre-boite* ('the Tin-opener'), in which he defined 'Abhumanism' as 'the world without man . . . the world as it is at the beginning, before it has been compartmentalised, classified, humanised . . . the sentiment which will allow man to cure himself of "man".' Bryen's first works are close to those of Wols. Bryen also exhibited with him in the first exhibitions of 'abstraction lyrique'. The crucial exhibitions were L'Imaginaire, 1947, Galerie du Luxembourg, H.W.P.S.M.T.B., 1948, Galerie Colette Allendy, Véhémences Confrontées, Galerie Nina Dausset, and Les Signifiants de

l'Informel, 1958, Studio Fachetti. The exhibition of Monet's water-lily series, 'Les Nymphéas', at the Orangerie in 1948 deeply impressed Bryen, and he moved in consequence towards increasingly subtle forms of 'Tachisme' – the painting of marks and blotches which constitute an independent universe.   G.V.

'Man fails as a measure of the universe, and the eye and ear often reach out into areas of form and sound which no longer emanate from purely human sources, from which human forms, human voices are excluded . . . Perhaps painting will judge itself tomorrow on the basis that it will be the most transparent expression of disaffection with the "human". It will have allowed to well up over its surfaces the calls, the signs, grimaces and outbursts of the great disintoxication, the great purge of "homo sapiens".'

Camille Bryen, *Parole Parle*, Paris, 1945.

117 Camille Bryen
Hépérile, 1951. *Oil on canvas, 146 x 81*
Musée National d'Art Moderne,
Centre Georges Pompidou

SAM FRANCIS

b 1923, San Mateo, USA

After studying science as a postgraduate at the University of Berkeley, Sam Francis joined the American Air Force during World War II, and it was during a period of hospitalisation for a serious injury that he began to paint. In 1950 he came to Paris and enrolled as a pupil of Fernand Léger. He discovered a close and stimulating friend in Georges Duthuit, the art critic and curator of the Petit Palais museum, who was also Henri Matisse's son-in-law. Francis' first paintings, monochromes of a pale transparent grey, present an expanded vision of space, where a cosmic and radiant energy seems to absorb the material body. This becomes transfigured, annihilated in the paint surface as the artist projects himself totally into his work. This vision was later confirmed by Francis' discovery of the Far East. He was closely associated during these years with Jean-Paul Riopelle and some of the American artists who were living in Paris including Al Held, Kimber Smith, Norman Bluhm and Joan Mitchell, while he maintained a great admiration for Bram Vah Velde, Philippe Hosiasson and Alberto Giacometti. After his first one-man show at Nina Dausset's Galerie du Dragon in 1952, he participated in the exhibitions organised by Michel Tapié: Signifiants de l'Informel and Un Art Autre. He showed in 1955 and 1956 at the Galerie Rive Droite. His extensive travels in 1957 and 1958 coincided with the recognition of his work in the more important museums of Europe and America. G.V.

HANS HARTUNG

b 1904, Leipzig, Germany

Born into a very musical, medical family, the young Hartung was passionately interested in astronomy and photography. He 'drew' the patterns made by lightning in his 'Blitzbücher' and even constructed a home-made telescope. Later, he became interested in painting: he admired Rembrandt, Goya, Franz Hals, and El Greco, and in 1921 and 1922 discovered Slevogt, Corinth and the German Expressionists, especially Kokoshka and Emil Nolde. In 1922, Hartung created a series of completely abstract watercolours, while his drawings in ink, charcoal and black and red chalks suppressed the image almost entirely, leaving marks whose interpretation became ultimately a matter of perception. The 'Dresden Altarpiece', in indian ink, is a good example: in retrospect it was completely prophetic of the 'Tachiste' movement of the 1950s.

Between 1924 and 1926, Hartung studied philosophy, psychology and art history at the University and Fine Art Academy of Leipzig, where a lecture given by Kandinsky in 1925 revealed the existence — and the long history — of other abstract experiments, including those of Paul Klee. Disregarding advice to go to the Bauhaus, Hartung transferred to the Academy at Dresden, where in 1926 the International Exhibition included a section on French Impressionism, Fauvism and Cubism. Rouault, Henri Rousseau, Braque and Picasso were of particular interest to him. Hartung was still teaching himself by copying reproductions, but in October 1926 he went to Paris, staying until 1931. He frequented the studios of André Lhote and Fernand Léger, but remained essentially solitary at this time. He travelled to the South of France, in Holland, Belgium, and back to Dresden in 1931 for his first one-man show. With his wife, Ana-Eva Bergman, he spent some time in southern Norway, but the death of his father brought him back to Paris and marked a period of grave

crisis. Leaving some work with Jeanne Bucher, Hartung went to Minorca, where he decided to return to the more instinctive style of his youth. Political and fiscal troubles that resulted from the situation in Germany drove him to Paris, Stockholm, Germany and finally back to Paris in 1936. He exhibited at the Galerie Pierre and at Origines et Développement de l'Art International Indépendant at the Jeu de Paume, which resulted in a certain notoriety. He met Hélion, Kandinsky, Mondrian, Magnelli, Domela, Miró and Calder, and Henri Goetz, with whom he lived for a year at the time of his divorce from Ana-Eva. Hartung then worked for a time with the sculptor Julio Gonzalez, whose daughter Roberta became his second wife. His iron sculpture of 1938 shows both Gonzales' influence and remains an attempt to give three dimensional expression to his graphic style in wire. The canvas 'T. 36-2' ('Toile', canvas, 1936, no. 2) was shown at the Exhibition of Twentieth Century German Art in the New Burlington Galleries, London.

In 1939, Hartung was interned in two French transit camps before he was sent to North Africa with the Foreign Legion. He was later imprisoned in Spain. After seven months of imprisonment he rejoined the Legion, but was gravely injured in November 1944, losing a leg.

Returning to Paris in 1945, where he assumed French nationality and received military decorations, he resumed his work as an artist and held his first one-man show in 1947 at the Galerie Lydia Conti. The following year Alain Resnais made a film about Hartung, which was shown in 1948 in Germany, and in 1950 at the Galerie La Hune, Paris. Hartung became friendly with Schneider, Soulages, Mathieu, Baumeister, and Rothko, and exhibited at the Centre de Récherches Cujas at the Galerie Denise René, and at the Salon des Surindépendants, the Salon de Mai and the Salon des Réalités Nouvelles. London saw his work twice during this period, at the Hanover Gallery in 1949 and the Lefevre Gallery in 1953.

In 1952 at the Gonzales retrospective at the Musée National d'Art Moderne he

XXXII Sam Francis
Other White, 1952. *Oil on canvas, 205 x 180*
Musée National d'Art Moderne, Centre Georges Pompidou

right
118 Hans Hartung
Composition, 1946. *Oil and pastel on canvas, 146 x 97*
Musée d'Art Moderne de la Ville de Paris

met Ana-Eva again and they remarried. Towards 1955, Hartung's 'psychographic' element subsided. His work became more static, meditative and harmonious. He was one of the most successful painters of the Ecole de Paris. s.w.

'Hartung's means of expression enrich themselves more and more: these basic elements are as varied as the use he makes of them. Curved, supple or violent lines, heavy or fine, rise like jets. His large colour-areas are opaque or transparent, heavy or light, and all the resources of a masterly technique are applied to them; matting, hatching, stippling, and contrast of light and dark twist the lines into networks and knots. His colours are also varied: he most often uses light greens, browns, lemon yellow, cerulean blue and black. 'The expressive power of this new language seems to have a larger field than has the traditional figurative language: it communicates directly, without detouring through a 'subject' in the painting; it avoids the confusion which arises too often between that which is represented (the object) and that which is expressed (the human, social, or cosmic reality), between the subject of the picture (accessory pretext) and the essential truth which the real artist comprehends and wishes to convey to others. And these abstract works in which man seems absent — because his appearance is not represented — are, nevertheless, charged with strong human feeling. Lines, as though drawn by restless anxiety, unroll, entangle themselves, draw into tight knots, meet at sharp angles or circulate in supple movement: their unstable grouping speaks of uncertainty, insecurity, confusion . . . There are heavy and hostile blots like insurmountable obstacles obstructing the horizon and areas of light behind the black barrier of present difficulties (T 48-19), aggressive lines which rise vertically as though in the act of revolt (T 47-12), or which dart towards the right as if for decisive action (T 48-15), prison bars behind which languish the unalterable desire to live (T 48-8, T 48-15), scattered spots which speak of man's infinite solitude in this world grown foreign to him (T 46-29). All the inner life of a sensitive and tormented man appears before our eyes, with its unfathomable complexity and the eddies which the slightest touch provokes in it' . . .

Madeleine Rousseau, in *Hans Hartung* (contemporary translation).

PIERRE KLOSSOWSKI

b 1905, Paris

Pierre Klossowski, the brother of the painter Balthus, and a disciple of Rilke and Gide, studied philosophy and theology at Lyons and in Paris. With Georges Bataille, Georges Ambrosino and Patrick Waldberg, he founded the esoteric Collège de Sociologie, and contributed to its review *Acéphale* (1936-7). The Collège proposed to study 'social existence in all its forms where the active presence of the sacred is manifest', and was interested in Nietzsche, Hegel and phenomenology. Klossowski's contributions to the Collège were republished as *Sade mon Prochain* in 1947. From 1948 to 1950 he collaborated with Sartre on *Les Temps Modernes*. *La Vocation Suspendue* (1950) demonstrates Klossowski's reasons for renouncing the priesthood while *Roberte ce Soir* (1953) becomes his manifesto, a perverse blend of the erotic and the mystic; through violation alone, the sexual act becomes a revelation of the spirit. It was for *Roberte ce Soir* that Klossowski, finding Balthus's illustrations unsuitable, offered six of his own pencil drawings, in order that a luxury edition could be produced, avoiding censorship on the basis of private subscription. Klossowski says that he has 'always drawn', but that, unlike Michaux, drawing for him has had to alternate with creative writing.

'Roberte, le colosse et le nain', 1953, neatly freezes a hallucinatory rape scene in *Roberte* into a pencilled tableau-vivant. These tableaux-vivants are described by Octave, the collector of the works of 'Tonnere' (Klossowski) in *La Revocation de l'Edit de Nantes* (1959), 'Life offering itself as a spectacle . . . in a moment of suspense.'

Just after *Roberte*, Klossowski undertook a series of large-format drawings, using his pencil to produce 'the silvery flickerings of the silent black and white cinema', but he himself refers us back to Seurat, whose stippled nudes were created with an equally laborious technique. These large-formats provoked the unstinted admiration of Bataille, Breton, Paulhan (who suggested his drawings should be included in the 'Art Brut' collection), Giacometti (who appreciated the sculptural quality of the large compositions), and Masson. They were first publicly exhibited at the Galerie du Cadran Solaire in 1967, eleven years after a single private showing, in Balthus's former studio in the Cour de Rohan. s.w.

. . . The type of woman who particularly appeals to our artist comes from the second half of the nineteenth century . . . the Second Empire beauty whose prototype was incarnate in the Empress Eugénie, or represented by the great 'Dame' of Manet's first period, or even better, the 'Demoiselles de la Seine' by Courbet . . . This type of beauty seems totally supplanted today by the industrialised pin-up, the film-star vamp, but here and there we see it reappear, emerging from certain social strata . . . and already it is exerting its attraction on the younger generation . . . We are returning to a taste for more reserved, more decent expressions, more classical, ultimately, because for us occidentals, inveterate heirs to Augustinian Manichaeism, the attraction lies precisely in the austere appearance of the face, which conceals – and this is where it matters – all the more exuberant charms . . . In the motifs of several paintings I have been able to salvage, we recognise a propensity for scenes whose violence is due to knowing unveilings, not to the unveiled, not to nudity, but to the instant which in itself is the least pictorial: the eye wants to linger on a motif without a story behind it, and our artist on the contrary seems to counter the eye's repose by suggesting to the mind what the painting dissimulates.

Pierre Klossowski, *La Revocation de l'edit de Nantes*.

. . . In this singular concept of an 'eternal return' that Klossowski elaborated through the study of Nietzsche, everything is fixed: Life is a ritual one cannot flee, a liturgical drama. The radical and thus obsessive problem of sex, where good and evil mingle inextricably to produce an ecstasy outside time, for its essence and its existence requires a representation: a language 'in itself'. . . . In the same dimension as Sade, but in a universe uniquely his own, Klossowski's descriptions are, frankly speaking, 'pictures', a gallery of horrors and theologico-sexual sublimities. . . . It is the postulation of a 'dark night', a real and silent communion, that Klossowski expresses with his theory of the regard or the voyeur: offering oneself to the 'regard' of the other so that he can 'behold' you. A tragic action that can end in the destruction of man. Klossowski expresses this in 'Le Bain de Diane', a work full of Alexandrian

119 Pierre Klossowski
La belle Versaillaise (Pretty Girl from
Versailles), no date. *Graphite on paper,
197 x 150*
Private collection

beauty and light . . . He develops this
problem in the hidden domain of
sexuality, a strange sexuality which
calls for respect and austerity: the
paradoxical coexistence of violation
and impotence. Because of these
spiritual problems, Klossowski makes
Roberte sometimes a fascinating and
monstrous sacred prostitute,
sometimes a strange and disconcerting
plurality of Roberte's.
. . . To my mind, painting offers
Klossowski a profoundly meaningful
solution: isn't it, after all, a silent and
sensual phenomenon that permits one
to give himself to the regard of the
other and the other to behold? Painting
is a real communication, via 'the spirit'
and 'the flesh'.

Franco Cagnetti, 'De luxuria spirituali', in
Les mines de plomb de P. Klossowski.

WIFREDO LAM

b 1902, Sagna la Grande, Cuba

Wifredo Lam's father was Chinese and
his mother of mixed African and Indian
blood. He studied painting in Havana
and lived in Spain until 1938, when he
moved to Paris.

He became friendly with Picasso,
who introduced him to Paul Eluard,
Max Ernst, Miró, and above all Pierre
Loeb, who put on Lam's first exhibition
in Paris. His friendship with André
Breton, whose poem *Fata Morgana* he
illustrated in 1940, led to his involvement
with the Surrealist group. Allying
primitive hieratic forms to a strong
influence from Picasso, Lam's work
achieved its greatest originality after his
exile to the Antilles in 1941. Here, he
found once more the spirit of the tropics
luxurious vegetation and the ancient
voodoo myths.

'Le Jungle' painted in 1942 and
exhibited in 1943 at the Pierre Matisse
Gallery in New York, achieves a
surrealistic amalgam: living reality
merges with other forces, the fantastic,
the erotic and the occult. Lam exhibited
again from 1945 onwards at the Galerie
Pierre, and returning to Paris in 1946, he
participated in the Exposition
Internationale du Surréalisme at the
Galerie Maeght in 1947, with an 'altar'
evoking Falmer's head of hair, from
Lautréamont's *Chants de Maldoror*.
With Matta and Victor Brauner, Lam
became one of the most influential
painters of the new Surrealist
generation. He embodied the principle
of a magical primitivism, which
affected Jackson Pollock as much as
Asger Jorn and the painters of the
Cobra group. In 1953 the Galerie Maeght
put on a one-man show of his work.

**'In a society where money and the
machine have widened the gap
between men and things beyond all
proportion, Wifredo Lam fixes on his
canvas the ceremony for which all
ceremonies exist: the ceremony of the
physical union between man and the
world. Deliberately engaging his
intelligence and his technique in a
legendary and unique adventure,
which lays bare with seismic shocks
the uttermost realms of the brain's
shell, Wifredo Lam celebrates the
transformation of the world into myth
and into complicity. Painting is one of
the rare weapons we are left with to
combat sordid history.
. . . 'Nurtured with sea salt, sun, rain,**

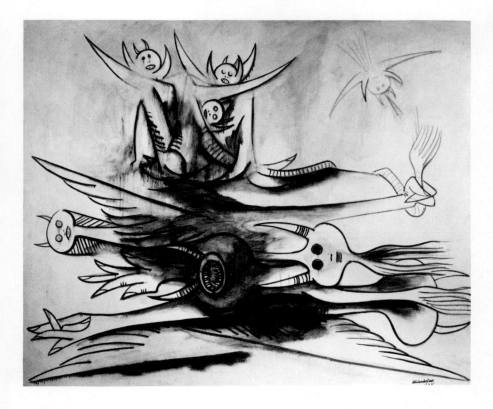

120 Wifredo Lam
Libération, 1947. *Oil on canvas, 127 x 160*
Private collection

wonderful and sinister moons,
Wifredo Lam is the man who summons
the modern world back to its original
terror and fervour.'

Aimé Cesaire, 'Wifredo Lam' in *Cahiers
d'Art XX-XXI.*

GEORGES MATHIEU

b 1921, Boulogne sur Mer

After studying English and Law at
university Georges Mathieu began his
first non-figurative paintings in 1944.
These were heavily influenced by
E. Crankshaw's study on Joseph
Conrad and the art of the novel. In
1945, he used his 'dripping technique'
for the first time in the painting
'Evanescence', and three abstract
canvases of 1946 were shown at the
Salon des Réalités Nouvelles in 1947:
'Survivance', 'Conception' and
'Désintégration'. Arriving in Paris in
1947, he discovered Atlan's paintings
at the Galerie Lydia Conti; he was
then completely overwhelmed by the
Wols exhibition at the Galerie Drouin:
'Forty paintings: forty masterpieces.
Each one more shattering, more
tortured, bloodier than the next: a
major event, doubtless the most
important since Van Gogh.' These

exhibitions confirmed Mathieu's own
development: moreover, he was
aware from an early date of the first
Abstract Expressionist paintings from
New York, thanks to his work in
public relations for the United States
Line. He organised the first exhibitions
of what he defined as 'lyrical
abstraction': L'Imaginaire (Galerie du
Luxembourg, 1947), H.W.P.S.M.T.B.,
(Hartung, Wols, Picabia, Stahly,
Mathieu, Tapié, Bryen, Galerie Colette
Allendy, 1948), and Blanc et Noir
(Galerie des Deux Iles, 1948). From
1948 onwards, he attempted to create
contacts between French and
American experimental painters and
their work, and was responsible for
the first exhibition of this nature at
the Galerie du Luxembourg in
October 1948. In 1951, he helped to
organise the exhibition Véhémences
Confrontées, presented by Michel Tapié
at the Galerie Nina Dausset. At a time
when Maurice Merleau-Ponty with his
Phénoménologie de la Perception, and
Gaston Bachelard with *La Terre et les
rêveries de la volonté*, were discussing
in philosophical and conceptual terms
the essential role played by the body
and the world of matter, Mathieu's
work embodied these concepts in paint.

The rapid, calligraphic gesture became
the emblem and the record of the body's
projection into another medium, paint.
A whole new world of signs was created.
Henceforth, Mathieu would be as
opposed to the formalism of geometric
abstraction as to the 'informel', the
painting defended by Michel Tapié,
with its wish to liberate the primitive
values of play, the sacred and the
profane. Mathieu's paintings, each one
a performance which risked failure,
were created at great speed, often
under the public eye, and gave rise to
many spectacular events, such as the
creation of the 'Cérémonies
commemoratoires de la deuxième
condamnation de Siger de Brabant',
realised with Simon Hantai at the
Galerie Kléber in 1957, and the 'Bataille
de Hakata', Tokyo, 1957.   G.V

'Hiroshima, Place Vendôme. An
exhibition which doesn't drag. A
lightning violence electrifies every
second. Georges Mathieu has clawed
his way over the walls of the Galerie
René Drouin. The alert would have
lasted two days. Eight canvases in all,
but one would have been enough. His
aim is perfect: bull's eye every time. A
shower of arrows, plate glass shattered
into splinters: the paint whistles along,
tracing the curve of an explosive
missile. A stroke of red howls and
writhes. A real firework display, the
colour rises and falls in black dribbles
on the world, a rearing insect's back.
With his aggression, Georges Mathieu
protects himself against theories and
formulas. He wants to stay vigilant for
this masculine adventure, where it's
difficult to distinguish cruelty from
love.'

Jean Caillens, on seeing the exhibition
Mathieu, Galerie Drouin, 1950.

XXVII Francis Picabia
Egoisme (Egoism), 1947-50. *Oil on canvas,
153.5 x 110.8*
Private collection

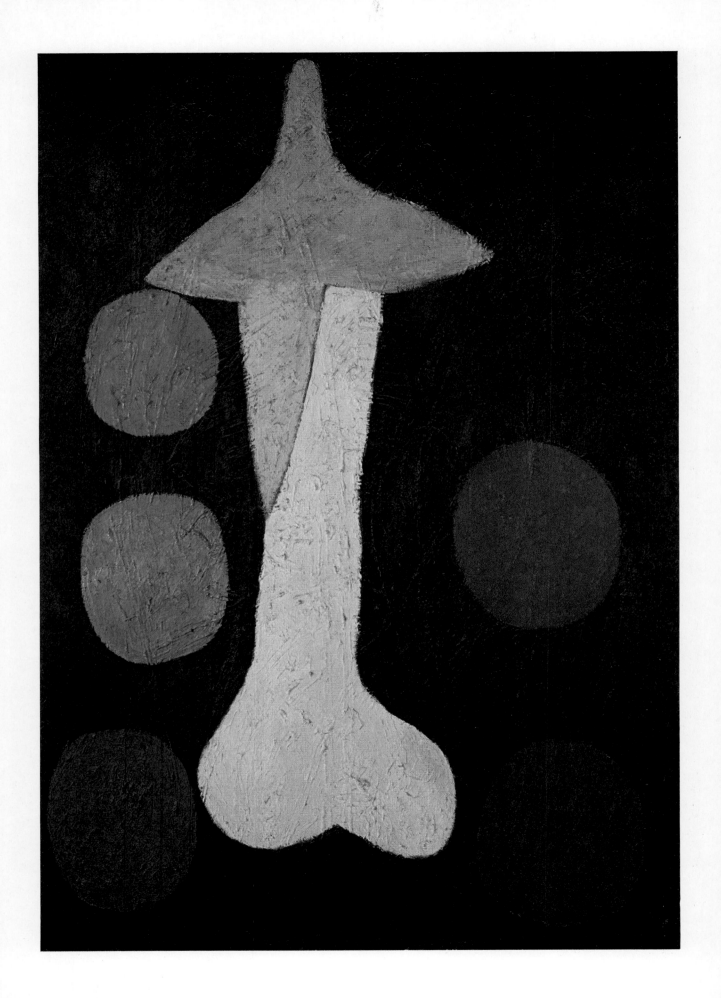

XXVIII Wols (Wolfgang Schulze)
L'Aile de la papillon (The Butterfly's Wing). *Oil on canvas, 55 x 46*
Musée National d'Art Moderne, Centre Georges Pompidou, gift of René de Montaigu

right
XXIX Wols
Sans titre (Untitled), 1947. *Oil on canvas,*
61 x 50
Private collection

XXX Matta
La Violence de la Douceur (Violence of Softness), 1949. *Oil on canvas, 200 x 297*
Artist's collection

121 Georges Mathieu
Conception, 1946. *Oil on canvas, 85 x 85*
Artist's collection

122 Georges Mathieu
Un silence de Gilbert de Nogent (Gilbert de Nogent in silence), 1950-1. *Oil on canvas, 130 x 218*
Fonds national d'art contemporain, Paris

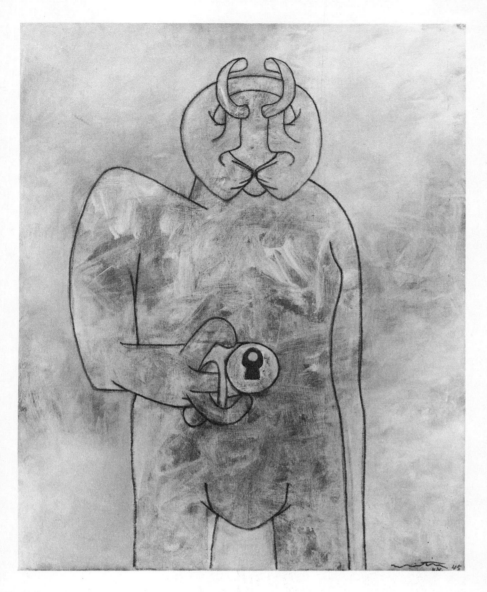

123 Matta (Roberto Matta Echaurren)
Poête (Poet) – Portrait of Andre Breton. *Oil on
canvas, 94.5 x 76.5*
Artist's collection

MATTA (Roberto Sebastian Matta Echaurren)

b 1911, Santiago, Chile

After studying architecture in Santiago
and working as a designer for Le
Corbusier between 1934 and 1937, Matta
met the poet Federico Garcia Llorca
during a trip to Spain. Llorca
recommended him to Salvador Dali,
who in turn introduced him to André
Breton. Thus Matta joined the Surrealist
group. The year 1937 saw his first
drawings, and he painted his first
canvases the following year, 1938, when
he also participated in the Exposition

Internationale du Surréalisme in Paris.

Influenced by Yves Tanguy, as was
his friend Gordon Onslow Ford, and
fascinated by the work of Marcel
Duchamp, he became, after his exile to
the USA in 1939, the most brilliant
representative of Surrealist automatism
with his 'psychological morphologies'.
From 1940 onwards, he exhibited at the
Galerie Julien Levy in New York, and
very soon appeared to be one of the
most fertile sources of the new American
painting. The works of Gorky, Mother-
well and Pollock all show his influence.

His art at the time, a lyrical explosion
of vertiginous spaces, at once

introspective and cosmic, for example
in 'La terre est un homme' (1942) changed
at the end of the war when the horror
of the concentration camps suddenly
became apparent. Man became a
mechanised figure in a metaphorical
theatre of cruelty, as in 'Etre avec', 1945-
6 and 'However', 1947. Henceforth Matta
would be divided between the 'vertige
d'Eros', the constant reference to the
erotic, and his work for revolutionary
political causes. In addition, he
participated in the post-war Exposition
Internationale du Surréalisme at the
Galerie Maeght. The Surrealists
excluded him from their group in 1948,
just when he had returned to France,
but he was readmitted in 1959. Having
spent the years 1950 to 1954 in Rome,
Matta returned to Paris for a time,
before finally settling in London. G.V.

'The "death instinct" has been given
every licence in these last few years, on
a quite unprecedented scale. It
abounds in unheard-of refinements
and only turns back when sure of
achieving complete annihilation next
time round. The sexual instinct, which
has developed with equal vigour
should, in effect, be opposed to this,
with its wish that the desire for
destruction should in each and every
case take on the form of a desire
diverted to the service of Eros. No
works of art [but Matta's] have ever yet
shown so perfectly, and so
"analytically" these two instincts at
grips with one another. Because of
this, they present nonetheless a certain
ambiguity to the spectator, with their
figures in plough-shaped boots, cross-
bow ties, whose faces are more like
moles than men (as though one ought
to be waiting to leave this era of
"shelters") yet who undertake, all the
same, a verbal and sexual intercourse
whose frenzy does not exclude a
punctilious precision. Matta's
explorations in work of this second
period have bearing, in psychoanalytic
terms, on the region lying between the
ego and the superego which is, above
all, the region which gives rise to
anxiety.
Matta was allowed to discover this
region, for it includes all the sources of
anxiety produced by the scruples of
conscience. Everything here attests to
its force: gestures of exorcism, the
elevation of people on trial, a narrow
compartmentalised world, bristling
everywhere with horror.
André Breton: Le Surréalisme et la Peinture,
N.R.F. Gallimard Paris, 1966. (Original
edition 1928.)

HENRI MICHAUX

b 1899, Namur, Belgium

After a difficult adolescence strongly affected by his reading of Lautréamont, Michaux began to write in 1920, and soon received the encouragement of Jean Paulhan. Arriving in Paris in 1925, he made the acquaintance of Max Ernst and Paul Klee; though still a writer he began to draw in his spare time. After much travelling he resumed this activity in 1937, with the creation of his first important series of gouaches and pastels on black backgrounds. These were exhibited in 1938 at the Galerie Pierre, and reproduced in 1939 in a small volume of poems entitled *Peintures* along with other works of the same period: ('Entre Centre et Absence', 'Au Pays de la Magie'). These were already perfectly characteristic of his universe: a realm of strange dream forms invoked from the depths of the unconscious.

In 1944 at the Galerie Rive Gauche, he exhibited the watercolours he had

124 Henri Michaux
Repos dans le malheur (Rest in Sadness), 1945. *Charcoal rubbing on paper, 31 x 24*
Musée National d'Art Moderne, Centre Georges Pompidou

125 Henri Michaux
Sans titre (Untitled), 1946-8. *Watercolour and ink on paper, 50 x 32*
Musée National d'Art Moderne, Centre Georges Pompidou

XXVI Henri Michaux
Sans titre (Untitled), 1945. *Watercolour and ink on paper, 65 x 50*
Musée National d'Art Moderne, Centre Georges Pompidou

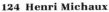

painted during the Occupation; landscapes reduced almost to signs, all forms seemingly drowned and annihilated in space. Two publications of 1946, *Apparitions* and *Peintures et dessins*, allowed the public to discover his very important article 'En pensant au Phenomène de la Peinture' and his 'frottages'. 'Dans le malheur' for example, is created by rubbing a pencil over paper laid on a rough surface. The violent death of Michaux's wife in 1948 gave rise to 'Nous deux encore', a series of large wash-drawings peopled with disquieting and phantasmagorical figures, and a book of lithographs *Meidosems*, all of which were exhibited in the same year at the Galerie Drouin. His watercolours and oils from 1949 to 1950 became violent and brilliantly coloured. They were followed by an indian ink series, 'Mouvements' (1950), where the drawing becomes a matter of innumerable repetitive signs. These were the precursors of the 'ink paintings' exhibited at the Galerie Drouin in 1954, and the drawings made under the influence of the drug mescaline.   G.V

'You're drawing for no special reason, scribbling mechanically, and nearly always faces appear on the paper. 'Leading an excessively facial life, we too are plunged into a perpetual fever of faces.
'As soon as I pick up a pencil, a paintbrush, they come to me on the paper, one after the other, ten, fifteen, twenty. And wild ones for the most part. Are they me, all these faces? Are they other people? What depths have they come from?
'Wouldn't they be simply the consciousness of my own head during its reflections? The grimace of a second face, in the same way that the adult man who suffers has stopped crying in his misery, from good manners, only to suffer more inside, he would have stopped grimacing, only to become more replete with grimaces inside. Behind the immobile face, deserted, a simple mask, another face, superlatively mobile, seethes, contracts, simmers in an unbearable paroxysm. Behind the rigid countenance, desperately searching for a way out, are the expressions, like a band of howling dogs.
'If I paint mad-looking heads, it's not to say that I'm mad in those moments, or that I propose to drive myself mad because for one reason or another it would please me. I begin on the contrary most often in a state of calm,

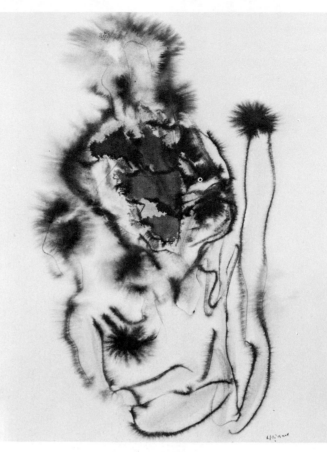

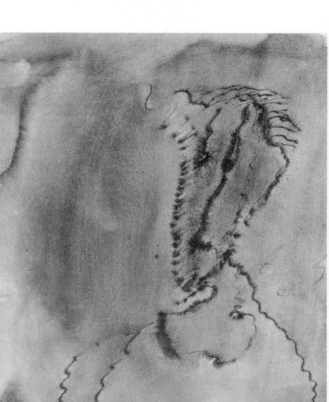

right
126 Henri Michaux
Personnage ton bistre (Person in Sepia), 1946-8. *Pen and wash on paper, 50 x 32*
Musée National d'Art Moderne, Centre Georges Pompidou

127 Henri Michaux
Sans titre (Untitled), 1946. *Watercolour and ink on paper,*
Musée National d'Art Moderne, Centre Georges Pompidou

128 Henri Michaux
Personnage sur fond sepia (Person on Sepia Ground), 1948. *Watercolour on paper, 24 x 30*
Musée National d'Art Moderne, Centre Georges Pompidou

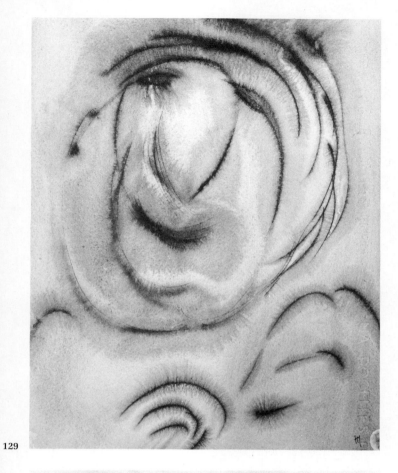

129

130

131

132

142

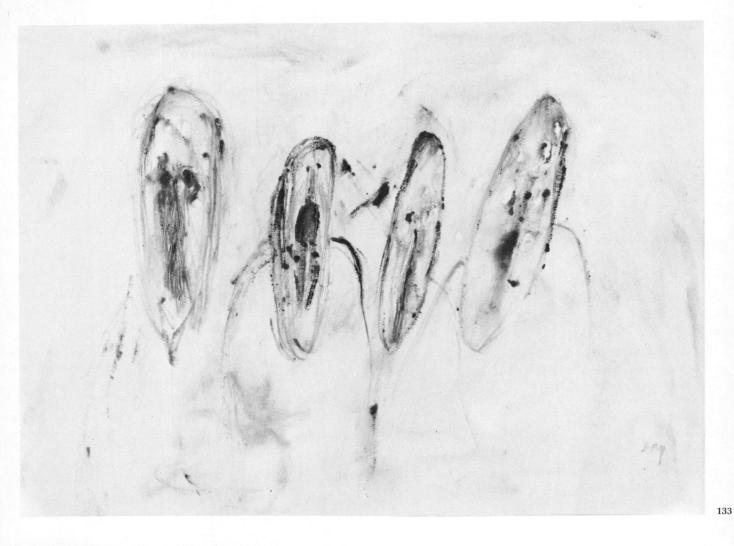

and determined to proceed with calm, but either the blotting-paper soaks up the ink too quickly or an unforeseen blot has formed, or an accident of a material nature — whatever it is, the madness (one of my propensities although I respect it in everyday life), the madness, then, of watching the paper soak up the ink too quickly, or the blot making me deviate from my original design, this madness calls up in me almost at once the echo of thousands of madnesses stemming from my none-too-happy past. The repercussions soon criss-cross with new "material mistakes" that I make in my annoyance, and the crossings-out I just can't help. Immense repercussions, now extending everywhere.'

Henri Michaux, *Peintures et Dessins*, Editions du Point du Jour, Paris 1946.

129 Henri Michaux
Figure jaune (Yellow Figure), 1948. *Watercolour on paper, 24 x 32*
Musée National d'Art Moderne, Centre Georges Pompidou

130 Henri Michaux
Sans titre (Untitled), no date. *Watercolour and ink on paper, 50 x 32*
Musée National d'Art Moderne, Centre Georges Pompidou

131 Henri Michaux
Sans titre (Untitled), 1948. *Watercolour and ink on paper, 32 x 24*
Private collection

132 Henri Michaux
Sans titre (Untitled), 1948. *Watercolour and ink on paper, 50 x 32*
Private collection

133 Henri Michaux
Sans titre (Untitled), 1949. *Watercolour and ink on paper, 38 x 54.*
Musée National d'Art Moderne, Centre Georges Pompidou

FRANCIS PICABIA

b 1879, Paris, d 1953, Paris

Immensely talented, intelligent and paradoxical, Francis Picabia saw the history of modern art unfold, from Impressionism to the post-war period. Deliberately provocative as playboy, dandy, virtuoso and wit, his intellectual curiosity was never satisfied, and he could at any moment turn accepted ideas about painting on their head, with his works — or his personal conduct. A brilliant exponent of Impressionism, his most successful period was between 1897 and 1909. It was at this time that he married Gabrielle Buffet, and designed his first large abstract canvases. In 1911 he met Marcel Duchamp and Guillaume Apollinaire, who included his work in the Orphism movement. Picabia became a member of the Puteaux group, exhibited with the Section d'Or group and, in 1913, participated in the huge Armory Show in New York. Here he met the photographer Alfred Steiglitz, and collaborated with him on *Camera Work* and *291*. From 1914 to 1916 he lived in New York where he exhibited his first 'mechanical' works; 1917 saw him in Barcelona, where he published *391*, then after brief periods in New York and Paris, he went to Zurich, where in 1919 he met Tristan Tzara. All the Dadaists at the time published in *Dada* and *391*, and Picabia, who had got to know André Breton, organised shows of Dada in Paris with Tristan Tzara, and published the review *Cannibale*. In 1921, Picabia left the Dada movement, and began his series of 'Monstres'. In 1925 he created a series 'Transparences', and exhibited them at the Galerie T. Briant in Paris in 1928.

In 1924 he had created *Relâche* for the Swiss ballet, and *Entr'acte* for the film producer René Clair. He presented *Ciné Sketch* with Marcel Duchamp at the Théâtre du Champs-Elysées. He was involved with the International Exhibitions of Surrealism in New York (1936), Mexico (1940) and Paris (1947). From the 1920s onwards, Picabia had a home on the Côte d'Azur, and during the Occupation he lived there, painting deliberately vulgar and commercial canvases, inspired by the kitsch of picture postcards and cinema posters. This 'anti-cultural' position was soon abandoned, however, and returning to Paris in 1945, he re-established his notoriety and influence. He had many exhibitions of work done in his new

134 Francis Picabia
Le masque et le miroir (Mask and Mirror), c.1930-45. *Oil on wood, 85 x 70*
Musée National d'Art Moderne, Centre Georges Pompidou, gift of Henri Goetz

XXVII Francis Picabia
Egoisme (Egoism), 1947-50. *Oil on canvas, 153.5 x 110.8*
Private collection

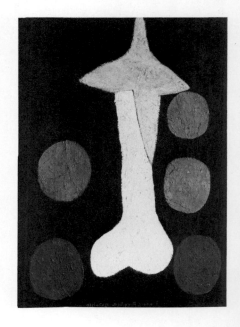

XXXI Maria Helena Vieira da Silva
La Bibliothèque (The Library), 1948. *Oil on canvas, 114.5 x 147.5*
Musée National d'Art Moderne, Centre Georges Pompidou

XXXII Sam Francis
Other White, 1952. *Oil on canvas, 205 x 180*
Musée National d'Art Moderne, Centre Georges Pompidou

'sur-réaliste' and abstract style, and participated in spirit with painters much younger than himself: he figured in the exhibition 'H.W.P.S.M.T.B.', for example, at the Galerie Colette Allendy in 1948. Picabia's recognition was complete after the State purchased 'Udnie' in 1948, and the Galerie René Drouin held a retrospective in 1949.   G.V.

'We only want a painting that may be a means of exchange of our sensibilities in the purest state, that may be the expression of what is the truest of our interior being. That is why there can be nothing figurative in this painting, because it is no longer an exploration of an external world but a more and more profound contact with an interior universe . . . For myself personally, I experience an imperious need for a dematerialisation of the universe in which we live, of this world of machines and formulas . . . Each sees there a different thing, and even something else every day according to the state of his spirit . . . each painting is for me a drama, passing through all the stages of my preceding production, forms, transparencies, super-impositions, in order to carry further and to touch at the end this fleeting but ecstatic instant when I know that I hold the unseizable which is reality.'

Colline, 'Un entretien avec Francis Picabia' in *Journal des Arts*, Zurich November 1945. [Contemporary translation]

JEAN-PAUL RIOPELLE

b 1924, Montreal, Canada

Riopelle was interested in painting and photography at an early age, and in 1939 became a pupil at the Ecole Polytechnique in Montreal. He was deeply impressed by the wild beauty of his native countryside, and his work also showed the influence of an older Canadian painter, Osian Leduc, and the intensity and expressionism of Van Gogh. From 1943 to 1945, he studied at the Montreal Académie des Beaux-Arts and the Ecole du Meuble. It was here that he met Paul-Emile Borduas, with whom he formed the 'automatiste' group. Their first exhibition was held in Montreal in 1946. That same year Riopelle visited New York for the first time and then went to France. He decided to live in Paris in 1947. In June, his Canadian group held the exhibition Automatisme at the Galerie du Luxembourg. He took part in the Exposition Internationale du

135 Jean-Paul Riopelle
Crépusculaire (Twilight), 1953. *Oil on canvas, 130 x 162*
Private collection

Surréalisme at the Galerie Maeght in July and August, and in December he was one of the painters at the L'Imaginaire exhibition organised by Georges Mathieu at the Galerie du Luxembourg. Adopted by the Surrealists, he became friendly with André Breton and Pierre Loeb, and signed Borduas' manifesto, *Refus Global*, in 1948. His first one-man show was held thanks to Nina Dausset at the Galerie du Dragon in May 1949. He was again at Nina Dausset's gallery for the group exhibition Véhémences Confrontées, and had further one-man shows in December 1951 at the Studio Fachetti, in May 1952 at the Galerie Niepce, in May 1953 at the Galerie Craven and the Galerie Pierre, and in December 1954 at the Galerie Rive Droite. His violently gestural painting, covered in splashes and drips, changed around 1952, when he started using a palette knife. Riopelle's 'action painting' now assumed its full forcefulness. With no direct reference to time or nature, and no indication of scale, he involved himself in the act of painting completely, falling into a state of trance, where he — and the spectator — seem to annihilate themselves before a vision of the absolute.   G.V.

SERPAN
(Iaroslav Sossountzov)

b 1922, Prague, Czechoslovakia
d 1976, Spain

Serpan began to write and to paint some time around 1940, during his biological and mathematical studies at university. In 1946, with Yves Bonnefoy, Eliane Cantoni and Claude Tarnaud, he founded *La Révolution la nuit*, a small dissident Surrealist review, which ran for only two numbers. Nevertheless, Serpan joined in various orthodox Surrealist activities, and in 1947, exhibited at the Exposition Internationale du Surréalisme at the Galerie Maeght. It was the year he published his poetry in *Les quatre vents* and *Les deux soeurs*, and met Michel Tapié at the Galerie René Drouin. From biomorphic, 'ectoplasmic' forms influenced by Yves Tanguy, Serpan's work evolved to suggest strange, proliferating growths with faces and devouring mouths in a cellular kind of space that evoked certain types of 'Art Brut', especially during his 'cachemire' period, from 1946-1947. Towards 1949, his painting became totally abstract, a projection of 'automatic' signs in the

136

137

fluid space of an infinite, biological universe. In 1950, Serpan founded the review *Rixes* with Max Clarac Serou and Edouard Jaguer: the contributors to the review were the abstract artists who had been influenced by Surrealism. Serpan's first one-man show was held at the Galerie Breteau in 1951, and Michel Tapié invited him to exhibit in Signifiants de l'Informel (1951-1952) and Un art autre (1952), both of which were held at the Studio Fachetti. With Tapié's support, he held regular exhibitions at the Galerie Stadler after 1955, and in the late 1950s and 1960s became known as one of the 'informel' painters preoccupied with the relationship between 'matière' and sign.　　　　　　　　　　G.V.

'Here we are far removed from the flowerings of painting at its finest. Here, leaving painting far behind us, we aim to reveal the identity of the painter himself, the man as he is. What? Doesn't the quality of the language we speak broadly gauge and determine the quality of our thought? Or even the phenomenal nature of our being? In this respect, out of all the non-semantic languages, the plastic arts are indisputably the most significant; with the additional support of man's everyday language they help (in vain) to bridge the gulf of our inalienable individuality. To force our way into the heart of the painting is to grant ourselves the liberty to enter the inmost regions of the painter's being.'

Iaroslav Serpan: 'Les dimensions de l'aridité, (Propos sur quelques peintures de F. Nieva), 'Numero', May-June 1953, p. 18. (Text written in 1952.)

'And so we can only mark the distance which separates us from all those who, claiming they were Surrealists, were simply tending to lead their revolt back to the exploitation of experiences alone, which one then agreed to treat as "literary" or "artistic". We cannot conceive of the practice of this critique in isolation from our total solidarity with the parties of the revolution. We know that no free man exists in a society where men are subjugated, and that liberty has its roots in daily life, which is subject to economic

136 Iaroslav Serpan
DOWHCH, 1947. *Ink on pasted paper, 146 x 126*
Private collection

137 Iaroslav Serpan
Peeschvercheus, 1949. *Oil on pasted paper, 146 x 126*
Private collection

determinism. We think that the most effective support that Surrealism can bring to the revolutionary cause is to put society's fundamental values on trial again in 1946. Our only regret is to see that militant revolutionaries have not adequately dissociated themselves from these values.'

Yves Bonnefoy, Elian Catoni, Iaroslav Serpan, Claude Tarnaud: *La Révolution la nuit*, no 1.

NICOLAS DE STAËL
b 1914, St Petersburg, Russia,
d 1955, Antibes

Exiled in 1919, de Staël went first to Poland with his family, and was then sent to Brussels. Between 1935 and 1937 he travelled in Spain, Morocco and Italy, before going to live in France in 1938. During the Occupation he was frequently in touch with artists who had taken refuge in the South of France: Arp, Sonia Delaunay, Le Corbusier and Magnelli. In 1949 he met Braque and Lanskoy, both of whom were to have an important influence on his work, and held his first one-man show at the Galerie Jeanne Bucher, where he exhibited again in 1945. In 1946 de Staël signed a contract with Louis Carré, and Jacques Dubourg began to take an interest in his work. Abstract from 1942 onwards, Nicolas de Staël's work began to seem violently expressive in its dynamic handling. The dense, sombre areas of paint pierced with sharp edges of light created a surface of very taut contrasts, such as we see in 'Les Toits', 1952. De Staël's focal position in the new Ecole de Paris evaded all critical classifications. He was at once trying to transpose his experiences into the autonomous language of paint, while using a non-figurative structure based on Cubism, to reaffirm the characteristics of the French tradition.

From 1948 onwards his palette lightened, soon becoming extremely brilliant, and his forms linked together with ample and powerful rhythms. After 1952 fragments of the real world began to show through the paint. The intrusion of figurative presences to his essentially abstract universe posed very serious questions for de Staël. He exhibited at the Galerie Jacques Dubourg in Paris in 1950, then in New York, and at the Mathieson Gallery, London, in 1952, but despite this increasing success, he took his own life at Antibes in 1955. G.V.

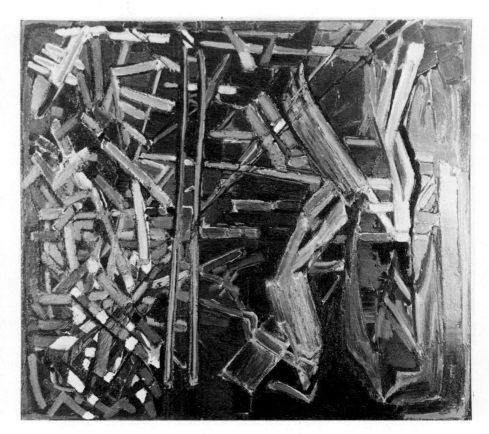

138 Nicolas de Stael
La vie dure (Hard Life), 1946. *Oil on canvas, 142 x 161*
Musée National d'Art Moderne, Centre Georges Pompidou

'In the corner of the bare, uncomfortable room labyrinthine drawings are spread on a stained table. In the middle, big white tin pots filled with colours await the moment, the dip of the paint brush, and the long frenetic hand which will mix and stir, and soon use up all they contain. I say frenetic because at the sight of these liquid pastes the painter, far from taking just a miserly brush-full, heady and elated, gives himself up to excess. The pleasure of painting! A sorcerer's concoctions! Immediately, Nicolas de Staël gets to the essential, what makes a painter a painter: the paint is touched, stirred, transfigured. In the patch of colour, the density of the substance spread in a layer, we imagine him hungry to devour his prey, to tear it into shreds with his teeth, the wild ferocity of a man who, besides, has the distinction of a highly civilised person, and lacking petty everyday morals, shows a great respect for the spiritual realms. From his first paintings onwards we have noticed him build up his work, as Utrillo did in his first landscapes. For Nicolas de Staël,

there's never enough: he applies the paint, he works it a little, and then puts on more. At his studio in Rue Gauget the other day I needed both hands to lift up a little canvas – it was so weighted down with colour.
. . . Nicolas de Staël's painting does not attempt to represent a particular, well-defined object; on the contrary, it is an organic whole which, as we have seen, dispenses with every element of description and the picturesque; it remains aloof from the painting the critics discuss. Staël – and he's right! – doesn't want people to talk to him about 'abstract art'. At the risk of losing an appreciation of different things, and even the possibility of his own evolution, he knows, he senses, that the painter will always need to have before his eyes – near or far away, the visible universe as a moving source of inspiration . . .'

Pierre Courthion, *Preface de l'exposition de Stael*, Montevideo, 1948

BRAM VAN VELDE

b 1895, Zoeterwoude, Holland
d 1981 Grimau

Though from an extremely poor family, both Bram and his brother Geer were to become painters and his sister Jacoba a writer. In 1907 he became apprenticed to a decorating firm, Kramers, where his employer, recognising the talent in some of Bram's naturalistic paintings which were influenced by Breitner, sent him to an artists' colony at Worpswede in North Germany. Here he discovered modernism and like his fellow artists at Worpswede was dominated by Expressionist influences. Although his painting remained figurative, his freedom and directness of attack, and his use of very bright colours, heralded the later abstract works. Leaving Germany in 1924, he settled first in Paris, where he exhibited annually with the Salon des Indépendants and then the Surindépendants, and after passing 1930 in Corsica, he spent from 1932 onwards in Majorca, until forced to leave because of the Spanish Civil War. His works from 1932 to 1940, in which a profound sense of colour animates dynamic abstract forms influenced by Picasso, laid the foundations for his post-war development. From 1940 to 1944 he lived in such abject poverty and depression that he stopped painting almost completely until 1945. In 1946, Edouard Loeb organised an exhibition of Van Velde's works for the opening of the Galerie Mai in Paris. Samuel Beckett hailed him as the sole artist with the rigour and the openness to confront the anxieties of the period. Despite two exhibitions at the Galerie Maeght in 1948 and 1952, and the support of Beckett and Georges Duthuit, it was not until 1958 that Bram van Velde achieved the recognition that was his due, with a retrospective exhibition at the Kunsthalle, Bern.   S.W.

'I have no other claim to introduce **Bram Van Velde** than that of friendship, that I knew him at the moment — devastating for me — when I returned to Paris, that I found hope again only in the presence of this weary man, living in a magnificent poverty. Amid all the remorse which is the only honourable thing we have left, nothing is more rending than the tense silence which surrounded this exceptional man. However fine they might be, the works

139 Bram van Velde
Peinture (Painting), 1947. *Oil on canvas, 130 x 162*
Galerie Maeght, Paris

of art created during these four years of disgrace, not one of them, to my mind, would be able to dominate Bram Van Velde's silence with its message. When one day I asked about the possibility of finally painting a human face, Bram answered "I would be too afraid". Today what can we expect of that mysterious construction, a face, with its monstrous, senseless resources, unlimited in every way? Of this liberation before the unknown?'

Edouard Loeb Invitation to the opening of the Galerie Mai, 21 March 1946

'Bram Van Velde is the first to admit that to be an artist is to fail as no other dare fail, that failure constitutes his universe, and to shrink from it implies desertion, art or craft, a happy household, in short, life. I'm not unaware that all we now need to bring this horrible affair to an acceptable conclusion is to make of this submission, this acceptance, this fidelity to failure, a new opportunity, a new term of the relationship, to make of this impossible and necessary act, an act of expression, be it just of itself, its impossibility, its necessity. And unable to go so far myself, know that I put myself, and perhaps an innocent

with me, into an unenviable situation. For what is this coloured plane which wasn't here before? I don't know, having never seen anything like it. It seems to have no connection with art in any case, if my memories of art are correct.'

Samuel Beckett, from a dialogue with *Georges Duthuit* originally published in *Transition*, 1949.

MARIA HELENA VIEIRA DA SILVA

b 1908, Lisbon

Arriving in Paris in 1928, Vieira da Silva began initially to study sculpture, first with Rodin's pupil, Bourdelle, and then with Charles Despiau. From 1929 onwards, she learnt engraving in William Hayter's studio, while with Fernand Léger and Roger Bissière she began to analyze form using Cubist principles. In 1930 she married the Hungarian painter Arpad Szenes.

Vieira da Silva's interest in applied art soon manifested itself in a series of carpet designs for Dolly Chareau, while in this field the influence of Joachim Torrés Garcia whose work she had first seen at the Galerie Pierre Loeb in 1932 was crucial. With the encouragement of Jeanne Bucher, who exhibited her first works in 1933 and then in 1937, she finally discovered her own style just before World War II. The essence of her work was an exploded concept of space, in which the human figure becomes imprisoned in a fine structural mesh, made up of multitudes of little squares subject to a play of opposing tensions. Inevitably, contemporary events lent a dramatic conviction to this vision of a universe progressively absorbing and annihilating its human element, as for example in 'Les Drapeaux', 1937, 'L'insurrection' 1939, 'La guerre' 1941-2, 'La Partie d'Echecs' 1943, and 'L'Incendie' 1944. During the war years, Vieira da Silva fled first to Portugal, then to Rio de Janiero, where with her husband, she assumed an important role among the Brazilian intelligentsia. She returned to Paris in 1947, and exhibited the same year with the Galerie Jeanne Bucher, while in 1949 and 1951 she had individual shows with the Galerie Pierre. In works such as 'La Bibliothèque' 1949, 'La Pluie' 1949, and 'Le Promeneur invisible' 1951, the space she creates is subject to a more masterly control. The opposing tensions are more integrated within the picture plane, and the paint is applied with a flexibility and subtlety of touch which emphasizes the mysterious lyricism of a universe whose boundaries Vieira da Silva seeks always to enlarge.   G.V.

140 Maria Helena Vieira da Silva
Les joueurs d'échecs (Chess Players), 1943. *Oil on canvas, 81 x 100*
Musée National d'Art Moderne, Centre Georges Pompidou

XXXI Maria Helena Vieira da Silva
La Bibliothèque (The Library), 1948. *Oil on canvas, 114.5 x 147.5*
Musée National d'Art Moderne, Centre Georges Pompidou

WOLS (Alfred Otto Wolfgang Schulze)

b 1913, Berlin, d 1951, Paris

Wols was brought up mainly in Dresden where his authoritarian father was a lawyer and a chancellor of Saxony. His childhood was unhappy and confused, but he was fascinated by botany and geography and was an excellent violinist. After some time as a car mechanic he worked with Leo Frobenius on an anthropological study of the history of music. Wols was for a brief period at the Bauhaus, where Moholy-Nagy gave him introductions to Léger, Arp, Ozenfant and Giacometti. He spent a year in Paris in 1932 and started to paint surrealist and abstract canvases, though he supported himself

as a photographer. After returning to Germany in 1933, he decided to emigrate for good and went to Spain. In 1937 he became the photographer for the Pavillon d'Elégance at the Exposition Internationale in Paris. At the onset of war, Wols suffered the humiliation of internment as a German citizen in six French camps, where he started to drink, and drew his strange and distressing watercolours incessantly by candlelight. Their claustrophobic density, and the overriding theme of imprisonment contrasts with the flying or submarine objects, and the delicate colours. The period after his liberation at Cassis and at Dieulefit (1940-2) was relatively happy and productive. Back in Paris, in 1945, an exhibition was held at the Galerie René Drouin, its catalogue crammed

with poems and aphorisms by Wols himself and his chosen philosophers – Lao Tseu, Tchouang-Tseu, the Bhagavad-Gita, Ecclesiasticus, Poe, Maeterlinck and many French writers.

His oil paintings, begun after the war, are symbols of explosion and disintegration, disturbingly ambivalent in their reference at once to external and internal worlds, the cosmic and the life of the microscope, the nerves, the sex, the brain; yet their sensitive use of often brilliant colour and the violent working of the paint in its trickles and scratches, make Wols perhaps the greatest of the 'informel' painters. Hounded by the authorities, living in poverty, creating in anguish for himself and no other, dying an alcoholic at thirty-eight in 1951, Wols was seen, at the time and afterwards, as the 'existentialist' artist par excellence.
                                  S.W.

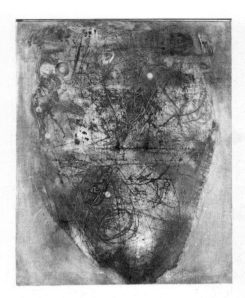

XXIX Wols
Sans titre (Untitled), 1947. *Oil on canvas,*
61 x 50
Private collection

141 Wols
Peinture (Painting), 1944-5. *Oil 81 x 81.5*
Museum of Modern Art, New York

142 Wols
Manhattan, 1948-9. *Oil on canvas, 146 x 97*
Private collection

'Objects shouldn't touch for they don't live: And yet they touch me: It's unbearable. I'm afraid of their coming into contact with me!'

Jean-Paul Sartre, *Wols*, Galerie René Drouin, 1945.

'The least phenomenon of nature for the wise man becomes an inexhaustible matter for reflection.'

Lautréamont, *Wols*, 1945.

'What does Wols do?
He lets himself plunge into the depths of his own being like a diver, and his hand sketches all that he sees:
Spiders webs, grasses, forests of seaweed, monsters, molluscs, Russian village-mountains, arks, islands, butcher-jewellers' shops, attractions fissures, focuses of fear.
All that and so much more.
He arranges his visions in a state of crisis.
I'm grateful to him for diving down and showing us his catch.
When, hunched in his bed, he takes up his thin pen and his gouaches, Wols doesn't know what he's going to draw.

While he's drawing he doesn't know what he's drawing.
When he's finished, he looks, and he doesn't know what he has done.
Of course you sometimes recognise towns and objects, but that's beside the point.
It's his prayer, his ecstasy, his malice which are the point.
. . . His love, his gratitude, his hate eddy together and make drawings.
The Beautiful, the Hideous disappear.
A hymn to Unity remains.

H.P. Roche, *Wols*, 1945.

. . . 'With the change in medium to oils however, Wols' universe changes and adapts, finds a resistance in this new technique which leads him on to more complex inventions. The minutiae disappear first of all. His style becomes more brutal, more disordered, colour and texture are used as hazard dictates. This time the drawing is often scratched or incised into the paint. But there is an underlying organisation of forms, which, finally, is extraordinarily present. It is rare to encounter such

proliferation and such equilibrium at once. Lines and colours irradiate and project outwards according to precise components of force. The tones are generally quite muted, blended, unobtrusive, and this doubtless to prevent anything from coming to distract us from what is happening, in the crucible of the painting, so that we are left entirely free to participate in the drama.'

René Guilly, *Wols*. Galerie René Drouin, 1947.

List of Artists

Roman numerals indicate colour plates
and bold numerals black and white
illustrations.

Photo Credits

pp 2-3: **MECV:** St Lô 1945
p 6: **Robert Doisneau:** L'Air d'Arceuil, 1945
p 8: **Willi Ronis:** L'Existentialisme, 1951
p 25: **Henri Cartier Bresson:** Matisse, Vence, 1944
p 43: **René Jacques:** Zone, La porte de Clignancourt, 1945
p 73: **Izis:** Impasse Traine, 1949
p 117: **Roaul Ubac:** La Nebuleuse, Brûlage, 1939
p 152: **Doisneau:** Valse du 14 Juillet 1949

Chronology

This chronology lists the events and activities for each year of *Aftermath* under the following categories: political events, new books **B**, films **F**, plays **P** and music **M** published or performed, major group exhibitions, one-man shows, and other events in the visual arts. Gallery and museum names are abbreviated (MNAM: Musée national d'art moderne).

For a more complete chronology, see the one compiled by Mme Annick Lionel-Marie in the PARIS-PARIS catalogue, pp 502-6.

1944

Allied landings in Normandy in June, Paris liberated in August. French provisional government is formed. French women obtain the vote for the first time.

P ANOUILH *Antigone*
B MESSAIEN *Technique de mon langage musical*
M BARTOK *Sonata for Solo Violin*
STRAVINSKY *Babel*
BRITTEN *Peter Grimes*

First exhibition by Front national des artistes.
Salon de la Libération *Gd Palais*
Maîtres et jeunes de l'art independant *Galerie de France*
Art abstrait *Berri-Raspail*
Dix peintres subjectifs *Galerie de France*
Peintures abstraits *L'Esquisse*

Vasarely *Denise René*

Commission de récuperation artistique formed. Death of Kandinsky. Galerie Denise René opens. The magazine Labyrinthe founded.

1945

Yalta conference. End of the war in Europe in May and in the Far East in September. Beginnings of nationalisation in France and Britain where the Labour Party wins the general election. In France, General de Gaulle becomes President and Marshal Petain is put on trial. In the USA, Roosevelt dies and is succeeded by Truman. In Germany, the Nuremberg trials begin.

B MERLEAU-PONTY *La Phénoménologie de la Perception*
MICHAUX *Epreuves, exorcismes*
PREVERT *Paroles*
SARTRE *Les chemins de la liberté*
F BRESSON *Les Dames du bois de Boulogne*
CARNÉ *Les Enfants du Paradis*
MALRAUX *L'Espoir*
M POULENC *Les Mamelles de Tirésias*
STRAUSS *Métamorphoses*

Sculptures d'aujourdhui *Drouin*
1er Salon de Mai *Maurs*
Naissance de la tragedie *Berri-Raspail*
Le Cubisme 1911-18 *Galerie de France*
Valeurs de France, plaidoyer pour l'art figuratif *Berri Raspail*
Art concret *Drouin*
Picasso & Matisse *Victoria & Albert Museum, London*

Matisse *Maeght*, Brassaï *Renou et Colle*, Fautrier *Drouin*, Wols *Drouin*

Death of Paul Valery. Sartre founds the review Les Temps Modernes. Galerie Maeght opens. Foundation of the review Arts de France.

1946

First session of the UNO opens in London. In France, General de Gaulle resigns. Despite the adoption, by referendum, of the constitution of the IVth Republic later in the year, this leads to a series of temporary and unstable coalition governments, between left and centre, that lasts until 1958. Start of the war in Indochina.

B ADAMOV *L'Aveu*
ARTAUD *Lettres de Rodez*
GENET *Les Bonnes*
ELUARD *Poésie ininterrompue*
SARTRE *L'existentialisme est un humanisme*
F Cocteau, *La Belle et la bête*, Clement, *La Bataille du rail*
M BOULEZ *1st Sonata*
CAGE *16 sonatas*
HONEGGER *4th Symphony*

Art et résistance *MNAM*
Oeuvres de malades mentaux *Hopital St Anne*
1er Salon des Réalites nouvelles *Palais des Beaux Arts*
L'Art contemporain français *Musée du Luxembourg*
Chefs d'oeuvres retrouvés en Allemagne *Orangerie*
Le noir est un couleur *Maeght*
Sur quatre murs *Maeght*
Peintures abstraites *Denise René*
Cubisme et art concret *Allendy*

Artaud drawings *Pierre*, Bonnard *Berheim Jeune*, Balthus *Galerie des Arts*, van Velde *Mai*

André Fougeron wins the Prix national des arts. Death of Gertrude Stein. Cahiers de la Pleiade first published. Tate Gallery partially re-opened after wartime damage.

1947

Establishment of the Marshall Plan and the IMF. Communist ministers forced to resign from French government. Independence of India and Pakistan. Partition of Palestine approved by UN.

B ARTAUD *Van Gogh, le suicidé de la societé*
CAMUS *La Peste*
MALRAUX *Le Musée Imaginaire*
QUENEAU *Exercices de style*
F AUTANT-LARA *Le Diable au corps*
CARNÉ *Les Portes de la Nuit*
CLAIR *Le Silence est d'or*
CLOUZOT *Quai des orfèvres*
M BRITTEN *Albert Herring*
SCHONBERG *Un survivant de Varsovie*

Exposition Internationale du surréalisme *Maeght*
Les mains éblouiés *Maeght*
L'imaginaire *Luxembourg*
Sur quatre murs *Maeght*
Automatisme *Galerie du Luxembourg*
Peintures abstraits *Denise René*
25 ans d'art sacré française *Galliera*

Hartung *Conti*, Chagall *MNAM*, Chaissac *Arc en Ciel*, Artaud *Pierre Loeb*, Miro *Pierre Matisse, New York*, Matta *Drouin*, Bissière *Drouin*, Atlan *Maeght*, Bellmer *Galerie du Luxembourg*

Pierre Bonnard and Albert Marquet die. Le Corbusier builds his first Unité d'habitation in Marseilles. Official opening of the MNAM in Paris. First Avignon Festival includes exhibition of contemporary art.

1948

Assassination of Ghandi. Communist takeover in Czechoslovakia. Blockage of Berlins begins. The Hague Congress on Europe. Creation of the State of Israel.

P BECKETT *Murphy*
B CENDRARS *Bourlinguer*
CHAMSON *La Suite cévenole*
JOUHANDEAU *Scènes de la vie conjugale*
SARTRE *Les Mains sales*
F COCTEAU *Les Parents terribles*
CHRISTIAN-JACQUE *La Chartreuse de Parme*
LEENHARDT *Les Dernières Vacances*
M BOULEZ *Le Soleil des Eaux*
MESSIAEN *Turangalila Symphony*
SCHAEFFER *Concert de bruits*
STRAVINSKY *Mass*

Les Mains éblouiés *Maeght*
HWPSMTB *Colette Allendy*
Tendences de l'art abstrait *Denise René*
Blanc et Noir *des Deux Iles*
l'Homme Témoin *Bac*
Prise de terre *Breteau*
Le Cadavre exquis: son exaltation *Dausset*
Tendences de l'art abstrait *Denise René*

Miro *Maeght*, van Velde *Maeght*, Picasso *Maison de la Pensée Française* – also in *1949, 1950*

Death of Francis Gruber. The COBRA group is formed, as is the Compagnie de l'art brut. Foundation of the review Critique.

1949

The Council of Europe is formed, as is COMECON and Nato. Berlin Blockade lifted. Adenauer becomes the first Chancellor of the new German Federal Republic. Devaluation of sterling and other European currencies.

B ARAGON *Les Communistes*
DE BEAUVOIR *Le Deuxième Sexe*
GENET *Le Journal du voleur*
SEUPHOR *L'Art abstrait, ses origines, ses premiers maîtres*
PICON *Panorama de la novelle littérature française*
F CLOUZOT *Manon*
DAQUIN *Le Point du jour*
TATI *Jour de fête*
M BOULEZ *Livre pour quattuor*
MESSIAEN *Quatre etudes de rythme*
SCHAEFFER & HENRI *Symphonie pour un homme seul.*

Les Mains éblouiés *Maeght*
L'Art brut prefere aux arts culturels *Drouin*
1er Salon de la jeune sculpture *Musée Rodin*
Eloquence de la ligne *des Deux Iles*
Les premiers maîtres de l'art abstrait *Maeght*

Hartung *Hanover Gallery, London – also in 1951,* Matisse *MNAM,*
Picabia *Drouin,* Vieira da Silva *Pierre – also in 1951.*

Penwith Society in St Ives holds its first exhibition. Art d'Aujourd'hui first published.

1950

Wave of strikes in France in March. In July, the USA intervenes in fighting in Korea.

B AYMÉ *Clérambard*
CAMUS *Les Justes*
CHAR *Les Matinaux*
DURAS *Une Barrage contre le Pacifique*
JOUVE *Ode*
P IONESCO *La Cantatrice chauve*
F CARNÉ *La Marie du port*
CLAIR *La Beauté du diable*
COCTEAU *Orphée*
OPHULS *La Ronde*
M AURIC *Phèdre*
POULENC *Stabat Mater, Jazz Plastique (First Salon de Jazz)*

Aspects de l'art d'aujourdhui *Denise René*
D'une saison à une autre *Colette Allendy*
Espaces nouveaux *Denise René*
Les Madis *Allendy*
Art sacré *MNAM*

Miro *Maeght,* Fernandez *Pierre,* de Staël *Jacques Dubourg,* Léger *Tate Gallery*

Le Corbusier builds the Chapelle Notre Dame du Haut at Ronchamps. Picasso awarded the Lenin Peace Prize.

1951

Churchill and the Conservatives win the General Election in Britain. Ceasefire in Korea. Unified European coal and steel pool approved.

B GIONO *Le Hussard sur le toit*
MALRAUX *Les Voix du Silence*
SARTRE *Le Diable et le Bon Dieu*
YOURCENAR *Les Mémoires d'Hadrien*
GRACQ *Le Rivage des Syrtes*
MONTHERLAUT *La Ville dont le prince est un enfant*
F BRESSON *Le journal d'un curé de campagne*
CIAMPI *Un grand patron*
M DUTILLEUX *1st Symphony*
STOCKHAUSEN *Kreuzspiel*
STRAVINSKY *The Rake's Progress*

1er Salon de Peintres Témoins de leur temps *Musée d'art moderne de la ville de Paris*
Cobra *Librarie 73*
Véhémences confrontées *Nina Dausset*
Signifiants de l'informel *Fachetti*
L'Art et la Paix *Lyons*
Presences 1951 *Denise René*
5 Peintres de Cobra *Pierre*
Formes et couleurs murales *Denise René*
La Fauvisme *MNAM*

Serpan *Breteau,* Villon *MNAM,* Laurens *MNAM,* Picasso in Provence *New Burlington Galleries*
Death of Andre Gide and of Wols. The collection of the Compagnie de l'Art Brut sent to the USA. Festival of Britain in London.

1952

Accession of Queen Elizabeth II on death of George VI. Eisenhower elected President of USA. French assembly adopts the Pinay plan. King Farouk of Egypt abdicates.

P BECKETT *Waiting for Godot*
B DURAS *Le Marin de Gibraltar*
SARTRE *St Genet*
TAPIE *Un Art Autre*
F BECKER *Casque d'or*
CAYATTE *Nous sommes tous des assassins*
CLAIR *Belles de nuit*
CLEMENT *Jeux interdits*
DUVIVIER *Le Petit monde de Don Camillo*
CHRISTIAN-JACQUE *Fanfan-la-tulipe*
M CAGE *Concerto*
POULENC *Four Christmas motets*

Les Peintres de la Nouvelle Ecole de Paris *Babylon*
Signifiants de l'informel II *Fachetti*
Une art autre *Fachetti*
Regards sur la peinture americain *Galerie de France*
La Jeune gravure contemporain *NMAM*
L'oeuvre du XXéme siècle *MNAM*

Rouault *MNAM,* de Stael *Mathiesen Gallery, London,* van Velde *Maeght,* Doucet *Ariel*

Death of Paul Eluard. Andre Breton opens the Galerie A l'Etoile scellée.

1953

Death of Stalin. In Indochina, build-up to the battle of Diem Bien Phu. Mendès-France fails to form a new French government.

B ANOUILH *L'Alouette*
BARTHES *Le Degré zéro de l'écriture*
KLOSSOWSKI *Roberte, ce soir*
LEBEL (ed) *Premier Bilan de l'art actuel*
ROBBE-GRILLET *Les Gommes*
SARRAUTE *Martereau*
VIAN *L'Arrache-Coeur*
F CLOUZOT *Le Salaire de la peur*
CARNÉ *Therese Raquin*
TATI *Les Vacances de Monsieur Hulot*
M JOLIVET *1st Symphony*
HONEGGER *Cantique de Noel*

12 peintres et sculpteurs américains contemporains *MNAM*
Salon d'Octobre *Craven*
Le Cubisme *MNAM*
Unknown Political Prisoner *ICA, London*
Parallel of Life and Art *ICA*
Lam *Maeght,* Miro *Maeght*

Francis Picabia dies. The magazine Cimaise & United States Line Paris Review (ed. Georges Mathieu) first published.

1954

Battle of Dien Bien Phu ends Indochina war. Following troubles in Tunisia and Morocco, war breaks out in Algeria. Nasser becomes leader of Egypt. Declaration of the People's Republic of China. In France, Abbé Pierre campaigns for the homeless, and Mendès-France becomes Prime Minister. Scheme for development of Barbican site in London proposed.

B DE BEAUVOIR *Les Mandarins*
LÉAUTAUD *Journal littéraire*
MAURIAC *L'Agneau*
MONTHERLANT *Port-Royal*
SAGAN *Bonjour Tristesse*
F AUTANT-LARA *Le Rouge et le noir*
CLÉMENT *M. Ripois*
CLOUZOT *Les Diaboliques*
GREMILLON *L'Amour d'une femme*
M MARTINET *Trois Mouvements symphoniques*
NONO *La Victoire de Guernica*
VARÈSE *Déserts*
Pierre Boulez founds the Concerts du Domaine Musicale

Phases *Fachetti*
Divergences: nouvelle situation *Arnaud*
Situations de la peinture d'aujourdhui *Ariel*
Le dessin contemporain aux Etats Unis *MNAM*
L'Ecole de Paris *Charpentier*
1er Salon de la sculpture abstraite *Denise Rene*

Kemeny *Fachetti,* Michaux *Drouin,* Rebeyrolle *Marlborough, London,* Pignon *Maison de la Pensée Française*

André Derain, Henri Matisse and Henri Laurens die.

Bibliography

GENERAL

Catalogues

Paris-Paris, créations en France, 1937-1957, Centre Georges Pompidou, Paris, *May-November* 1981, *Director: Germain Viatte*. German edition, Prestel Verlag, Munich, 1981. *Westkunst, Zeitgenossische Kunst seit 1939*, Messehalle, Cologne, *May-August* 1981, *Director Laslo Glozer*. Du Mont Buchverlag, Cologne.

ALOISE – see ART BRUT

ANONYMOUS – see ART BRUT

KAREL APPEL

Catalogues

Appel Studio Paul Fachetti, Paris, 1954. (Preface by Michel Tapié). *Karel Appel*, Stedelijk Museum, Amsterdam, 1955. (Introduction by Michel Tapié).

Monographs

Christian Dotremont, *Appel* Eds. Ejnar Munksgaard, Bibliothèque de Cobra no. 3, Copenhagen, 1950. Hugo Claus, *Karel Appel, painter*, Harry N. Abrams, New York 1962. (Preface by Herbert Read). Peter Bellew, *Karel Appel* Fratelli Fabbri, Milan, 1968. Alfred Frankenstein, *Karel Appel*, Harry N. Abrams, New York 1980.

ANTONIN ARTAUD

Catalogues

Portraits et Dessins, Antonin Artaud, Galerie Pierre Loeb, June 1947. *Antonin Artaud, 1896-1948, Dessins*, Musée de l'Abbaye Sainte-Croix, July-September 1980. (Preface by Henry Claude Cousseau, with complete bibliography to 1980).

Other

Antonin Artaud, *Artaud le Momo*, Editions Bordas, Paris 1947. It includes eight original drawings and the poem 'L'Exécration du Père-Mère'. Antonin Artaud, *Oeuvres Complètes*, N.R.F. Gallimard, Paris, 1956.

ART BRUT

Catalogues

Exposition des oeuvres exécutées par des malades mentaux, Centre Psychiatrique de Sainte-Anne, Paris, 1946. (Preface by Waldemar George). *L'ArtBrut préféré aux Arts Culturels*, Galerie René Drouin, Paris, 1949. (Preface by Jean Dubuffet). *Outsiders*, Arts Council of Great Britain, Hayward Gallery, London 1979.

Books

L'Art Brut, Fascicules de la Compagnie de l'Art Brut nos. 1-10, Paris, 1964 – Lausanne, 1977. Edited by Jean Dubuffet. Roger Cardinal, *Outsider Art*, Studio Vista, London, 1972. Michel Thévoz *l'Art Brut*, Albert Skira, Geneva, 1975.

JEAN-MICHEL ATLAN

Catalogues

Atlan, Oeuvres récentes, Galerie Maeght, Paris 1947, with an introduction by Jacques Kober. *Atlan*, Musée National d'Art Moderne, Paris, January 1963, with a preface by Jean Cassou. *Atlan*, Musée National d'Art Moderne, Centre Georges Pompidou, Paris, January 1980.

Monographs

Michel Ragon, *Atlan*, Eds Ejnar Munksgaard. Bibliothèque de Cobra no. 4, Copenhagen 1950. André Verdet, *Atlan*, Musée de Poche, Eds Georges Fall, Paris 1957. Michel Ragon, *Atlan*, Eds Georges Fall, Paris 1962. Bernard Dorival, *Atlan*, Eds Pierre Tisné 1962.

Other

Atlan, *Le Sang Profond*, Editions L'Atelier de la Salamandre, Paris 1944. Franz Kafka, *Description d'un Combat*, with lithographs by Atlan, Eds Maeght, Paris 1946. Saint-Juste, *Pour la défense de Robespierre*, lithographs by Atlan, with a note by Jacques Kober, Eds Réclame, Paris 1949.

BALTHUS

Catalogues

Balthus, Pierre Matisse Gallery, New York, 1949. *Balthus*, Musée des Arts Décoratifs, Paris, 1966. *Balthus*, Tate Gallery, London, 1968. *Balthus* Eds. La Biennale di Venezia, Venice, 1980.

Monographs

Jean Leymarie, *Balthus, dessins et aquarelles* Galerie Claude Bernard, 1971, Eds. du Chêne, Paris, 1976. *Balthus, paintings and drawings*, 1934-1977, preface by Frederico Fellini, New York 1977. Jean Leymarie, *Balthus* Albert Skira, Geneva, 1978.

HANS BELLMER

Catalogues

Hans Bellmer, Dessins 1935-1946, Galerie du Luxembourg, Paris, 1947. (Preface by Joe Bosquet). *Bellmer*, Galerie Daniel Cordier, Paris, 1963. (Text by Patrick Waldberg). *Hans Bellmer*, Cnac Archives, Paris, 1971 (on the occasion of an exhibition at the Centre National d'Art Contemporain).

Monographs

André Pierre de Mandiargues, Nora Mitrani, Gisèle Prassinos, Jehan Mayoux, Jean Brun, Jacques de Caso, Yves Bonnefoy, *Hans Bellmer, vingt-cinq reproductions, 1934-1950*, 1950. Alain Jouffroy, *Hans Bellmer*, William and Nora Copley foundation, Chicago, n.d., Lund Humphries, London 1959. Constantin Jelenski, *Les Dessins de Hans Bellmer*, Eds Denoel, Paris 1966. Sarane Alexandrian, *Hans Bellmer*, Eds. Filipacchi, 1971. Ed. Roger Borderie 'Bellmer', special number of the review *Obliques*, Eds. Borderie, Nyons 1975. André Pierre de Mandiargues, *Le Trésor cruel de Hans Bellmer*, Eds. Le Sphinx, Belgium 1979.

Other

Hans Bellmer: *La Petite Anatomie de l'Inconscient Physique, ou l'Anatomie de l'Image*, (1941-1945), Editions le Terrain Vague, Paris 1957 and 1978.

ROGER BISSIÈRE

Catalogues

Bissière, Galerie René Drouin, Paris 1947, *Bissière*, Musée des Arts Décoratifs, Paris, 1966.

PIERRE BONNARD

Catalogues

Pierre Bonnard, Royal Academy of Arts, London, 1966. *Pierre Bonnard, Centenaire de sa naissance*, Orangerie des Tuileries, Paris, 1967.

Monographs

Antoine Terrasse, *Bonnard*, Albert Skira, Geneva, 1964. Jean Clair, *Bonnard*, Henri Screpel, Paris, 1975.

GEORGES BRAQUE

Catalogues

Georges Braque: Tate Gallery, London 1956 *Georges Braque:* Orangerie des Tuileries, Paris 1973-1974

Monographs

Douglas Cooper: *Braque, paintings 1909-1947*. Lindsay Drummond, London 1948. John Russell: *Georges Braque*, Phaidon, New York – 1959.

BRASSAI

Catalogues

Language of the Wall, Parisian graffiti, photographed by Brassai, Museum of Modern Art, New York, 1956, and Institute of Contemporary Arts, London 1958 (Preface by Roland Penrose). *Brassai*, Bibliothèque Nationale Paris, 1963. *Brassai*,

Museum of Modern Art, New York, 1968. (Introduction by Lawrence Durrell).

Books by Brassai

Les sculptures de Picasso, Eds. du Chêne, Paris 1948, London 1949. *Brassai*, Eds. Neufs, Paris, 1952 (Introduction by Henry Miller). *Graffiti*, Chr. Belser Verlag, Stuttgart, published in English, 1960, and in French, Editions du Temps, Paris 1961. *Conversations avec Picasso*, Gallimard, Paris, 1964.

VICTOR BRAUNER

Catalogues

Victor Brauner Paintings from 1932 to 1958, Richard L, Feigen & Co., Chicago 1959. (Texts by Brauner and their translation accompany each painting). *Victor Brauner*, Musée National d'Art Moderne, Paris June 1972. (With an essay by Dominique Bozo). *Les Dessins de Victor Brauner au Musée National d'Art Moderne*, Centre Georges Pompidou, 1975 (Preface by Dominique Bozo).

Monographs

Alain Jouffroy, *Victor Brauner*, Musée de Poche, Georges Fall, Paris 1959. Sarane Alexandrian, *Victor Brauner, l'Illuminateur*, Cahiers d'Art, Paris 1954.

CAMILLE BRYEN

Catalogues

Camille Bryen, Galerie des Deux Iles, Paris 1949. (Preface by Jacques Audiberti). *Camille Bryen*, Musée National d'Art Moderne, Paris, 1973. (Preface by Jean Leymarie).

Monographs

R.V. Gindertael, *Bryen*, Raymonde Cazenave, Paris, 1960. Yvon Taillander, (preface) *Carte blanche a Bryen* Librarie Connaître, Paris, 1964. Daniel Abadie, *Bryen abhomme*, Eds. La Conaissance, Brussels, 1973.

BERNARD BUFFET

Catalogues

Cent Tableaux de 1944 à 1958 par Bernard Buffet, Galerie Charpentier, Paris 1958. Bernard Buffet, *Les Horreurs de la Geurre*, Eds. Orfea, Paris 1955.

Monographs

Jean Giono, *Bernard Buffet*, Fernand Hazan, Paris, 1956. Pierre Berger, *Bernard Buffet*, Eds. Pierre Cailler, Geneva 1958.

MARC CHAGALL

Catalogues

Marc Chagall, Tate Gallery, London, 1948.

Marc Chagall, Musée des Arts Décoratifs, Paris, 1959. *Hommage à Marc Chagall*, Grand Palais, Paris, 1969-1970.

GASTON CHAISSAC

Catalogues

Gaston Chaissac, Musée National d'Art Moderne, Paris 1973. *Gaston Chaissac, 1910-1964*, Galerie des Ponchettes et de la Marine, Nice 1976. *Gaston Chaissac, 1910-1964*, Cahiers de l'Abbaye Ste-Croix no. 29, Les Sables d'Olonnes, 1978-9 (Introduction by Henry Claude Cousseau).

Monographs

Anatole Jakovsky, *Gaston Chaissac, l'homme-orchestre*, Presses Littéraires de France, Paris 1952: Dominique Allan Michaud, *Gaston Chaissac, puzzle pour un homme seul*, Gallimard, Paris 1974. Henry Claude Cousseau, *Gaston Chaissac, 'cordonnier in partibus'*, Jacques Damase éditeur, Paris 1981.

CONSTANT

Catalogues

Constant, Stedlijk Museum, Amsterdam, 1978.

Monographs

Christian Dotremont, *Constant*, Eds. Ejnar Munksgaard, Bibliothèque de Cobra no 6, Copenhagen, 1950. Pierre Cailler, *Constant*, Eds. Pierre Cailler, Les Cahiers d'Art Documents, no. 54, Geneva 1957, Van Haaren, *Constant*, Amsterdam, 1967.

CORNEILLE

Catalogues

Corneille, Galerie Colette Allendy, Paris, 1954. (Preface by Charles Estienne). *Corneille*, Stedelijk Museum, Amsterdam, 1956. (Text by Edouard Jaguer.) *Retrospective Corneille*, Charleroi, Palais des Beaux Arts, 1974. (Preface by Christian Dotremont).

Monographs

Christian Dotremont, *Corneille*, Eds. Ejnar Munksgaard, Bibliotheque de Cobra, 1950. Jean Clarence Lambert, *Corneille* Eds. Georges Fall, Musée de Poche, Paris 1966.

FLEURY-JOSEPH CREPIN — see ART BRUT

JACQUES DOUCET

Monographs

Jean Laude, *Jacques Doucet*, Eds. Ejnar Munksgaard, Bibliothèque de Cobra, Copenhagen 1950. René Passeron, *Jacques Doucet*, Galerie Dina Vierny, Paris 1973.

JEAN DUBUFFET

Catalogues

Catalogue intégral des travaux de Jean Dubuffet – Catalogue raisonné by Max Loreau, vols. 1-21, Eds. J.J. Pauvert, Paris, 1964-1968, Eds. Weber, Paris, 1968-1971. *Jean Dubuffet 1942-1960*, Musée des Arts Décoratifs, Paris, 1960. *Jean Dubuffet, a retrospective*, The Solomon R. Guggenheim Foundation, New York, 1973. *Dubuffet retrospektive*, Academie der Kunste, Berlin, 1980.

Monographs

Georges Limbour, *Tableau bon levain à vous de cuire la pâte, l'Art Brut de Jean Dubuffet*, Eds. René Drouin, Paris and Pierre Matisse, New York, 1953. Daniel Cordier, *Les Dessins de Jean Dubuffet*, Eds. Ditis, Paris, 1960. Max Loreau, *Delits, Deportements, Lieux de haut jeu*, Weber, Lausanne, 1971. Gaeton Picon, *Le travail de Jean Dubuffet*, Albert Skira, Geneva, 1973.

Books illustrated by Dubuffet

Francis Ponge, *Matière et Mémoire, ou les lithographies à l'école*, Eds. Fernand Mourlot, Paris, 1945. Eugène Guillevic, *Les Murs*, Eds. Du Livre, Paris, 1950. Jean Paulhan, *La Métromanie, ou les dessous de la Capitale*, Ed. by the authors, Paris, 1950.

Other

Jean Dubuffet, *Prospectus et tous écrits suivants*, writings compiled and presented by Hubert Damisch, Gallimard, Paris, 1967. *Jean Dubuffet*, 'Cahier' directed by Jacques Berne, Ed. de l'Herne, Paris, 1973.

ETIENNE-MARTIN

Catalogues

Etienne-Martin, Palais des Beaux-Arts, Brussels, 1965 (Preface by Jean Dypréau). *Etienne-Martin*, Musée Rodin, Paris 1972.

Monographs

Michel Ragon: *Etienne-Martin*, Eds. La Connaissance, Brussels 1970.

JEAN FAUTRIER

Catalogues

Fautrier Oeuvres 1915-1943, Galerie René Drouin, Paris 1943 (Introduced by Jean Paulhan). *Fautrier – Les Otages*, Galerie René Drouin, Paris 1945 (Preface by André Malraux). *Fautrier 1928-1958*, Institute of Contemporary Art, London 1958 (Introduction by Herbert Read). *Jean Fautrier, retrospective*, Musée d'Art Moderne de la Ville de Paris, 1964. *Jean Fautrier*, Josef-Haubrich-Kunsthalle, Cologne, 1980.

Monographs

Michel Ragon, *Fautrier*, Musée de Poche, Paris 1957, English trs. Golden Griffin books,

New York, 1958. Palma Bucarelli, *Jean Fautrier, pittura et materia*, 11 Saggiatore, Milan 1960. (The definitive biography, with the first attempt at a catalogue raisonné.) Edwin Engelberts, *Jean Fautrier, oeuvre gravé, oeuvre sculpté, essai d'un catalogue raisonné*, Galerie Engelberts, Geneva 1969.

LOUIS FERNANDEZ

Louis Fernandez, *Cnac archives*, no. 4, Paris 1972, published for the exhibition *Louis Fernandez* at the Centre National d'Art Contemporain, Paris.

AUGUSTE FORESTIER – see ART BRUT

ANDRÉ FOUGERON

Catalogues

Les Pays des Mines, contribution a l'élaboration d'un nouveau réalisme français, edited by the Fédération des Mineurs du Nord et du Pas de Calais on the occasion of the exhibition at the Galerie Bernheim Jeune, Paris January 1951. *André Fougeron*, Neuer Berliner Galerie, East Berlin, August 1967 (Introduction by Jean Milhau). *Fougeron, 1943-1973*, Peintures et dessins, Salle de Cordeliers, Ville de Châteauroux, June 1973 (with full bibliography).

Monographs

André Fougeron, *Album de Dessins*, Les Treize Epis, Paris, May 1947 (Preface by Louis Aragon). Anatole Jakovsky, 'Fougeron', in 'Desnoyer, Walch, Tal Coat, Pignon, Gruber, Fougeron', *Le Point*, no. 6, Souillac, November 1947. Jean-Albert Cartier, *A. Fougeron, Les Cahiers d'Art*, Documents no. 7, Ed. Pierre Cailler, Geneva 1955.

Articles

Sarah Wilson, '*La Beauté Révolutionnaire?* . . .' *Oxford Art Journal*, vol. 2, no. 3, 1980.

SAM FRANCIS

Catalogues

Sam Francis, Centre National d'Art Contemporain, Paris, 1968, (Preface Pierre Scneider.) *Sam Francis, paintings 1947-1972*, Albright Knox Art Gallery, Buffalo, New York, 1972.

Monographs

Peter Selz, *Sam Francis*, Harry N. Abrams, New York, 1975.

ALBERTO GIACOMETTI

Catalogues

Alberto Giacometti, Museum of Modern Art, New York 1965 (Introduction by Peter Selz). *Alberto Giacometti*, Tate Gallery, London. (Essay by David Sylvester).

Giacometti, Orangerie des Tuileries, Paris 1969 (Introduction by Jean Leymarie). *Alberto Giacometti*, Stadtliche Kunsthalle, Mannheim, 1977-8 (Essays by James Lord and Michael Berenson). *Alberto Giacometti*, Fondation Maeght, St Paul de Vence, 1978 (Text by Michel Leiris). *Giacometti*, Serpentine Gallery, London, 1981 (with a conversation between Giacometti and David Sylvester).

Monographs

Jaques Lupin, *Alberto Giacometti*, Paris 1962. Jean Genêt, *L'Atelier d'Alberto Giacometti*, Marc Barbezat, Decines, 1967. Franz Meyer, *Alberto Giacometti, Eine Kunst existenzieller Wirklichkeit*, Frauenfeld and Stuttgart, 1968.

STEPHEN GILBERT

Monograph

Edouard Jaguer, *Gilbert*, Bibliothèque de Cobra, no. 10, Ed. Ejnar Munksgaard, Copenhagen, 1950.

MADGE GILL – see ART BRUT

FRANCIS GRUBER

Catalogues

Francis Gruber, Tate Gallery, London 1959. *Francis Gruber 1912-1948*, Musée d'Art Moderne de la Ville de Paris, 1976-7.

Monographs

Tristan Tzara: 'Francis Gruber' *Le Point, no. 36*, Mulhouse, 1947.

HANS HARTUNG

Catalogues

Salute to Hans Hartung (in celebration of his seventieth birthday), Lefebre Gallery, New York, 1975 (Essay by Werner Haftmann). *Hans Hartung, Oeuvres sur Papier, retrospective 1922-1978*, Cahiers de l'Abbaye Ste-Croix, Musée des Sables d'Olonne, 1978 (Preface by Henry Claude Cousseau). *Hans Hartung, Oeuvres de 1922 à 1939*, Musée d'Art Moderne de la Ville de Paris, March 1980.

Monographs

Madeleine Rousseau, James Johnson Sweeney, Ottomar Domnick, Hans Hartung, Domnick-Verlag Stuttgart 1949 (in English, Franch and German). R.V. Gindertael, *Hans Hartung*, Paris 1960. Umbro Apollonio, *Hans Hartung*, O.D.E.G.E., Paris 1967. Pierre Descargues, *Hartung*, Cercle d'Art, Paris 1972.

Other

Hans Hartung, *Autoportrait*, compiled and edited by Monique Lefebvre, Bernard Grasset, Paris 1976.

JEAN HELION

Catalogues

Hélion, Dessins 1930-1968, touring exhibition, Centre Georges Pompidou, Paris 1970.

Monographs

Daniel Abadie, *Hélion où la Force des Choses*, La Connaissance, Brussels 1975.

ASGER JORN

Catalogues

Asger Jorn, Kestner Gesellschaft, Hanover 1973.

Monographs

Guy Atkins, *Jorn in Scandinavia, 1930-1953*, Lund Humphries, London 1968. *Cobra*, the review republished by Jean Michel Place, Paris 1980.

ZOLTAN KEMENY

Monographs

Michel Ragon, *Zoltan Kemeny*, Eds. du Griffon, Neuchâtel 1960. Gaeton Picon, Ewald Rathke: *Kemeny, Reliefs en Métal*, Maeght, Paris 1973.

PIERRE KLOSSOWSKI

Catalogues

Les mines de plomb de Pierre Klossowski, Le Cadran Solaire, Paris 1967 (Preface by André Masson). *Pierre Klossowski*, Galleria Schwarz, Milan, April 1970. *Pierre Klossowski, Simulacra*, Kunsthalle, Berne, June 1981 (with a complete bibliography).

Others

Pierre Klossowski – *La Revocation de l'Edit de Nantes*, Eds. de Minuit, Paris 1959. *Klossowski*, ARC, Revue trimestriells, no. 43, Paris 1970.

WIFREDO LAM

Monographs

Michel Leiris, *Wifredo Lam*, Harry N. Abrams, New York, 1970. Sebastian Gasch, *Wifredo Lam à Paris*, Galeria Joan Prats, Barcelona, 1973. Max Pol Fouchet, *Wifredo Lam*, Eds. Cercle d'Art, Paris, 1976.

Articles

Aimé Cesaire and André Breton, 'Wifredo Lam in *Cahiers d'Art XX-XXI* 1945-6, Wifredo Lam, *Oeuvres récentes de Wifredo Lam*, in *Cahiers d'Art XXVI*, 1951.

CHARLES LAPICQUE

Catalogues

Lapicque, Musée National d'Art Moderne, Paris 1967. *Les Dessins de Lapicque au*

Musée National d'Art Moderne, Centre
Georges Pompidou, 1978.

Monographs

Jean Lescure, *Lapicque*, Flammarion, Paris
1956. Bernard Balanci & Elmina Auger,
Charles Lapicque, catalogue raissoné de
l'oeuvre peint, Eds. Meyer, Paris 1972.

HENRI LAURENS

Catalogues

Henri Laurens Grand Palais, Paris 1967.

Monographs

Maurice Raynal, Pierre Reverdy, Georges
Limbour, Michel Leiris, Francois Leibowitz,
Balthazar Lobo, 'Laurens', *Le Point* no. 33,
Souillac, 1946. Werner Hoffman, *Henri
Laurens, bildhauer*, Verlag Gerb Hatje,
Stuttgart, 1970. Patrick Waldberg, *Henri
Laurens, ou la femme blessée en abîme*, Le
Sphinx-Veyrier, Paris, 1980.

FERNAND LEGER

Catalogues

Fernand Léger, Musée des Arts Décoratifs,
Paris, 1956 (with complete bibliography).
Fernand Léger, Grand Palais, Paris 1971.

Monographs

Jean Cassou & Jean Leymarie; *Léger,
Dessins et Gouaches*. Eds. du Chêne, Paris,
1972.

Books

Claude Roy: *Fernand Léger, Les
Constructeurs*, Paris, Falaize, 1951, with
poems by Blaise Cendrars and Paul Eluard,
published on the occasion of the exhibition
of 'Les Constructeurs' at the Maison de la
Pensée Française, June 1951.

RAYMOND MASON

Catalogues

Raymond Mason, Pierre Matisse Gallery,
New York, 1968. *Raymond Mason,
Sculptures et dessins*, Galerie Claude
Bernard, Paris 1977.

ANDRE MASSON

Catalogues

André Masson, Museum of Modern Art,
New York, 1976, and Galeries Nationales du
Grand Palais, 1977.

Monographs

Michel Leiris and Georges Limbour, *André
Masson et son Univers*, Eds. des Trois
Collines, Geneva & Paris 1947.

GEORGES MATHIEU

Monographs

François Mathey: *Georges Mathieu*,
Hachette, Paris, 1969.

Other

Georges Mathieu, *Au delà du Tachisme*,
René Julliard, Paris, 1963; *De la Révolte à la
Renaissance, (Au delà du Tachisme)*, N.R.F.
Gallimard, Paris 1975.

HENRI MATISSE

Catalogues

Henri Matisse, exposition du centenaire,
Grand Palais, Paris 1970. *Henri Matisse,
paper cut-outs*, Saint Louis Art Museum
and Detroit Institute of Art, 1977.

Monographs

Alfred H. Barr Junior, *Matisse, his art and
his public*, Museum of Modern Art, New
York 1951, and London 1975.

MATTA

Catalogues

Matta, Galerie René Drouin, Paris, 1947.
(Preface by André Breton). *Matta*, Museum
of Modern Art, New York, 1957. (Text by
William Rubin). *Sebastian Matta*, Museo
Civico, Bologna, 1963. (Texts by Francesco
Arcangeli, Franco Solmi and Max Clarac-
Serou. *Matta*, Hanover Kestner-Gesellschaft,
1964. (Preface by Wieland Schmied).

HENRI MICHAUX

Catalogues

Henri Michaux, Galerie René Drouin, Paris,
1948. (Preface by Henri Pierre Roché and
Michel Tapié). *Henri Michaux*, Musée
National d'Art Moderne, Centre Georges
Pompidou, Paris and The Solomon R.
Guggenheim Museum, New York, 1978,
with complete bibliography.

Monographs

René Bertelé, *Henri Michaux*, Seghers,
Collection 'Poètes d'aujourd'hui', Paris,
1949; revised edition 1975. *Henri Michaux*,
'Cahier' directed by Raymond Bellours, Ed.
de l'Herne, Paris 1966. Geneviève Bonnefoi,
Henri Michaux peintre, Abbaye de
Beaulieu, 1976.

Other

Henri Michaux, *Apparitions* (drawings and
'frottages'), Ed. du Point du Jour, Paris,
1946. Henri Michaux, *Peintures et Dessins*,
Ed. du Point du Jour, Paris, 1946. Henri
Michaux, *Meidosems* (lithographs), Ed. du
Point du Jour, Paris, 1948.

JOAN MIRO

Monographs

Roland Penrose, *Miró*, Thames & Hudson,
London 1970. Jacques Dupin, *Miró*. José
Pierre & José Corredo-Matheos, *Miro et

Artigas, céramiques, Galerie Maeght,
Paris 1974.

HEINRICH ANTON MULLER – see ART BRUT

FRANCIS PICABIA

Catalogues

Francis Picabia, Galeries Nationales du
Grand Palais, Paris 1970.

Monographs

Michel Sanouillet, *Picabia*, L'Oeil du Temps,
Paris 1964. William Camfield, *Francis
Picabia*, Eric Losfield, Paris 1972.

PABLO PICASSO

Catalogues

*Picasso – oeuvres reçues en paiement des
droits de succession*, Grand Palais, Paris,
1979-80. *Pablo Picasso, a retrospective*,
Museum of Modern Art, New York, 1980.
(Edited by William Rubin). *Picasso's
Picassos*, Arts Council of Great Britain,
Hayward Gallery, London 1981. *Pablo
Picasso. Werke aus der Sammlung Marina
Picasso*, Haus der Kunst, Munich, Prestel
Verlag, Munich, 1981.

Monographs

Roland Penrose, *Picasso, his Life and
Work*, Victor Gollancz, London, 1958,
revised edition 1981.

Other

Claude Roy, *La Guerre et la Paix*, Eds.
Cercle d'Art, Paris, 1954. Dore Ashton,
Picasso on Art, A Selection of Views, New
York, 1972. Kirsten Hoving Keen, 'Picasso's
Communist interlude: the murals of 'War'
and 'Peace', in *The Burlington Magazine*,
no. 928, vol. CXXII, July 1980.

EDOUARD PIGNON

Catalogues

Ostende et les Mineurs, Edouard Pignon,
Galerie de France, Paris, March 1949.
L'Ouvrier Mort, un tableau et ses Dessins,
Galerie de France, Paris, June 1952.
Edouard Pignon, Musée National d'Art
Moderne, Paris, July 1966 (Essay by Bernard
Dorival).

Monographs

Henri Lefebvre, *Pignon*, Collection Musée
de Poche, Eds. Fall, Paris, 1956, 2nd Edn,
1970. Jean-Louis Ferrier, *Edouard Pignon,
50 Peintures de 1936 à 1962*, Galerie de
France, Paris 1962. Jean-Louis Ferier
Pignon, Les presses de la Connaissance,
Paris 1976.

Others

Edouard Pignon, *La Quête de la Réalité*,

Eds. Gonthier, 1966. Edouard Pignon, *Contre-Courant*; Eds. Stock, Paris 1974.

PAUL REBEYROLLE

Monograph

Pierre Descargues: *Rebeyrolle*, Eds. Maeght, Paris 1970.

GERMAINE RICHIER

Catalogues

Sculptures of Germaine Richier, engravings, studio of Roger Lacourière, Anglo-French Art Centre, London, 1949 (Text by René de Solier). *Vieira da Silva, Germaine Richier*, Stedelijk Museum, Amsterdam, 1955. Germaine Richier, Musée Nationale d'Art Moderne, Paris 1956. (Preface by Jean Cassou). *Germaine Richier 1904-1959*, Galerie Creuzevault, Paris, 1960. (Text by Jean Cassou).

Monographs

Jean Cassou, *Germaine Richier*, Eds. du Temps, Paris, 1961.

JEAN PAUL RIOPELLE

Catalogue

Riopelle, Peinture 1946-1977, Musée National d'Art Moderne, Paris 1981.

Monograph

Pierre Schneider, *Riopelle, signes mêles*, Eds Maeght, Paris 1972.

GEORGES ROUAULT

Catalogues

Paintings and prints: Georges Rouault, Museum of Modern Art, New York, 1945 (Text by James Thrall Soby). Rouault, oeuvres inachevées données à l'Etat, Musée du Louvre, Paris, 1964. (Preface by Bernard Dorival). *Rouault. An exhibition of paintings, drawings and documents*, Arts Council of Great Britain with the Edinburgh Festival Society, 1966. *Georges Rouault, exposition du centenaire*, Musée d'Art Moderne, Paris. (Preface by Jean Leymarie. Catalogue by Michel Hoog and Isabelle Fontaine).

Monographs

Lionello Venturi, *Georges Rouault*, Eds. Skira, Paris, 1948. Pierre Courthion *Georges Rouault*, including a catalogue of works prepared with the collaboration of Isabelle Rouault, Thames and Hudson, London, 1962. Francois Chapon. *Oeuvre gravé, Rouault*, with a catalogue by Isabelle Rouault assisted by Olivier Nouaille-Rouault. Ed. Andé Sauret, Montecarlo, 1978.

Other

Georges Rouault, *Sur l'Art et sur la Vie*, Denoël, Paris 1971. (Preface by Bernard Dorival).

IAROSLAV SERPAN

Monograph

Geneviève Bonnefoi, *Serpan*, Centre d'Art Contemporain de l'Abbaye de Beaulieu, Beaulieu, 1977.

NICOLAS DE STAEL

Catalogues

Nicolas de Stael, Grand Palais, Paris and Tate Gallery, London, 1981.

Monographs

André Chastel, Germain Viatte, Jacques Duborg, *Nicolas de Stael*, Eds. Le Temps, Paris 1968.

BORIS TASLITZKY

Boris Taslitzky, *III Dessins de Boris Taslitzky faits à Buchenwald*, La Bibliothèque Française, Paris 1946, reprinted by the Assocation Française de Buchenwald-Dora, Eds. Hautefeuille, Paris 1979. 'Les Travaux et Les Jours, Jean Amblard et Boris Taslitzky', in *Arts de France* nos. 13-14, c. Marcxh 1947. Mireille Miailhe, Boris Taslitzky, *Algérie 1952*, Eds. Cercle d'Art, Paris, 1952. Boris Taslitzky, Mireille Miailhe and Jacques Dubois, *Deux Peintres et un Poète, retour d'Algérie*, Eds. Cercle d'Art, Paris 1952. Boris Taslitzky, *Tu parles*, Les Editeurs Français réunis, Paris 1959.

BRAM VAN VELDE

Catalogues

Bram van Velde: Archives de l'Art Contemporain no. 12 published by the Centre National de l'Art Contemporain, on the occasion of the retrospective exhibition at the Musée National d'Art Moderne, Paris, December 1970.

Monographs

Samuel Beckett, Georges Duthuit, Jacques Putman, *Bram Van Velde*, Eds. George Fall, Musée de Poche, Paris 1958, and Grove Press, New York, 1959. Jacques Putman: *Bram Van Velde*, Catalogue raisonné Edizioni Pozzo, Turin, Guy le Prat, Paris, and Harry N. Abrams Inc, New York 1961. Jacques Putman, Charles Juliet, *Bram Van Velde*, Eds. Maeght, Paris 1975.

Articles

Samuel Beckett Bram van Velde in *Les Cahiers d'Art*, Paris, 1945-6; Bram van Velde *Derrière le Miroir*, Paris, June 1948.

MARIA HELENA VIEIRA DA SILVA

Catalogues

Vieira da Silva, Germaine Richier, Stedelijk Museum, Amsterdam, 1955. *Vieira da Silva, peintures 1935-1969*, Musée

National d'Art Moderne, ed. by the Centre National d'Art Contemporain, Paris, 1969. (Preface by Jean Leymarie).

Monographs

Pierre Descargues, *Vieira da Silva*, Presses Littéraires de France, Paris, 1949. Guy Weelen, *Vieira da Silva*, Fernand Hazan, 1960, revised an enlarged edition, 1973. Antoine Terasse, *L'Univers de Vieira da Silva*, Henri Screpel, Paris, 1977. Dora Vallier, *Vieira da Silva*, Weber, Paris, 1971. Jacques Lassaigne, Guy Weelen, *Vieira da Silva*, Poligrafa, Barcelona, and Eds. Cercle d'Art, Paris, 1978.

JACQUES VILLON

Catalogues

Jacques Villon, Musée des Beaux Art, Rouen, and Grand Palais, Paris, 1975. *Jacques Villon*, Fogg Art Museum, Harvard University, Cambridge, Massachusetts, 1976. (Edited by Daniel Robbins).

Monographs

Paul Eluard, Rene-Jean, *Jacques Villon ou l'art glorieux*, Louis Carre, Paris, 1948. Dora Vallier, *Jacques Villon. Oeuvres de 1897 à 1956*, Cahiers d'Art, Paris, 1957.

ADOLF WÖLFLI — see ART BRUT

WOLS

Wols, Galerie René Drouin, Paris 1945 (principal texts by Camille Bryen, Sylveire and H.P. Roché). *Wols*, Galerie René Drouin, Paris 1947 (Text by René Guilly). *Wols 1913-1951*, oils and gouaches, Gimpel Fils London, 1951 (Introduction by Will Grohmann). *Wols, Peintures, aquarelles, dessins 1913-1951*, Musée d'Art Moderne de la Ville de Paris, Paris 1973-4. *Wols Photographs*, Kestner-Gesellschaft Hanover, June 1978, and Centre Georges Pompidou, Paris 1980 (with text by Laszlo Glozer).

Monographs

Wols: Aphorisms and Pictures, ed. Peter Inch, Arc Publications, Gillingham, 1971 (with English and French texts of the aphorisms). *Circus Wols, The Life and Work of Wolfgang Schulze*, ed. Peter Inch, Arc Publications, Todmorden, Lancashire 1978 (with essays by Jean Tardieu, Dore Ashton, Claire van Damme, Peter Inch, Roger Cardinal, Oyvind Fahlström).

Articles

Will Grohmann, 'Das graphische Werk von Wols', *Quadrum*, no. 6, Brussels, 1959. (The complete graphic work, including illustrations to Bryen, René de Solier, Sartre, Artaud, Paulhan, Kafka, etc.)